Dearest Michael

Thankyou for being an important
part of my journey and the work!,

Lots of love

The Healing Power of Chanting

An Inspirational Journey of Freeing the Inner Voice

Nikki Slade

NIKKI SLADE
FREE THE INNER VOICE PUBLISHING

"The first time that I read Nikki's account of her life story, I welled up with tears. I remember being deeply moved as Nikki took me on a journey through the twists and turns of her spiritual awakening. I remember feeling that Nikki was (and still is) one of the most extraordinary women that I have had the honour of meeting. I remember healing a part of me the more Nikki revealed herself to me in the pages of this book. This book changed me for the better.

Nikki and I have both worked consistently to create this title for you, but there is no doubt in my mind that Nikki has worked infinitely harder. Over the years, I witnessed Nikki pouring herself and her love into every chapter—tirelessly refining the words that you are about to read. Her persistence and effort comes from her heartfelt intention—to see you unfold and find your own inner voice through her story. It is for you to connect with the deepest part of who you are and bring it out into the light. It is for you to unlock your truest, free expression through embracing the power of chanting – and all the gifts it brings – into your life.

I could not be prouder of Nikki for entering into the world of an unfamiliar song – writing – in order to share her story here in this book, The Healing Power of Chanting. I know that it will touch your life in special ways. Enjoy it, for all that it is, as you are about to experience the gift that is Nikki Slade.

Join Nikki on the chanting journey—and free YOUR inner voice."

Emily Gowor
Author mentor to Nikki Slade

"Nikki Slade is an inspiring force for peace and an ambassador of sacred sound and voice.

Her courageous life is a testimony to the life-changing role singing can play in the awakening of self-awareness and wisdom. She is a remarkable singer and voice teacher with an outrageous sense of humour, empowering diverse audiences across the globe through the devotional power of chant and song.

Since our first collaborations in the early 1990s, I have been privileged to witness and to enjoy Nikki's remarkable facilitation skills sourced from a life dedicated to sound as a spiritual practice. Nikki Slade's book and life story are an essential and unique wake-up call, reminding all those who have ears to hear of the unique purpose and presence of sacred sound at this critical time in the evolution of life on Earth."

Chloe Goodchild
Founder of The Naked Voice Foundation
Sound Visionary, International Singer & Author
www.thenakedvoice.com

"Listen, okay? I never chanted. The whole thing about chanting in a Buddhist way (car, career, success, love, jewels, flat screen TV, bigger body parts, etc.) seems a perversion of the original purpose.

So I never did that kind of thing. Then I kept losing my voice; who knows why? Not me, that's for sure. My voice would freeze, or get sore, or simply refuse to work. Nikki talks about the work sinking deep foundations into your voice work – enabling you to last longer, sing stronger and feel good about it, too. It's all about a vibe. There are mantras and chakras to work through also, and even if you're a little sceptical about this stuff – I say – try it.

I'm near the end of a year of performing in a play and was worried about several moments where I have to break into song due to the stress of per- forming eight shows a week. Since I've been working with Nikki, my voice has handled this stress level with no problem.

I say give the whole thing a try – the only thing you have to lose... is your voice!

Peace."

Sir Lenny Henry
Comedian, Actor, Writer, Television Presenter

"I love Nikki's chanting and the way the resonance was raised in the room during the conference. I felt inspired and that helped me to move out of my own chrysalis and turn me into a butterfly. Sound is a powerful force. I believe Nikki is one of the most evolutionary sound magicians on the planet."

Barbara Marx Hubbard
Author of "Conscious Evolution: Awakening the Power of Our Social Potential"

"Nikki Slade is an inspiration—this is teaching at its very best!"

Sarah Kent
Time Out Magazine

"After six months trying to get to know people here, I feel I knew everyone better and quicker after just an hour with Nikki than after all the preceding months put together. The session really created some bonds through shared experience and broke down barriers too."

Anna Hellyer
M&C Saatchi Business Director

"Fab inspired entrepreneurs evening with Nikki Slade – if you ever need someone to energize an event through voice, she's your woman!"

Nick Williams
Inspired Entrepreneur

"I was introduced to Nikki Slade. Her style and expertise has the power to bring individuals and groups together very quickly, which then allowed us to work more effectively with our programmes. She has been an asset through-out our banking client list and I would highly recommend her to anyone who is interested in the transformation of teams and individuals."

JC Mac
Working Voices

"I returned for some more sessions with Nikki and since then my confidence has definitely grown. I trust my instincts much more during client presentations and I've got much better at listening to the sound of my inner voice and acting on it. If I could think of a symbol to describe Nikki, it would probably be a tuning fork."

Graham Fink
Former Executive Creative Director, M&C SAATCHI

"Working with Nikki is a life-changing experience. Through her work, I was able to uncover and heal old soul patterns around the fear of speaking out and expressing myself as authentically and courageously as possible. Whether you are feeling the pull to attend a Kirtan, hire her for a blessing, or work with her one-on-one, I cannot recommend Nikki enough."

Rebecca Campbell
Author of "Light is the New Black"
www.rebeccacampbell.me

"Nikki Slade: This woman really does understand the power at the heart of vibrational medicine and that is the energetics of chant and actualization of your true voice."

Melvyn Carlile
Managing Director

"I have been particularly impressed with Nikki's highly developed personal and professional skills, with her focus, experience, insight and unique ability to support me moving from vulnerability into strength and confidence, enabling me to express myself more powerfully, and indeed to find and express my voice more clearly."

Dr. Kim A. Jobst
MA. DM. FRCP. MFHom.
Functional Shift Consulting Ltd

Dedicated to Julian Slade –

My uncle and beloved godfather who championed my singing voice.

Foreword

I n this incredible book, Nikki gracefully takes you on her journey, which is everyone's journey – the journey of being human. It is the evolution from darkness to light, from repression to freedom and self-expression. It is an awakening into wholeness.

The freedom to *be* is what so many people are looking for, but so often they are looking in the wrong place – they are waiting for *others* to change, or for circumstances to change, so that they can feel free. One definition of freedom is "the power or right to act, speak, or think as one wants." *Who* is stopping us from doing this? We think it's "them" – but is it? Time and again people discover that once they find physical freedom, or the law changes and they get freedom of speech or whatever. Although this is an important first step – it's not enough.

It seems that until we give ourselves that freedom – the permission to act, speak or think as we choose – and that until we free ourselves from within, the world out there won't change very much anyway. Even if it does, we won't feel free; it won't be enough. Once we *understand* this, then comes the big question: *How do we find freedom? How can we free ourselves?*

The answer is in this book and the practical wisdom it contains.

There are certain stories that do more than entertain – they transform you as you read. This book is one of those – it's alchemy – and when you participate in the chants provided, you are guaranteed to experience a shift in your life. This sounds like a bold statement, and it is. But it's accurate. I am in a privileged position to have seen the profound difference Nikki's work has made to thousands of people's lives, including my own.

Nikki has the incredible ability to bring out the best in people. She believed in me long before I believed in myself and this kind of unconditional vision is what puts her in the highest league of true teachers. She's coached many leaders in all areas of life – the results speak for themselves. In other words, you can trust the guidance you will discover in this book.

It's those "challenges" that evolve us to be the best in life – and you will see from reading this book how perfect the specific challenges Nikki encountered were to develop her to be the great leader and teacher she is. Whilst you read, you too will realize the perfection of your own journey – no matter what it looks like from your current vantage point – and also gain hope and encouragement that you can accomplish your unique purpose in life.

The real freedom we are all seeking is the freedom from the tyranny of our internal dialogue – the constant commentary of doubts, criticisms, and worse. When we can rise above this relentless "false self," we connect, instead, with the affirming voice of who we really are. This is the Inner Voice Nikki refers to in the title of this book. Nikki's chanting, as I have shared in my own work, is one of the best ways I know to find freedom from this mind-chatter that

so many people think is their identity, and discover our Real Self. Once we become our Real Selves – the authentic self that doesn't think, but knows – then the adventure really starts. We live life fearlessly, and the life we were born to live unfolds perfectly in a way far more wonderful than we can conceive.

So, get yourself a cup of tea, or whatever you need to get comfortable, and settle in and enjoy.

Michael James
Author, Speaker & Teacher

Contents

In gratitude to Emily Gowor, who brings out the buried talent of newborn writers and unleashes the unspoken word in their souls. I could not have done this without you.

Preface

I t never occurred to me that I would write a memoir about the impact that chanting has had on my journey, but when prompted by a few respected close allies and friends who encouraged me to write my journey down, I agreed. I am so pleased they did encourage me, for it has been a truly enriching and rewarding process.

In the summer of 2011, my first "book angel" appeared. I was on a business development course led by my dear friend and inspired entrepreneur, Nick Williams. There were sixteen of us on the course, including Julia McCutchen, a prior publishing consultant at Random House and founder of the IACCW (an organization dedicated to intuitive writers). Julia and I had lunch one winter's day in Marylebone, 2011. Over our meal, Julia, completely unprompted, said three things to me: "I feel that it is really important that you get your chanting and voice work message out into the world", "I feel guided to encourage you to write a book", and "If you are challenged at this prospect, I would also be willing to mentor you through your first draft."

I have enormous respect for Julia and I was in awe of her generosity. Julia is a sharp and astute woman of high integrity. I, therefore, trusted what she said and paid close attention to her words. I was initially confronted by the idea, as I had never written a book before. My initial reaction was to be anxious at the prospect of taking on a project like this. I didn't express this out loud, however. Instead, I boldly said, "Yes, I will do it!" with the obedience and reverence you would show a teacher that you dare not decline.

I walked away from lunch that day, and in the coming weeks all I did was resist putting pen to paper. One month later, my second angel appeared. I was in Cheltenham leading a chanting event when, right there in front of me in the front row, was a good friend of mine who I hadn't seen for ten years, Amba Gatherum. Amba had been living in Australia and worked as a personal assistant to Brandon Bays (founder of *The Journey*). Amba is an extremely intuitive woman. At the end of the gig, she approached me and said, "Nikki, I am inspired to tell you that you must write a book. It's very important you do this." Now, where had I heard that before? I thought to myself, "That's two bells!"

The third angel came in the form of another close friend, Sarbdeep Swan. He said, "Ma," as he affectionately calls me, "it's time you wrote a book. There are people out there who will benefit from your experience," he said. I felt an intense command from deep within to listen and obey, and so it was that I began the process of writing *The Healing Power of Chanting* in January 2012.

Four years later, my whole writing journey has been both a revelation and an enormously enriching experience. The process has felt like revisiting old rooms in a house where I once lived. Each room that I have entered along the way has brought the whole experience attached to it back to me vividly. It is amazing how we can live our lives forward and understand them deeply in retrospect. I have cried again and laughed again, but overall I have felt deep gratitude to all of the souls on my journey.

Ironically, in looking back, I can see that the people who made it tough for me gave me the gift of strength to be who I am today. In other words, I have come to realize that, in the end, there is no such thing as a bad experience. Everything that has happened in my life has been an opportunity for growth and has been perfect for my soul's evolution. I have learned so much by writing, but, in particular, I have gained a deeper understanding of the relevance of darkness – which has been a necessary part of my journey. In fact, it has been a gift – a treasure to be mined.

My commitment with this book is to reach out to those people who are asking the questions, "Who am I?" and "Surely there must be something more to life than this?" For me, the life-changing discovery of the practice of chanting was the answer to those deep questions I had been asking all my life. For years, I realized that I had been looking for my answers in all the external places. Chanting was the secret key to freeing my inner voice.

I am excited to pass this key on to those of you who are new to chanting. And for those of you who are already familiar with the power of voice work, may this book inspire you to deepen your chanting practice.

My deepest wish is that you experience the joy of connecting with your inner voice through chanting and are, therefore, fully self-expressed in the world.

Nikki Slade
Transformational Voice Facilitator
Global Western Kirtan Leader

Introduction

"Imagine the time the particle you are returns where it came from."

Rumi

I n a global society that is thick with the pressures of social conditioning and wearing of personality masks, it is easy to get pulled out of our own center by the current from the rivers of the people around us. These personality masks we often wear are our attempts to survive and belong in a world where it is safer to pretend to fit in rather than "to thine own self be true" (Shakespeare). In my case, the search for my real identity led me down a path of abusing alcohol and drugs before I experienced profound and true healing.

I am committed to sharing my transformational journey through the power of chanting and through the pages of this book in order to bring hope and relief to those who are moving through their own darkness or dark night of the soul. This is so that they may express their own fearless voice in the world and expand into a space of limitless possibility through sound. Most people, if they are honest, have experienced moments in their lives when they have swallowed the natural flow of their true voice in order to avoid negative feedback from the people around them. This can be a stifling and, at times, even desperate experience when you know that there is something that you want to express but your inner being is metaphorically tied in knots out of fear.

Imagine being offered a precious tool to help you navigate through those constraining moments – a tool that left you expanded, empowered and free to speak whilst, at the same time, remaining connected to the power of love. Being introduced to chanting gave me a miracle tool to work with no matter what interactions I had to face. I gained an eternal friend in chanting that has brought me comfort in my darkest hours.

When I was introduced to the power of chanting (otherwise known as Kirtan) in 1987, I encountered a spiritual awakening that literally transformed my perception of life from within and forever changed my experience of being alive. Chanting has given me the strength and wisdom to carry me through so many storms. This ecstatic practice awakened me and has led me to all the people, places and things that have brought me greater clarity and ultimate fulfillment on my spiritual path on Earth. My commitment is to reach seekers who, like me, had questioned, "Who am I?" and "Where am I going?" and to have them discover, too, that chanting is the key to their inner freedom and full self-expression.

My story strikes me as a modern day *Peer Gynt*, the play by Henrik Ibsen. In this classic tale, we follow the main character (Peer) and his intense search for his true self. In paradox, we witness how he, instead, loses himself over and over again in selfish pursuits – hedonism, ambition, lust, and the depths of insanity. These are realms that I, too, have visited in my life through my own intense – and sometimes desperate – search for inner freedom. To this day, I know that I only have a daily reprieve from these delusions based on my surrender to staying connected to my inner voice. I am a human being and I still have challenges in my life (naturally), but by staying close to the practice of chanting, I have the chance to see the way through them more clearly.

As destiny would have it, I was actually cast as an ensemble member in a production of *Peer Gynt* at the Royal National theatre in London after my spiritual awakening in 1991. It was whilst acting in this show that I saw the parallels in Peer's story with my own life. As I look back now, at the age of fifty-three years, I see the perfect synchronicity of those earlier events in my life. I appreciate today that if I had not endured certain trials, I would never have discovered chanting. I am now extremely grateful to my past, for it has made me who I am today. The power of chanting has opened up a whole new destiny for me. I have realized that happiness is an inner job, regardless of the outside, and that the world is a mirror of my own inner state. Therefore, even in days of resistance, I am no longer a victim in this world.

A whole new career opened up for me through chanting. My practice revealed that there is a thirst in this world for people to have a place where they can authentically express their voice in a non-judgmental space. My most fulfilling work has been with recovering addicts for over twelve years at the Priory Hospital in North London. This subject is naturally close to my own heart, as I know in my bones that if I hadn't discovered chanting, I would have surely died of alcoholism. It has been phenomenal to witness patients in deep states of depression being uplifted and connected through the chanting practice, and for the majority of them to continue with the practice after they leave by chanting along with a CD of mine.

These results happen because, through chanting mantras, we connect directly to the vibration of the inner SELF. In this space, there is an inner sanctuary away from the incessant fluctuations of the mind and emotions. When we chant regularly, we feel more alive. We have more energy. We have a better relationship with our SELF and, therefore, with others. The more we chant, the more connected we are and the more likely we are to fulfill our potential, providing we follow up on the inspired actions that inevitably arise in the practice. We are essentially provided with a map for fulfilling our destiny.

I am committed that you, too, recognize that the gift of chanting is natural, it belongs to all of us, and it is the key to our inner nature in the same way that outer nature belongs to everyone. The vibration of chanting transcends the high and low, good and bad, and better or worse. It connects us to the bliss of the true self, which is eternally free and beyond duality. It is not a "woo-woo" pursuit, but rather a grounded and transformational tool for connecting to our inner voice that rapidly expands the quality of our daily life.

With this book, I have included for you a chanting mix that provides four key chants along with a bonus chant to start you on your chanting journey. The information to download these chants will be provided for you as you immerse yourself in my journey. My invitation is that you jump on the chanting train today. Allow these chants to be your companion through the pages of this book, regardless of whether you are sitting still, cooking, cleaning, driving, or listening with headphones on the tube. I just invite you to add a little chanting to your life!

Continue on with the full conviction that whatever darkness or obscurity you may face, there is a hidden treasure that is waiting to be discovered through your voice. Everything you have ever wanted to know about chanting will be revealed in your practice as your own unique experience unfolds.

May chanting be your golden key to inner freedom.

Prepare to Free your Inner Voice

This book and my story has been written in four parts. My intention is to take you on a three-dimensional journey, where in one moment you are reading about the power of chanting and in the next you are immersed in a real-life chanting practice. In each section of the book, I invite you to absorb the experiences I share with you and receive them as an inspiration to reflect upon your own life and where chanting could make a difference for you.

At the beginning of each part of the book, you will be introduced to a new chant. You will also be given the opportunity to download that chant for free by following the website link provided. Throughout the part, you will then be invited to chant with me by listening to the track as the story unfolds. At other times, you may choose to play the chant quietly in the background as you read. But, regardless of whether you chant out loud or simply listen to the chants, I encourage you to receive the magic of your own chanting practice. Go deeply within your own being and allow yourself to open during each track. After you have finished chanting in each part, I invite you to pause and imagine what life could be like for you if chanting was your constant companion.

In the first two parts of the book, I share my experiences of inner darkness and its twists and turns throughout my upbringing and young adult years. In parts three and four, I share my dramatic spiritual awakening through the power of chanting and the many gifts this practice has brought to me. After plunging into the depths of my soul, I reveal what emerged for me on the other side – an awakening that connected me to the guidance of my own inner voice. Each part of my story is named after, and accompanied by, the chant that reflects the significant events of my life at that time.

It is my deepest wish that you continue to embrace chanting in your life once you have finished reading the book. The following is a gentle guide to help you to get the most out of your practice and also from the free tracks that accompany this book:

> Sit comfortably. If you are on a chair, keep your feet firmly on the floor or sit cross legged on a cushion. Rest your hands easily in your lap or place one hand on your heart and one on your belly. Listen to the calling line as I chant it and then please join in with the response group. Notice your experience as you chant, but do not try to produce or control it. You may notice tingling sensations in the body, and you may have visions or see colours. If your mind is agitated and you are having restless emotions, this is simply inner purification – just keep coming back to the mantra. You will, ultimately, feel expanded and blissful inside and feel a sense of coming home. Saints and sages over centuries have said, "The self is already attained." In other words, there is nowhere to get to – just a reconnection to who you truly are.

Please note that, with a selection of the significant people in my story, I have used pseudonyms to honour and protect their privacy. These names are indicated with an asterisk the first time I introduce them in the book.

ॐ नमः शिवाय

Part 1: Om Namah Shivaya

Om Namah Shivaya is a primordial Sanskrit mantra. Sanskrit is the ancient language of mantra – word formulas that were discovered by sages of India centuries ago as being a particular combination of sound vibrations that, when chanted or meditated upon, had a specific result on the mind, psyche and environment.

Om Namah Shivaya literally means "I bow or I merge with my own inner SELF." It is a panchaskara mantra, meaning it is made up of five syllables, or the five holy letters (na-mah-shi-vaa-ya). The five holy vowels are the seed sounds of the five elements of creation – earth, water, fire, air, and ether. It is preceded by OM or AUM, which is the sacred primordial sound. Chanting the mantra cleanses limitations in the mind and body and elevates the psyche to awaken to higher states of consciousness.

Om Namah Shivaya has been an anchor for me through countless storms. Whenever appearances are bleak and internal states are unstable, repeating the mantra connects me to who I truly am, which is at one with my inner SELF.

My invitation to you is to repeat Om Namah Shivaya at the start of each day. The mantra has the power to free you from the bondage of troublesome thoughts and turbulent emotions. As you chant, you will notice a sense of calm flowing into the cells of your being, bringing greater clarity and openness to your mind. Whenever you feel unsettled during the day, bring your attention back to the mantra and repeat it silently inside. Notice how your day starts to flow easily when you stay close to the mantra.

I was four years old and lying in my bed, my face burning hot, with a voice that appeared to come from deep within me. It was saying, "What if there was nothing?" "What if there was no-thing?"

"What?" I thought. "No parents, no sky, no cars, no trees, no aeroplanes?" I sat bolt upright in bed, quivering with fear. If all these things that I knew as my world were suddenly taken away, what would happen to me? Who would I be? Where would I live even, if there weren't houses? I started clinging in my mind to the forms of both of my parents. I was totally terrified at the idea of being alone without anything or anyone. It was too overwhelming to bear, that perhaps everything I knew as my reality didn't exist. I forced myself to stay awake until the black velvet universe with tiny stars in my mind, and the inner voice pulsating inside me eventually disappeared, leaving me in peace, at last to finally fall asleep.

I was an unusual child. I always felt uncomfortable and out of place in most social circumstances. I also felt strange being born as a girl. I identified much more with boys, and so I spent much of my childhood feeling like a tomboy – albeit one with long blonde hair. I hoped that any minute an alien would appear and say, "It is okay, Nikki. You've been here long enough now; it's time to go home." I soon realized that perhaps I was the alien. My journey was to spend the next several years having no clue about who I really was.

Every day during this passage of time, I had this insatiable longing to feel truly at home inside my own skin. I grew up in Putney, South London, in the 1960s and '70s with my middle-class liberal parents and my brother, Rupert, who is three years younger than me. My family seemed to move through their lives without the need to ask pressing questions like: "Who am I?" and "Where am I going?" I would constantly observe them living their lives whilst

I would feel like I was the outsider – the black sheep of the family – looking on and wondering what was wrong with me. Why I didn't fit in?

Mealtimes around the family dinner table were predictable. There was always humour present, which I enjoyed, and the conversations would invariably include the current news of the day, politics, our cat and dog, my brother's chaotic dressing habits, or who was coming to visit us next week – particularly my grandmother. There was definitely something deeper missing in the conversation for me, although I couldn't quite put my finger on it at the time. I thought to myself, "This can't be all there is to life." As I sat at the dinner table listening to them talk, I would zone out of the conversation into my own fantasy world thinking, "Yeah, yeah, yeah. Okay, now what?" I would feel dry and disconnected inside whilst listening to their words; I just didn't resonate with what they were saying. However, I never dared to voice my existential questions about the universe, in case they were dismissed. My family appeared to be happy talking about their everyday existence, so who was I to disrupt or judge them?

I concluded that there must be something strange going on with me. Each day, I would feel an enormous pressure of a yearning building inside me asking, "Where am I going?"

Every day, from the age of four until the moment I left home for college, I questioned life. I would often stand in my pyjamas before bedtime and gaze out of my bedroom window. I would look out at the night sky and the stars or at the clouds floating by in the day-time and wonder, "What is the meaning of all this?" I would then create future dreams in my head and ponder both the depth and intricacies of life's design.

I would think to myself, "God, did you really create all of this?" (Apparently he did, according to Grandma, my dad's mother.) Her father, my great grandfather, was the Sub-Dean of Westminster Abbey cathedral in the early 1900s, so he must have had the answers, I thought. I kept wondering, "If God really exists, then what does he look like?" In my childhood, I always imagined God as a young man in a suit, with the appearance of a studious choirmaster. I can't imagine why. Perhaps it was because we attended St. Margaret's – our local church – in Putney. At St. Margaret's, all the Christians looked spindly, geeky, and boring to me, so perhaps God looked the same.

On other days, I deepened my contemplation of "Where am I going?" Instead of studying the sky, I would sit for hours in front of my bedroom mirror, staring at my face and my long blonde hair that surrounded it, asking, "Who am I?" whilst wild thoughts circulated in my mind. I wondered if my contemporaries had asked this question, too. It wasn't until much later in life that I came to realize these are actually some of the biggest questions that people who are seekers ask at various points in their lives. It became evident to me that we are all seekers of truth, and we simply ask these questions at different stages because we have a sense that something is missing. We feel separated from the experience of our inner fulfilment and happiness, even if we don't actually realize that this is what we are, in truth, seeking in our pursuit of a myriad of external achievements.

ॐ नमः शिवाय

At my first primary school, all the children there seemed to me to be engaged in ordinary play. They were passionate with the latest toy trends and fads in a way that never interested me. My games, on the other hand, were intense ones that I would play by myself. They were centred on in-depth fantasy worlds where I would create characters for myself that would connect me to my dreams of being someone else. I felt that if I could be someone else, perhaps I would then feel more at ease.

When I was six years old, I became obsessed with the musical theatre artist Tommy Steele. I wanted to be just as carefree as his character Arthur Kipps was in the movie *Half a Sixpence*. Wherever Tommy was in that film, an orchestra would suddenly strike up and Arthur Kipps would break into song. Sometimes he was in the streets in the pouring rain. Other times he was in a fairground or a boat race. Tommy Steele was magical to watch. I quite fancied myself being dressed like his character, Arthur Kipps, wearing a cream suit and a summer boater (a flat-topped straw hat). This felt more like my style than the stupid frilly dresses that his girlfriend, Anne, wore in the film.

When I was seven, I had a great friend named Sebastian. Sebastian had a fantastic house in the woods that backed off the edge of his garden. His parents were well known in the film and theatre industry. I loved to go exploring in the woods behind his house because there I could sing freely and wildly without anybody hearing. I would recreate all the characters of the musical *Half a Sixpence* with my voice. The character that I, of course, loved the most was Arthur Kipps. I modelled myself on Tommy Steele. He had so much charisma and joy when he performed. He was a major inspiration for me. He had a great identity – he sang, he danced, he was charismatic and he smiled. One afternoon when I was in the middle of singing my lungs out in the woods behind Sebastian's house, unbeknown to me, Sebastian's mother, Jane, was listening to me.

When my mother came to pick me up, Jane said to her, "Have you heard Nicola sing? She seems to love Tommy Steele. She's got quite a voice you know." "Really?" my mother asked. A week later, I came out of school and Jane had given my mother a fully autographed photo from Tommy Steele to give to me. I didn't know that Jane knew him in real life. This was like winning the lottery for me! For the next five years, Tommy was both my hero and starboard for life. One day, my parents even bought tickets for me to see him live at the London Palladium theatre. I was so excited. He was phenomenal in the show. He made everybody in the audience happy by singing and dancing – getting everyone to sing and clap along. As I watched him, my heart burst open, and I knew, deep within me, that was what I wanted to do, too – to make people happy by inspiring them all to sing along.

And thus, I began my twenty-year journey of looking for my SELF through performance. My father played the piano by ear and could pretty much pick up any song. "I gather from Jane that you can sing?" he remarked. He promptly sat at the piano and said, "Sing something you know and I will play it." I sang *Half a Sixpence* to him whilst he searched for the notes. "You're rather good," he said. From then on, a pattern emerged that every time we had guests to our house, I was invited by my dad to sing in front of them. This was an invitation I often resisted, as singing in front of others was always intimidating for me. However, despite my fears, I did sing on numerous occasions for my parents' friends and family throughout childhood.

One Sunday, my grandmother and Uncle Julian came to lunch. Uncle Julian listened intently to my voice with great interest. He was the late Julian Slade, composer of the great British musical, *Salad Days*. He encouraged my singing from very early on. He would often have a new Christmas musical show being debuted at the Bristol Old Vic theatre. I would go with my family and watch the actors singing and dancing. At six years old, I thought to myself, "This is it! This is what I want to do with my life!" I couldn't see the point in doing anything else with my time. I was ready to fully express myself on stage – singing, dancing and feeling great. In retrospect, I recognize now as I look back that, in truth, I was seeking the bliss of consciousness through song and dance, although I certainly didn't recognize this then.

I continued to love acting and losing myself in characters. My brother, Rupert, and I loved creating adventure games. He and I had about 100 plastic miniature animals. We played with them in the bath when we were four and seven years old. I loved giving each one a name, a character and an accent. I loved mimicking the voices and got completely absorbed in creating voices and scenarios for them.

ॐ नमः शिवाय

When I was nine years old, Justin (my best friend Janie's brother) had some action men. He was selling them for half a crown back in the 1970s. Now, this was good news! I loved boys' stuff. I was very much the tomboy. I also wanted to dress the same as my two friends, Rupert and Blair. Then, there were the Hazel boys (three handsome brothers who lived around the corner from us) who dressed the best as far as I was concerned. I wanted to wear what they wore – Polo neck sweaters made of crushed velvet material and corduroy trousers from Colts (a boys' store in Richmond). I even made my mum take me there so I could be just like them. She bought all my clothes there until I reached puberty.

At home, one of my indoor hobbies was drawing. As a child, I loved to draw with my Caran d'Ache pens. I didn't draw dogs, cats, horses or houses, but men! I loved creating male characters on paper. Some with beards, some with long hair, and some played in bands influenced by my watching *Top of the Pops* in the 1970s on a weekly basis. I got great joy from naming these bearded men and giving them an identity. I would name them with popular names at that time, like Jake or Steve, and then I would interview them out loud whilst drawing them. I attributed each one with a unique accent, dialect and age written by their name. At the tender age of eight, I would find myself content for hours sitting at the end of my mother's kitchen table drawing away. Our beloved house cleaner, affectionately named Obin, would be cleaning the kitchen whilst I drew, and she always took a keen interest in my drawings. She had a teenage son, Edward, who she said had albums of a band called *The Moody Blues*, who looked just like my drawings.

Obin was a special friend to me throughout my life. I always felt uncon-ditionally listened to and heard by her, which felt deeply precious to me. She used to knit teddy outfits for my brother's and my teddies, who were respectively named Andrew and Richard. I was proud of their intricately knitted outfits. I loved Obin; she always had time for me and my creations. Obin lived on a council estate. She was poor but I never heard her complain. Rupert and I would visit her at her flat on Christmas Eve every year without fail to take her a present. I remember years later, when I was about thirty-two years old, taking Obin out for her 80th birthday with my teddy, Richard, in his knitted outfit to honour her special occasion. We ate at a Greek restaurant on the Fulham road, drank 20 tonic waters between us, and stayed talking and laughing until two in the morning! Obin was extremely fit for her age.

I put this down to her avid commitment to swimming up and down in the pensioner's lane four times a week at the Putney baths.

Nine years later, Obin died just one month before her ninetieth birthday. I went to see her in hospital four days before she passed away. I remember standing in the doorway on my way out saying goodbye and she said to me, "You look so beautiful standing there, Nikki. Bye bye, darling!" I was in Edinburgh for the weekend standing on a train platform when the text came from my mother saying, "Obin died peacefully in her sleep last night." The tears rolled down my cheeks as my great friend left this earthly plane.

ॐ नमः शिवाय

I was filled with joy when my father gifted me with a brand new cassette tape recorder for my tenth birthday. This brought about hours of exploration. I created characters and made-up plays I recorded in which I lost myself in all of my characterizations, especially the male roles. It was such a fabulous outlet to fulfil my creative urges. I would write plays and, when I had completed the play, I would let my parents and visiting adults listen to the whole thing on tape. I had a hunger for their feedback and, most especially, their praise.

As I reflect back now, I can see that my self-esteem was invested in the approval I received for my plays and the creative performances that I put on for my parents, friends and relations. If my father liked it, I somehow felt I was good enough. I can see now that if the characters I played were part of my identity, then it was critical to me that my parents validated my creations, as this instantly meant they were validating (and therefore appreciating) me. It clicked around seven years old that I seemed to get more love, attention, and approval when I was good at something. Simply being me didn't occur to me as being enough. My father would consistently affirm my singing and vocal impressions by the way he smiled approvingly – sometimes he would even laugh. He also enjoyed the made-up characters that I invented. I would make up plots for them with different scenes and record these scenarios on my new cassette recorder.

I played the tape to him afterwards, and he would praise me highly for having such a creative imagination.

"I think this play is really very good," he said. "Maybe one day it will be on the radio!"

As I look back on it now, it is easy to see that I made a core decision in those early years, which could be summed up as, "I am only worth something when I receive outer approval." This belief remained with me for many years and, although it was something I had made up and was not based in reality, my decision to need male approval (in particular) has shaped so much of my life and ignited a longing within me to free my own voice.

ॐ नमः शिवाय

The world of inventing famous and imaginary characters was all mine for ten years, until one dreaded Sunday lunch when my younger brother, Rupert, age seven, stole my thunder. He began to mimic Frank Spencer (a well-known seventies TV sitcom character) at the table. "That's my party piece!" I thought to myself furiously. "I always do impressions of Frank Spencer. He's just stolen my act! How dare he do that!" My parents praised him because he did it well – even I could see that. In that moment, I physically felt a big chunk of my confidence and identity disappear.

It was then that I made my second defining core decision in life, which was, "There is no room for me. I have been replaced." This decision created a stressful environment of competition that dogged my life for years and played out over and over again in a wide range of relationship dynamics, both personal and professional. Looking back, I could literally have decided anything about my relationship with Rupert, such as, "How much fun it would be for us both to mimic together!" However, instead, I chose to bury the limitless and free self-expression that I enjoyed so much in my early childhood. Nonetheless, it was impossible to suppress my intense imagination entirely. I was still highly creative, but I wasn't bold about it in the same way that he was. Rupert was naturally bold, and I recognized that I was cowardly and scared of life.

My relationship with Rupert was, in retrospect, a critical catalyst for my journey. The tension between us, as with most siblings, caused me to long for freedom of self-expression. He always modelled for me a complete absence of self-consciousness that, for years, I was in awe of. Rupert was also popular, and he was great at getting along with anyone – something I definitely struggled with. When I was eleven years old and my brother was nine years old, we were kicking a football in an empty playground during the school holidays. Suddenly a bunch of eleven- and twelve-year-old kids appeared, threatening us to give them our ball. I pulled my brother over and said, "We should give it to them – they might beat us up!" Rupert yelled at them, "Go away, you stupid idiots!"

I was in awe of how at ease my brother was in asserting his voice in any environment. He was only nine at the time and he had instantly stopped four older kids in their tracks from laying a finger on him. To my horror, their focus then switched towards me. They could tell that I was definitely the victim. One of the bullies said to me, "You told him to say we were stupid, didn't ya?" "No!" I said. I was petrified as they advanced towards me. "We don't believe ya!" I screamed to my brother, "Run!" Rupert fled down the road.

I wasn't fast enough, but just as they were about to pull me over, by pure grace, my mother just happened to be driving past. She saw us and screeched the car to a halt. My mother could be quite draconian on occasion. "What do you think you're doing?" she bellowed out in her plummy voice, at which point the bullies all fled for shelter. Thankfully, we escaped in one piece – well, physically at least. As I look back at that event, I realize that right there I made my third defining decision, which was, "I can't stand up for myself."

In fact, years later, when I was thirteen years old, I actually was beaten up in the street by two rough girls in Putney when I refused to give them my tennis racket. One of them, I distinctly remember, had a deformed hand, which she shoved in my face. She was clearly the boss, as she coaxed the other girl to knee me in the face until my nose bled. From that point forward, I became fearful of walking alone in the middle class suburban area of Putney where I lived. When I did venture out, I would often feel there was someone coming up behind me to hurt me. Rupert, on the other hand, took all confrontation on the chin. In fact, he progressed to travelling on the underground aged eleven years, all the way to watch his favourite football team, Arsenal, and he remained fearless.

In retrospect, this was one of many perfect early life experiences that the universe gave me to strengthen me to seek inner freedom. I learned very early on that talent alone wasn't enough in life. For many years, I thought that live performance was my route to inner fulfilment and happiness. I would often wonder if performance was so important to me, why I always went through such incredible anxiety before going on stage. I really wasn't naturally at ease with this. I would always flinch when asked to sing in front of people. Rupert definitely out-shone me in self-confidence, even if his talents were initially less obvious than mine.

I clearly remember that, when I was ten, my lack of confidence took a turn for the worse. My parents had a Sunday lunch party with all their Putney friends. At some point during that afternoon, I was called to sing – and I was dreading it. My heart was thumping, yet a part of me wanted to face the fear and do it. I came down the stairs to the sounds of clapping as they all encouraged me to sing. I chose the comedy song *I Cain't Say No* from the Hollywood musical *Oklahoma*. My father struck the C note on the piano and

I burst into song with the first phrase in my best American accent. I sang, "It ain't so much a question of not knowing what to do..."

ॐ नमः शिवाय

At the end, they all applauded. I was completely relieved that it was over. My brother, Rupert, suddenly appeared from nowhere dressed hilariously as a fairy with flowers in his hair and my father began to play *We'll Gather Lilacs in the Spring Again* by Ivor Novello. Rupert sang his rendition fearlessly out of key, yet triumphant. His comedic performance brought the house down. I overheard one of the guests at the party say "I don't know about *Oklahoma*, but that boy has made my afternoon!"

At that point, I gathered more evidence to my core decision that I had been replaced and that there was definitely no room for the two of us in this world. My parents would often say, "He's completely fearless, that one!" Rupert was awarded etheric medals for his confidence by family, friends, and schoolteachers. This must have made a great impression on him, the fruits of which are apparent to me in his adult life to date, as Rupert has achieved outstanding success in the business world. He has taken incredible risks in travelling the world and making lifelong friends in every city, from Warsaw to New York.

It is important for me to say here that when Rupert and I were not in the competitive arena of performance with one another, we had hours of fun talking, laughing and playing together, and watching 1970s sitcoms. I remember crying when my brother – my playmate – was packed off to boarding school aged only eight years. I missed him hugely. I am both inspired and proud of my brother today, and I can see how the decisions I made about our childhood relationship provided me with a firm foundation for my spiritual journey.

School was a character-building experience for me. Except, this time, I am not referring to the characters that I mimicked or the ones I invented, but rather in developing myself in how to function in the jungle called life. This jungle was ferocious and it had every creature in it.

After leaving nursery (which I loved), it all went downhill for me. I went to a private school called Hurlingham School in Putney, South London. We had a spinster headmistress called Miss Whitehead, and she employed six other spinsters to run the school with her – one of whom was called Miss Savage, and she was true to her name. One day at school dinner, I remember feeling very left out as all the children were chatting to each other at the table. Suddenly, the girl next to me asked me for a beaker of water. I seized the opportunity for attention and deliberately dropped the beaker into her semolina pudding. I wanted attention so badly because none of the kids were speaking to me, and I thought that surely this would make them all laugh. It had the reverse effect. They all bellowed out my name as, "Nicola is stupid!" The girl screamed at the nearest teacher to come to her rescue. The teacher duly summoned the deputy head Miss Savage to come to the table.

Miss Savage came roaring in and dragged me from my seat into the junior dining hall next door. She told me I was very bad. She forced me to stand before all the junior school children who were eating their lunch right in front of the French windows that overlooked the playground. All the juniors stared at me, sniggering, because Miss Savage had announced to them how shamefully bad I was. I was so scared that I nearly wet myself! It felt like I was enduring some kind of medieval humiliation. At six years old, I formed my earliest core decision about authority figures. I decided that, "If I unleash my self-expression before these people, they will kill me off." I felt stifled as I stood there swallowing my voice and chewing my hair at the same time as the junior children continued to stare on. I remember clearly the life force leaving my body as I spun out into a fantasy world at the front of the room in an attempt to escape the shock.

The following week in the school playground, I found myself struggling to join in with the other children and make friends when suddenly I saw some junior boys kicking a football in the junior playground below. I knew football a little and decided to see if I could join them. It took a lot of courage to approach them. I ran down three flights of steps to join in when, from nowhere, the ball hurtled towards me. To my astonishment, I managed to kick it back into play. My heart jumped for joy. "At last!" I said to myself. "I'm part of a game!" Suddenly, a boy called Marcus appeared. He shoved his face and glasses into mine and said, "You're ugly. You'll never be part of our game. GO AWAY!"

ॐ नमः शिवाय

I will never forget that moment. I leaned backwards and totally froze. Right then and there I decided "I am not wanted. People are mean and nasty and you can't trust them. I am never joining a group again because it's not safe." I am clear that this decision attracted the event with the bullies in the playground near my home with my brother three years later. So, at six years old, I was already building evidence that it wasn't safe to join in groups and that I was better off on my own. The decision that I didn't belong stayed with me throughout my school days. To compensate for it, I would habitually stick to having one best friend and would do everything and go everywhere with her rather than risk school playground group activity. I did, however, know that I wasn't ugly. I had exceptionally thick, long golden hair that was almost Rapunzel-like, and blue-grey eyes. I had received many positive affirmations from my family about my looks, which contributed to my lifelong confidence in my outer appearance. Unfortunately, this rarely helped me to have inner confidence.

I chose to wear my hair loose to school and, as long as I live, I will never forget the day I was singled out by the dastardly Miss Whitehead who had said that the school standards of appearance were now being addressed. "I have gathered you all here today about our school dress code." She stared out across the hall at us all. We were all under extreme scrutiny. To my horror, she pointed sharply to me to come to the front of our morning assembly. My heart sank. "Surely she is not pointing at me?" I thought. Miss Whitehead beckoned persistently to me to walk to the front. I walked forward, shaking and scared. She abruptly announced, "See this girl here! Nicola! Her hair is an absolute mess!"

Her tone was one of shattering disdain. I was only six years old and I quivered in shame. My knees were wobbling terribly with fear.

"Nicola!" she said. "I don't know why you think this is an acceptable way to attend school! I suggest you either cut this mess or scrape it off your face!"

This was the end for me. My hair had always been a winning formula for me. Now, even that trophy had been destroyed. At home that afternoon, I begged my parents to take me away from this horrific experience. So my parents agreed to move me to a new school, which was good riddance to Hurlingham School.

The new school was called Roehampton Church Primary School. It was actually a very nice school in many ways. However, I now had an expectant pattern engrained within me that attracted bullying. There were two teachers in particular at Roehampton who were harsh to me – one was Miss Cowie, and the other was Mr. Ayling. By now, all I wanted after having finally moved schools was to fit in and avoid repeating the same mistakes. I vividly remember walking into my new class for the first time with my hair pulled back in a ponytail, as I didn't dare now to wear it loose. I walked in behind another tall girl, who was also new, called Georgie. I heard all the kids whispering about us.

"She looks all right, the tall one!" a couple of girls mumbled.

"Don't like the look of the one with the ponytail!" sniggered some boys.

I cursed Miss Whitehead under my breath for leaving me with this hair legacy. "They would have liked me if my hair was loose," I thought to myself. I knew I looked pretty with my hair loose because all the Spanish waiters used to flirt with me when we went on our family summer holidays to Spain!

I took my seat at the desk. The ringleader of the class, Anita, who was a heavy girl, began making jibing comments under her breath about my appearance. My new teacher's name was Miss Cowie, and she definitely lived up to her name. I distinctly remember one time when we were in maths class. She drew two columns on the board – one column for single objects and another for doubles (e.g., one cat then two cats). We had to draw them and I didn't understand the exercise.

When I asked her to explain, she said, "Nicola, are you stupid or something? All the others get it, why don't you?" The class all laughed at my stupidity.

Later that week, we went to Heathrow Airport on a school trip to watch the aeroplanes taking off. When we came back, we were asked to make a large airport out of toilet rolls and cereal packets. I was uncoordinated with my hands and I failed to contribute to the model. Miss Cowie thought there was something wrong with me. From then on, she would regularly single me out as the odd one. When she was explaining the rules of the gym apparatus one day, she repeated everything loudly just for me. This echoed my early traumas of being reprimanded by Miss Whitehead. Miss Cowie duly asked my parents to send me for hearing tests. She thought perhaps that I was deaf because I never seemed to understand what she was saying. In my hearing test, I sat listening to marbles falling into a tray and I heard every single one! I was very musical, so I knew I wouldn't have a problem.

ॐ नमः शिवाय

I was finally liberated in my early thirties when I discovered the root of my learning difficulties. It had nothing to do with being either deaf or stupid. I went to a specialist, where I was officially diagnosed with dyspraxia, a motor coordination disorder. The way in which we compute and sequence information is often complex. Put simply, it makes understanding and undertaking the practical area of life very difficult. This explained my not being able to cut with scissors at school, tie my shoelaces, or get dressed easily after swimming. Art classes at school were a practical nightmare for me. As a result of the symptoms of dyspraxia, I was continuously getting lost on the underground train, as I was unable to comprehend maps.

Travelling in general, especially abroad, was horrendous. In my case, I constantly needed a practical person with me to translate how new and foreign structures worked. For example, years later when I was in New York working, I couldn't use the subway on my own. I relied intensely on my colleague, Mark, who happened to be the son of a policeman. Although he wasn't a copper himself, he had immense dexterity in moving through the practical world. He made me feel grounded and was always armed with maps and an iPhone. He cleverly programmed the directions into the phone to get us around. He was a total dream travel companion for someone with dyspraxia. When he wasn't there, I would take cabs everywhere at a vast expense – I simply couldn't face getting lost.

The other symptom for dyspraxia is poor time management and organizing systems. It is often difficult to know and see how to organize time so that it works for you, and this results in frequently being late. It especially shows up for me when trying to put my study papers in order – it is virtually impossible for me. The end outcome is a huge muddle with files that are upside down and jutting out. For the record, most computers annoy me. I just want to throw them out the window. They are as far removed from my comprehension as reading the telephone directory in Ancient Greek! I didn't realize that I had lived with this condition for thirty-five years and never knew there was a diagnosis for it. Throughout my life, I was teased and judged as being either deaf or thick by family, authority figures, and colleagues. In retrospect, I am clear now that this was my soul's choice not to relate heavily to the manual domain and not to get caught up in things material, as my future (as revealed later in life) was to study the metaphysical and vibrational realms.

I remember the day I was diagnosed by a specialist called Mr. Bennett, referred by my friend Steven (who also had dyspraxia). I went for an appointment in which Mr. Bennett asked me to complete a series of tests. These tests were a sequence of physical coordination exercises, none of which I was able to complete successfully. It came as a deep relief to me when he confirmed my condition. I'd imagine it would be the same relief for those who are recognized as having dyslexia for the first time as they, too, have difficulty sequencing information and sustaining attention for long periods of time. Upon my diagnosis, I experienced a flashback to a junior school report I had received once that said, "Nicola has poor coordination in netball." Suddenly, it all made total sense to me.

I often dealt with my school challenges of dyspraxia and bullying by fantasizing about singing and feeling free as I sang. I liked to imagine where singing might take me in the world. As Miss Cowie was rattling on about stuff that didn't compute with me, I would gaze out the window and imagine myself bursting into song with hundreds of people joining in. As I watched the rain splash against the windowpanes, I was suddenly Tommy Steele again. I was singing, *If the rain's gonna fall, let it fall on Monday*! By the time I returned from that dream, the lunch bell had gone. I would charge into the playground after gulping down my sponge and custard dessert singing Tommy Steele songs one more time.

I was really happy and content in those fantasy moments. One day, during our break time, Georgie (the other new girl) started talking to me. She was a foot taller and immaculately turned out. In fact, she won the school prize for best-turned out girl. This registered with me as impressive, especially as I had been singled out in the past as the worst turned out in my previous school.

"Shall we be friends?" she asked.

"Okay!" I said. Georgie was to be one of my first significant best friends. We stuck together like glue – which, for me, served my nervous reservations about playing in groups – and became unhealthily inseparable.

Georgie was a dominant character. She was a friend and bully all rolled into one. She never permitted me to play with anyone else. If ever I tried to approach other children, she would instantly bully me. When she was being nice, we had a lot of fun together. We were both tomboys and we used to play football, cricket and croquet at her house. We would wear all her elder brothers' kit, which we pinched from their drawers! She had two elder brothers, called Francis and Stevie, who were both at Eton, where uniform was of the essence. I wanted to be like them and wear the boys' kit daily. Being a girl was a rough deal for me.

The problem with Georgie was that she was very possessive. I remember one day at school, while attempting to join in a French skipping game with a group of girls, Georgie abruptly grabbed hold of my arm and pulled me up the grassy bank at the side of the playground behind a tree where no one could see us. It was a hideous and dark experience. She squeezed my arms really tightly until they bruised.

"Don't ever play with them again, do you hear me? Do you understand? You're *my* friend remember!" she growled. In the end, I felt like I couldn't wait to get away from that friendship. My prayer was answered because, at the end of that term, Georgie was moved to a private school just like her brothers.

ॐ नमः शिवाय

Meanwhile, back at home, I had two best friends in all the world. My first love was my beautiful black cat with huge green eyes named Tushy. Tushy was there for me through all the ups and downs of my childhood. He would wait for me every day on the front wall of our house until I came home from school. He would crawl into my bed at night, cuddle into my arms and lick my neck whilst purring loudly and kneading his paws into my nightgown. I loved him with all my heart.

Years later, a man who did space clearing came to my house. I had a photograph of Tushy by our front door sitting magnificently on top of a tree stump. The man glanced at the photo and said to me, "Who is that?" "My beloved cat in childhood," I replied. "He was more than that, Nikki. He was your guardian. Very strong energy around him, indeed!" he replied. I was forty-three years old when he told me this, and I cried uncontrollably as I knew what he said was true. Tushy passed away at the royal age of twenty years in my mother's airing cupboard. He was scrawny with battered ears by then from all the scraps he got into with the big ginger tomcat next door, called Gandolph, who bullied him daily. Although, eventually, my parents moved houses, Gandolph took his toll on Tushy. I felt so sad not to have spent more time with him at the latter end of his life, as by then I was away in repertory theatre. I will never forget the call from my mum whilst I was in Liverpool that Tushy had passed away. I howled because I felt I had lost my most beloved companion.

My first best friend outside of school was Janie, who lived two doors up from me. Janie and I were inseparable from the age of two and three. We played every day at each other's houses. I loved her; she was my first true friend. We played with teddy bears, dolls, and action men and built camps in our gardens. I would often imagine that I was Arthur Kipps and she was Anne from *Half a Sixpence*.

She had five older brothers whose names all started with the letter J. There was Johnnie, Jeremy, Jimmy, Jeoffrey, Justin and her folks Jack and Joan. And Johnnie married Judy! I loved studying this family, mainly because all the brothers were grown men except for Justin (who was a teenager). They had soup-strainer moustaches and long hair with side burns, like the men I loved to draw. Jeremy was into the Beatles. He looked like John Lennon and Johnnie looked like George Harrison from the Sergeant Pepper album. I began playing the Beatles albums when I was eight years old. I loved their music, especially the song *Lucy in the Sky with Diamonds*. At that age, I didn't lyrically understand the words, but it just sounded magical to me.

When I joined Roehampton Church School, Janie was already in the same school, but in the year below me. I will never forget one Sunday lunch at home; I was sitting at the family dinner table in the dining room. I happened to glance out of our window to see Janie (aged ten then) with her new best friend from class called Vicky. They were walking up the road, linking arms together. I was mortified. I felt completely replaced. Right there I made another core decision: "It's not safe to love people because eventually they will leave you."

I was strongly attached to Janie. I was devastated that she had found a new best friend. One day, when she did finally come around to my house to play, after a couple of hours she wanted to go home, but I didn't want her to leave. I stood in front of my bedroom door and locked her in. I begged her to stay and pleaded with her: "Why aren't you my best friend anymore? Do you prefer Vicky to me now?" Janie was upset that I had locked her in and she said, "Yes, I do prefer Vicky." I was to discover later on in life that my possessive attitude towards Janie ran deeper. Janie and I used to play mother and father games, where we would each role-play pretending to be snuggled up in bed together. I always played the father, and I clearly remember enjoying the game much more than Janie did.

ॐ नमः शिवाय

Throughout the storms of my life, singing continued to be my saving grace. When I was eight years old, my class teacher, Mrs. Stewart, announced that there would be a talent contest. We all had to bring something to the contest that we were talented at, whether it was a drawing, model making, or perhaps a written poem. I knew this was my chance to sing for real, not just in my fantasy world. Georgie nudged me and said, "Go on, you can do it!" My heart thumped as we had already seen ten drawings brought forwards for show. "Has anyone got something that isn't a drawing?" asked Mrs. Stewart. I found myself floating forwards to the front of the room. I stared at everyone, frozen with fear. I knew that I had to find my voice. The whole class stared at me. "Not Nicola!" muttered one of them.

I was determined to break through this ordeal. I stood at the front of the room, looking out at the sceptical faces, and opened my mouth, hoping that sound would come out. Lo and behold, out popped the song *It's a Fine Life* from the movie *Oliver!* – at full throttle! People looked through the window from the neighbouring classroom to see who was singing. As I sang my last note, a rapturous applause sounded loudly from everyone.

"Wow, they all seem to suddenly like me now," I thought. "This singing thing is powerful. It brings me love." And hence, another core decision was formed: "When I sing, I am heard, but when I speak my truth, I am ignored."

My last year of primary school turned out to be the happiest year of my junior school journey. Georgie had left by then and I gave myself permission to join in and play with the other children. I began to French skip with the other girls every lunch break. I even invited all my girlfriends to tea for my eleventh birthday where my dad wrote a hilarious calypso song about all of them. He pre-recorded it and played it for us after we cut the cake.

That same year, I remember when something very special and extraordinary happened to me. I was singing my heart out in the playground during lunch break when I encountered an exciting thought: "Wouldn't it be incredible if all the pupils came together to sing and dance right now? Just like they do in the musicals?!" In that moment, I boldly began to sing in a loud voice. I sang my favourite song from *Half a Sixpence*, *If the Rain's Gotta Fall*. My new best friend, Carrie, started to join in with me, followed by two other girls. We held hands and started flowing through the playground like a locomotion train. We gathered more and more people, linking hands as we skipped around and sang.

Against all odds, even the boys started joining in. Before long, everyone in the junior school had joined our huge singing circle. Everything was suddenly in slow motion for me, and my heart was bursting at the sense of belonging. For the first time in my life, I was not the outsider. My dream had come true – to be in a musical in real life. This was by far my happiest early memory. It was truly a defining moment for me. As I look back, it was, in fact, the first seed I had sown towards my destiny to work with the power of chanting.

My favourite teacher, Miss Gotto, witnessed the whole event and approached me. She said, "I saw that, Nicola. You have a lovely voice. Would you like to sing in the end of term church service? I would like you to sing *Amazing Grace* from the pulpit. What do you say?" In that moment, I felt heard and recognized for my true soul note. It felt rather similar to the Matilda character, in the book *Matilda*, when Miss Honey champions her literary talents, her genius, and her then-unseen destiny to bring people together.

My face lit up and I said, "Yes!" I then immediately felt scared that I would now have to deliver a performance.

That moment came for me on the last day of term. I went up to the pulpit and waited for the organist to strike her first chord. I looked out onto the congregation of parents, pupils, and teachers – and I began to sing. In that moment, I was truly myself. I felt free. After the concert finished, all the parents came bounding up and praised my performance. It felt incredible to be seen and heard simultaneously. Years later, I made a recording of the song *Amazing Grace* to be played at Miss Gotto's funeral. I thank her for recognizing the passion I had inside of me all those years ago, and for opening my first public singing performance opportunity. Miss Gotto will always hold a special and important place in my heart. In 1973, I left my primary school with a mixture of rich memories, both joyful and painful, and much to reflect upon. My last year there was, by far, my happiest.

My secondary school turned out to be my Armageddon trial. As I write this book, I share my perception of my experiences only. I am, ultimately, not here to judge anyone. I am clear today that everyone in my life, whether they are aware or not, has influenced my evolution. All the wisdom teachings through the ages say, "Keep your enemies close to your chest," or "With friends like these, who needs enemies?" The classic Vedic text *The Bhagavad Gita* illustrates how the central player, Arjuana, came face to face with his enemies on the battlefield. It was through having the courage to face them in the name of Lord Krishna that his eventual enlightenment came. Krishna reveals to him that everything in this universe is moving us towards the supreme goal of liberation. All the episodes I am about to relate build a panoramic view as to what inspired me to free my inner voice.

ॐ नमः शिवाय

The first day at my comprehensive, secondary school in South London was terrifying. The school was called Pimlico School, but it could just as well have been named the Jungle School. The building was new and modern and looked like a hideous concrete greenhouse. It sunk low beneath pavement level. It won a 1970s award for its revolutionary design. I moved back to that area years later as a woman in her forties. During that time, the building was pulled down and a new one was resurrected. I felt, somehow, that the building was a reflection of my own inner reconstruction.

I will never forget the first day I walked through this submarine-like building with its linoleum floor concourse. There were hundreds of kids barging through the doors. As a middle-class white girl, I noticed that there was every nationality, culture and class under one roof. The overwhelming first impression I had was, "This place is rough." The vibe I picked up was survival; a dog-eat-dog energy.

"How on earth will I survive here?" I uttered under my breath.

My father was a political man, a staunch Liberal Democrat. He chose Pimlico School for me mainly because the music department was renowned as the best in London and I was a gifted French horn player and singer. Therefore, he genuinely felt it was the best school to support my talents. My feeling was that it was also important for him to have at least one of his children go through the state school system in alignment with his political liberal views. It wasn't going to be Rupert who, at six years old, was already showing signs of rebellion by chewing his hat and blazer, and who also struggled to write his name properly. My brother, thus, was sent to private preparatory school in Oxford.

Back in the jungle school, I was in a class of forty children. I remember the sneers from the class when my new teacher, Miss Greenhead (at least it wasn't Whitehead this time – my old headmistress), announced that there were eight special musicians in the class, of which I was one, who would not be attending sports classes, but rather music theory sessions instead. I took note of who the other musicians were, but I wasn't sure I wanted to go with them. It felt safer not sticking out from the rest. Two of the girls, Ericka and Shelley, were also French horn players.

It was very unusual to have three girls who all played the French horn. Ericka came from an affluent yet edgy background. Her mother worked for a celebrity ballerina and they lived in a large house in Chelsea. Chelsea was where aristocrats, affluent artistes, and TV personalities wined and dined in posh restaurants and wine bars. Ericka, from the get-go, was determined to rebel and not focus on her music. She hung out with the Chelsea and Battersea trendy middle-class kids. This clique would spend their evenings and weekends buying fashionable clothes at BIBA, a fashionable clothes store at that time. By the time she was thirteen, I suspected she was already experimenting with drugs. Ericka had it in for me. She didn't like it that I refused her invitations to bunk off from school and forget homework.

I felt caged in. If I was focused and disciplined, the rebels hated me, but if I joined the rebels, I was sabotaging my future. This became a dilemma for me throughout secondary school and most of my early adult life. The most important questions for me were, "How do I fit in?" and "Will they like me?" My opinion of myself was, "I am not wanted" and "I am definitely not the popular one!" The scars of being shamed in front of the school at age six followed me into secondary school. Living with this dilemma, I was neither successful academically nor socially at school. I remember buying lemon sherbet bonbons for Ericka and her friend Grace. I wanted to prevent them from mentally torturing me on a daily basis.

The last straw came when Grace rang me one weekend. She asked me if I really liked Ericka. Grace was being very friendly and told me that she'd had enough of Ericka. I succumbed to her charms at the end of the phone and voiced my feelings about Ericka.

"You bitch!" said Ericka (who had been listening on the end of the other receiver). I had been snared. I put the phone down shaking. My mother, like a tiger, demanded that I give her their phone number. She snatched the phone from me and called Grace. She threatened Grace verbally on the phone. "If this ever happens again, I will go to the head teacher!" she roared.

After that call from my mother, they both backed off for a short while. Every day from then on involved me finding strategies for dodging the two of them. There were also paradoxes in this painful situation. In my second year, at thirteen, I was invited to sing an African spiritual song at our school concert. Once again, I was saved by my singing voice. Grace came to the concert with her mother. The song was called, *Oh By And By, I'm Gonna Lay Down My Heavy Load!* I sang it and there was a loud stillness in the audience. You could hear a pin drop.

Later that evening, Grace's mother rang me. She said, "Nicola, I wanted to call and say how beautiful your voice is. You really moved me this evening. I want you to know that Grace cried when she heard you."

"Thank you!" I replied. I felt surprised by the warmth of her words. I would like to say at this point that "grace" has been a very important word for me in my life. In my late twenties, I had a spiritual awakening when the power of grace touched my life. As I reflect back now, I can see the perfection of that girl named Grace. She was my teacher in the dark and I know that, on a soul level, there is great love between us. I heard thirty-five years later, when I ran into an old school contemporary, that Grace had ended up in prison for drug-related crimes. May God bless you, Grace.

ॐ नमः शिवाय

After the performance of the African spiritual song, Mr. Spencer (the head music teacher) approached me.

"You have quite a voice there, Nikki!" he said. "I'm thinking of having you audition for the junior opera company at Glyndebourne, the esteemed opera company in the UK." I knew in my gut this wouldn't work out for me, as my voice didn't suit classical singing. My range was very low and, if you can't hit the C above Middle C easily, you are in trouble with opera. My late grandfather on my mother's side was a professional opera singer. I am sure he passed some of his vocal talents on to me. But opera wasn't my destiny. I failed the Glyndebourne audition miserably when I croaked on the high notes.

I was to discover several years later that my inability to sing high was due to holding onto a lifetime of suppressed emotions, some of which were ancestral. There is a history of bronchial vulnerability on my father's side, which contributed to my father and me both having mild asthma. In adulthood, I was able to unlock that space and gain an extra octave of my singing voice through the work of a talented and natural voice coach from Canada named Edwin Coppard. Edwin passed on a modality called Tap for Health or EFT (Emotional Freedom Technique). He combined tapping the body with making sounds of release. I will never forget the day that my inner trauma was released. These high notes that I had never sung before came flying out of me, off the top of my head like a bird soaring higher and higher.

The journey through my secondary school turned out to be a perilous seven-year search for my identity. I had the title Special Musician. But somehow, this privileged title didn't fit me at all. I looked around at all the other classical Special Musicians and felt bored by their company. They were focused, studious, and downright dull to me. I knew in my gut that being a classical horn player was not my vocation either, despite the fact that for one season I graduated to being principal horn of the London School Concert orchestra. A humourless conductor eventually fired me for messing around in the rehearsals. I noticed that, from a young age, I always seemed to be the one who was singled out for being bad – much like the episode with the semolina and Miss Savage (making me stand in shame before the juniors).

At thirteen, I was hauled in for a meeting with the senior directors from The Centre of Young Musicians. I didn't realize why I had been summoned forth until I got into the office. Mr. Edney and Mr. Hinton were normally quite friendly to me (especially Mr. Hinton). However, on this occasion, they were both frowning and the atmosphere was grave. I was both scared and surprised. The previous year I had a really happy experience playing horn in the London School concert band. I played with 110 other state school kids with Mr. Hinton conducting. I loved that project. All the trombone players gave me loads of flirtatious attention with my loose, long-flowing blonde hair.

They used to call me Pepsi because my name was Ni-"cola". Neil and Charlie used to smile at me as I turned around in rehearsals, but Terry was the one I fancied. Eventually, he found out I liked him. He obviously found it confrontational because he shyly ignored me. Ivor, on the other hand, was crazy about me. He was desperate for me to go out with him.

"Oy, Pepsi! Let me buy you a drink?" he would pipe up when we all went to the pub after rehearsals. I was too young to drink at the time (but looked old enough). I used to order vodka and lime which would ignite in me a guaranteed surge of inner confidence. I felt like a spark was lit inside me. I became bold and free. I felt like I could do anything. It was like the difference between night and day for me.

I remember Ivor (the bass trombonist) taking me down into the car park under the school after our end of term concert.

"I've always fancied ya, Pepsi! Give us a kiss!" he exclaimed. He leaned forward and tried to snog me. I pulled back awkwardly. He looked a bit like the singer Leo Sayer – cute in a way, but not my type at all. When I declined, he tried a few more times and then he gave up. I couldn't help but wish it were Terry who had taken me down to the car park.

Back in the office, Mr. Edney said, "Nicola! I don't suppose you know why we have called you here?"

"No," I replied uncertainly.

"We have had negative reports from Mr. Storey about your behaviour as principal horn in the training orchestra. He says you were very disruptive in rehearsals. What do you have to say about that?" I shrank inside, but internally I was shouting. "It's not fair. Why am I always blamed when there are lots of other musicians involved?" Instead, I remained silent and shamed.

"Your silence says it all," said John.

I really liked Mike Hinton and I knew, in truth, that he had a soft spot for me, too. When I had played in the happy summer project, he piped up. "You see Nicola, I know you are a good girl really. This kind of report isn't you! Now listen: get back out there and be on your best behaviour. We want to promote you to a higher orchestra." Somehow, I knew in that moment that classical music was not in my heart. The environment seemed too serious; it wasn't exciting enough for me. Jazz, soul, and blues were much more my style. However, my real passion always lay in theatre and acting.

ॐ नमः शिवाय

I was attracted to the theatre. I had always loved the element of make-believe and characterization. I felt that going onstage would enable me to express myself and to channel all the repressed self-expression I had inside. My main talent was my strong singing voice, but I had always longed to be an actor. That first year at secondary school, I joined an outside drama club in Putney called Group 64. There was a fantastic man called Will who directed our group. He encouraged us to write our own play and perform it. I loved improvisation, so I was excited about this project. I felt alive and free every time I went to rehearse at the club. I vividly remember collaborating with about four other girls on this one piece. We created the story of a drunken toyshop owner who was often too inebriated to open his store. I was delighted to have the lead role. It gave me a golden opportunity to escape into this edgy role. I couldn't wait for my parents to come and see it. I was really nervous, however. They had heard me sing many times before but had never seen me act.

The curtain rose and I immersed into the full flow of the character, playing my half-cut (drunken) toyshop owner. I felt so alive and in my element up there. Here I was, fulfilling my dream to be an actor. At the end, I proudly came outside. To my horror, I saw pale expressions on my parents' faces.

"Let's speak in the car!" they said. They praised every girl in the cast (in particular, one girl called Lizzie), but said nothing about my performance.

"What about what I did?" I asked nervously. There was an ugly pause.

"You're definitely not an actress, Nicola! You're certainly a singer, though. Maybe you should stick to that," said my parents.

was absolutely devastated at his response. The impact their feedback had was shattering, and I definitely allowed it to destroy my confidence in acting for years. Upon reflection, I have wondered perhaps whether my mother was not at all comfortable about my portrayal of being an alcoholic on stage. This was a sensitive subject for her as her own mother (my grandmother) had suffered that way.

As I reflect on these critical moments, I see clearly a lineage of criticism being passed down through the family that I was next in line to inherit. In retrospect, I see that my father passed a lot of the critique on to me that he had personally received. He grew up in the artistic and academic shadow of his two older brothers. Both his brothers were awarded scholarships to Eton. They also became Oxford and Cambridge first class graduates. His brother, Julian, was also a talented childhood actor which attracted a lot of praise. My father, Adrian, also enjoyed acting as a boy. However, he was never praised as an actor and performer the way his brother Julian was. I often felt that his resistance to encourage me as an actor was perhaps more connected to his own past experience than my future.

I definitely share my father's striving and yearning to achieve something great in life. Ironically, just like my father, I have compared myself far too harshly with my brother and peers. He did not rate me as an actor because he felt I wasn't good enough. Upon reflection, I am sure his criticism was, inevitably, to protect me from future failures. However, when you want to do something that badly in life, it is extremely hard to hear criticism as contribution.

Despite the lack of affirmative feedback from my parents, I was still determined to be an actor. I chose to ignore their views and, in doing this, I auditioned for the part of Mrs. Pankhurst in a school production of *Oh What a Lovely War*. My parents came to see the show with my cousin, Humphrey. By this time, I had a self-fulfilling prophecy of their critical feedback. My cousin was a TV producer at the time, and he confirmed my critical expectations and told my folks after the show that I should stick to singing. I was inwardly raging at my family. I passively blamed them for crushing my aspirations to be an actor before I had been given time to develop the potential I felt was there.

From then on, I would run this pattern every time I came to act on stage. I was cast as Sally Bowles in the musical show *Cabaret* at school. This time the director was to blame. She would praise my singing and then follow up by saying, "It will be great when your acting is as exceptional!" Once again, my negative expectations of my acting skills were fulfilled. In later years, I learned that the sub-conscious mind will continue to create the experience of what we most fervently believe and expect to happen in life.

ॐ नमः शिवाय

I remember the terror I felt before my first night on stage as Sally Bowles. I woke up at 2:00 a.m., unable to sleep, and my Dad found me crying on the stairs.

"What is the matter, darling?" he asked with concern. I told him I was too scared to go on stage. He sat in his dressing gown with his arm around me until I calmed down. "You'll be great!" he said. That moment meant the world to me and stood out as being special. I can now see, in retrospect, what a perfect cosmic set-up this was. I am clear now that the universe set my father up to give me just enough criticism to ensure that I pursued the path of sound, song, and voice. He probably wasn't aware of how instrumental he was in guiding me towards my destiny.

The musical *Cabaret* went brilliantly. *The Chelsea News* gave me electric reviews for my performance as Sally Bowles. I would come off stage and the ripple effect was bizarre – I was suddenly a star in the school for two whole weeks. Everyone was talking about me. It was an identical reception to when

I sang *It's a Fine Life* at age seven to my primary school class, and the African spiritual song in front of my secondary school. After the show, we held a cast party in a school classroom. Some of the teenage girls who had played Kit Kat Club girls went off to the pub in their false eyelashes and all of a sudden my heart sank. I felt completely alone. I had experienced being someone as Sally Bowles, but who on earth was Nicola Slade and what did she have to say? The existential questions from early childhood came back to haunt me.

"Who am I? And where am I going?"

I was generally unhappy at Pimlico School as I felt extremely isolated but chose not to tell my parents how I felt. I didn't want them to think they had failed by sending me to the Jungle School. Things were also sensitive at home. My father was extremely busy running an advertising agency – fighting general elections and standing on various community boards – and my mother would frequently turn to me for solace when she was on her own in the evenings.

When I was thirteen, I pursued my first boyfriend, Simon. He was very pretty. He had long blond hair, green eyes, and a sexy waist from competitive swimming. He was tall and mature for his age – eleven going on fifteen. He also played trumpet, so we played in the orchestra together. I told my best friend, Tracey, that I fancied him and she went straight to tell him one break time when he was standing in the concourse. He was flattered that an older girl liked him, and I was thrilled when he asked me out. We entered into an eight-month relationship, which mainly consisted of buying jubilees or triangular raspberry ice lollies together after school. Having sucked the lollies dry, we would go down into the underground station and snog for hours on the tube platform. We experimented way too young and I thank God today that I drew the line at sex. The fear of my large family tribe finding out if I suddenly got pregnant exceeded any desire for further experimentation.

Unfortunately, Simon's curiosity couldn't wait any longer. The dreaded Lizzie – a girl even older than me – pursued him and fulfilled his desires. Much to my dismay, Simon was gone.

I confronted him one day and asked him, "Why did you leave me?"

"You are too possessive," he replied, which was partially true. I am clear that temptation played its part in our break-up, too. Simon was the only boy I ever truly loved in a romantic way. We would reconnect sporadically at mutual parties over the years, sometimes intimately, until I was twenty-one. Our parents became great friends, and still are today, and so our paths have overlapped. As I reflect on my love for Simon above other boys I encountered,

I think he was, perhaps, the closest version of what I might have looked like had I been born a boy.

From the age of fifteen upwards, I started to have strong lesbian crushes. If I am honest, these crushes unconsciously started at seven years old with my best friend Janie from next door. I had a massive crush on both my German teacher and my hairdresser. Both of these obsessions kept me going through much of my secondary school years until I met my greatest friend, Nousjka. Her parents were Dutch and her father was a journalist based in the UK. She was absolutely gorgeous, with a perfect figure and a very keen eye for fashion. We were inseparable. For her, it was a deep friendship, like sisterhood – her own sister was back in the Netherlands. But for me, I had definitely fallen in love. The feelings I had for her were hard for me to contain, and so I eventually confessed the extent of my attraction to her when I was seventeen.

At that time, I could only admit to being bisexual, which was true based on previous experience. One stressful evening, when Noush was staying at my family home, it took all my courage to admit to her that I had a crush on her, which was excruciating for me to do. I ran out of the room and up and down the stairs three times before I could say it out loud. I knew not to have any expectations of her; there was no chance of anything happening between us, as Noush was most certainly straight. She was very gracious when I came out to her and expressed all my feelings in earnest, saying that she was very flattered that I felt that way about her and that, of course, it would never affect our friendship as far as she was concerned. I was relieved that I had told her, but also resigned and sad that there was no romantic future between us.

The end of our sixth form came and we were both eighteen. Noush was accepted into a university to study journalism following the footsteps of her father in Maryland. I will never forget the day she left for the airport. I felt like my heart was breaking as I drove home after having waved goodbye. It was pouring rain and it felt like the windscreen wipers were there to wipe my tears away. I realize, in retrospect, that these felt like the tears of a lover who had been left behind.

ॐ नमः शिवाय

It felt strange leaving sixth form and, particularly, my close friendship with Noush. The last two years at secondary school were definitely my happiest. I also have vivid memories of having my first ever secondary school party to celebrate my seventeenth birthday. I was paranoid about who to invite, as I was a different person with each of my friends. I was an avid people pleaser with no real identity of my own, so I would often attach to strong personalities at Pimlico School for validation, regardless of whether they were rebels or swatters. My need to be popular had me drawing up a list of 100 people for my party – some of whom weren't even my friends. This tied in with my chronic need for external approval.

In those days, I felt that if everyone liked me on the outside, all was well. I could never quite relax internally without that outer validation. I invited everyone from sixth form and all my friends and acquaintances from my drama group outside of school, plus my cousins who I normally talked posh with. I was now confronted with being at my own party and having to change my personality between cockney, posh and theatre luvvie talk all in one night. It felt like a nightmare situation. I remember drinking several miniature vodkas before the party even started!

My parents insisted on being in the upstairs flat in case of emergency and, sure enough, there was an emergency. We were gate-crashed in my middle class south London home in Putney by five punks who arrived with spray cans and tried to ambush the back gate. They were two infamous punk brothers who were renowned troublemakers, plus another punk called Danny and a couple of others who I didn't recognize.

My mother was brilliant. She came down the stairs with her draconian voice and yelled out of the back door, "If you step in here an inch further, I will hose you down!" at which point she grabbed the hose pipe. The five spikey peacock haircuts were drowned like rats as they slid off the back garden gate and out into the street. They yelled abuse at her. However, the hose pipe trick worked and they never came back!

To avoid further catastrophe, my dad assigned a skinhead guest called Clitos to be his bouncer for the night.

"No problem, Mr. Slade," Clitos replied (in between burping from too much lager and then promptly throwing up in our front garden!). The rest of the night completely rocked, with tipsy guests playing frisbee in the garden. Everyone talked about that party for weeks at school, and I had the experience of being popular for about two weeks – which was a huge reward for me, having invested so much energy to fit in there.

However, my glory soon dissolved as I became paranoid for several days that the infamous punk brother gate-crashers would come to get their revenge on me. When I next saw them at school, I approached them. In true people pleaser fashion, I apologized to them that they had gotten wet being hosed down on my mum's gate.

"Your mum's a character. We thought it was funny!" they chuckled. My fears were instantly deflated. As I reflect now, many of my worst fears in life have never come to pass, but the projection and paranoia internally strangled me and constrained my self-expression for years.

By the time I finished sixth form in 1980, I was eighteen and very clear that I wanted to pursue a vocation in acting. That summer, my applications to drama school began in earnest to all the mainstream drama schools. In between auditions, I worked as a bar girl in a wine bar, where I enjoyed drinking large amounts of alcohol as well as serving it. The wine bar was in up market South Kensington, and they had a traditional jazz band there, which used to play on Wednesday nights. One day, the leader of the band, a Frenchman called Guy, invited me to join his band spontaneously to sing one number. I was nervous. However, I managed to sing the whole of a Fats Waller number without a microphone, and my voice could still be heard. I received a great response from the customers and, as a result, Guy invited me to be a guest with his band at the 606, a well-known jazz club in Chelsea, on Friday nights.

This was an exciting, though daunting, opportunity, as my childhood fears of being in front of people singing hadn't transformed. I remember dressing up on Friday nights, putting on my makeup and shaking as I got into the car to drive to the 606 across Putney Bridge with my heart thumping. My experience was that anytime I was invited into the outside world to be visible in front of others, I was petrified unless I could have a few drinks inside me. My fantasies of performing were so much easier — just imagining I was singing in front of people was a breeze. As I arrived at the 606 on Friday nights, the intense fear inside me was so great that I remember taking a whole bottle of cheap red wine to the toilet and slugging the entire contents down. "Phew." I could feel the Dutch courage begin bubbling up inside me. Now I was ready to sing!

ॐ नमः शिवाय

As I look back, I can closely relate to the late Amy Winehouse for using Dutch courage to get her through the ordeal of performance — may God rest her soul. Ironically, years later I was on holiday in the Caribbean where there was a piano bar in the resort. It was a resort on St. Lucia where, apparently, Amy Winehouse used to go on holiday. I sang classic jazz songs there spontaneously one night — stone cold sober — and a woman there said to me afterwards, "I have only ever heard one singer match your performance here tonight and that was the late Amy Winehouse. There but by the grace of God go I."

The fire of red wine was throbbing inside me as I walked downstairs to the basement of this cosy 606 club, where the four trad jazz musicians were playing. Guy was on clarinet and Bernie on the piano with his goatee. Then Alan played guitar; he was a dear old boy with a bald head who would constantly chirp up with his nasal cockney accent, "What key we in?" I can't now recall the drummer's name. They were all very welcoming to me and I felt somehow like Snow White and the seven dwarfs with these guys, as they were such an eccentric crew. The number finished and my heart thumped as Guy invited me up to sing. Everyone applauded to encourage me, especially white haired Michael O'Brien, who spoke like Prince Charming, and his peroxide blonde girlfriend, Hazel, who had piercing blue eyes and a warm smile.

I stood up and hummed the key into Bernie's ear. He knew immediately from my voice what note to start on.

"*I Got Rhythm* in F," he piped up, and we were off! His fingers on the keys were magic in the intro and I felt a rush of excitement as the rhythm section piped up. I sang the first few bars and, once I got going, I was flying. I attracted a great reaction from people who became loyal fans in that well-known basement. One was Michael O'Brien, whom I mentioned earlier. He definitely was an eccentric, with his thick, almost yellowing white hair. He always wore gumboots with his trousers tucked in at the top. Michael was keen to mentor me because he knew that, with the right support, I could be very successful in the jazz world. One Sunday at lunchtime, he took me up to Soho – the wild club and bar land of the West End of London.

Michael took me to a restaurant called Kettners. A great jazz pianist called Keith Sawbridge played there. Peter Boiseau, was the restaurant owner and he also owned Pizza on the Park. Michael encouraged me to sing a number with Keith accompanying me. I was extremely nervous again, however, I managed to stand up and sing *I Got Rhythm* by Gershwin in the F key. My rendition got a lovely response from Keith and the customers that day. Keith then invited me to sing with him in an illustrious restaurant in Knightsbridge where he had, on occasion, accompanied Barbara Streisand. Peter Boiseau, the owner (another eccentric Englishman), arrived riding his bicycle straight into the restaurant. He was the man behind the pizza and jazz tradition in the West End of London. He turned to me and took me to one side and said, "Very good my dear – you've got real talent there!" I felt excited that day that the response had been so strong. My challenge was having the confidence to keep up this performing in public. I definitely relied on alcohol.

The time came for my drama school auditions, which were a nerve-wracking experience for me. Every time I stepped in before the panel, my inner critic would be super loud telling me that I wasn't good enough. Sure enough, the rejection letters would come back one by one from each school, fulfilling my inner most destructive belief.

I remember one audition for the Guildhall, where I shook so badly that a lady wearing a black turban had to calm me down before I could even speak. Each day that a rejection letter came, I slipped into a decline of disappointment, giving enormous power to what these panellists thought of me. Another six months passed and a very good friend of mine called Sophie, from my amateur dramatic group where we met in a production of *The Boyfriend*, told me about a theatre school called The Guildford School of Acting.

"I'm going to audition for it," she said, "why don't you?" I ran into the kitchen and asked my parents if they would pay for my audition just one more time. They agreed, and I will never forget that train journey down to Guildford. My heart was thumping expectantly and I prayed inside that I would get in this time. I stepped into the audition room, once again, and stood before the panel.

This time, I had plenty of practice. My Portia speech from Julius *Caesar* went well, followed by Josie's speech from Nell Dunnes's *Steaming*.

"Thank you, Nicola," said the Scottish director. "And now would you please sing?" I sang *Wouldn't it be Loverly* from *My Fair Lady*, which went down very well. "You have a great voice," the director said, "what's your dance like?" My heart sank, as this was a struggle for me. I had two left feet. Once in an amateur production of the musical *The Boyfriend,* I had played Madame Dubonet, who sings a song called *Fancy Forgetting*, which has a waltz in it. When I rehearsed the waltz, I used chalk lines drawn on the floor to help me follow the steps – another echo of my dyspraxia. I used to dread the waltz scene every night.

ॐ नमः शिवाय

The dance audition was dreadful. I prayed I hadn't blown it. Two weeks went by, when finally a letter from Guildford arrived. It lay on our doormat. I ran upstairs to open it (similar to Billy Elliott and the Royal Ballet School). With nervous anticipation, I read the words: "We are pleased to inform you that you have a place here at the Guildford School of Acting for September 1980."

I leapt up and down on my bed. I couldn't believe it – I'd gotten in! I phoned Sophie and she had been offered a place, too. Sophie and I were really close friends and have remained so for over thirty-five years. She is truly a loyal and wonderful person. We had such laughs at Heatham House during the production of *The Boyfriend*. Sophie played Polly Browne to my Madame Dubonet. As actresses, we would dream of our ideal future on the stage and big screen. It was totally thrilling to think that we would both be going to drama school together.

Sophie and I wound up in digs together with three other students (Carol, Alison and Suzanne). Hence, our three-year journey began. Sophie took to Guildford like a duck to water. In fact, after thirty years, she still keeps in touch with her drama school friends. I had a very different journey there. The whole reality of being in a connected group was challenging for me. I liked all the students, but I held back socially. The old scars of being an outsider at school were still with me. Here I was at the age of seventeen having made it to drama school, my big dream, feeling insecure and acutely aware of my sexuality. I was a young bisexual, possibly lesbian girl, with many horizons to explore. I couldn't transform my doubts about my acting ability, and it came as a complete shock when I was offered the lead in the Greek tragedy *Medea* in my first term at Guildford.

The whole production was a nightmare for me. Our director was extremely unhelpful in guiding me with this huge part. My lack of confidence and his lack of direction contributed to my terrible performance of *Medea*. I was terrified on that stage and the inner strain showed on my face. My Uncle Julian sent me a telegram for good luck, which I felt totally undeserving of. I received terrible feedback throughout the school and wondered how I would ever continue acting. Ironically, Sue Rassay, a fellow student and one of my strongest critics of that performance, is my greatest advocate today. She supports my Free the Inner Voice work and employs my services with her drama students annually. She is the resident drama director of the London School of Musical Theatre. My life has been full of divine set ups and cosmic coincidences all along. I truly believe that my critics have made me who I am today.

After *Medea*, I wondered if I would ever land a lead role again. At least I could depend on my singing voice, I thought. We had our first singing class with Mrs. Veal that morning. We called her Ma Veal as she personified classical and old school vocal training. She would praise all the sopranos, especially Barbara from America. Everyone sang a brief solo. My heart thumped with anxiety until it was my turn. I sang a ballad from *Half a Sixpence* called

I Know What I Am. All the students applauded enthusiastically until Ma Veal demolished my performance on poor technique. There was nothing left of my self-esteem at that point. I went to the Scottish director, Ian Dewar, who I knew affirmed my singing talents. I asked him to have a word with Ma Veal. Still, to this day, I don't know what he said, but she was never that harsh again.

In my early thirties, I realized that I had harboured a long-term resentment towards Mrs. Veal, and I wanted to make amends to her for my holding judgement and blaming her for all those years. Although I didn't agree with her judgement of my singing voice, I could accept that she had a different singing style than mine, which was mainly classical. I arranged to visit her in Guildford at her home where we met for an amazing tea together. I made a bold apology to her for my attitude to her teaching, and I acknowledged the value of what she had taught. I also shared with her the transformation I was having in my voice with my new teacher who was, ironically, also classically trained. The miraculous result was that she offered me two terms of teaching a postgraduate singing course at the Guildford School of Acting, my old drama school. Another miraculous circle had completed. During those two terms teaching, I began to recognize that I had a talent for empowering people. I encouraged the students to express their voices with confidence. Thanks to Ma Veal, a powerful seed was sown for my future as a voice facilitator.

The last two years of my time as a student at The Guildford School of Acting became less focused on rehearsals and more on drinking, drugging and exploring my sexuality. I did put energy into rehearsals, but was also very much preoccupied with my newfound friend, Melvyn. He was an actor in the year below me. He was gay and very much out, which I found both bold and daring – especially back in 1981. He dyed his hair jet-black and wore colourful clothes. He hung out with another gay guy called Andy, who was less extroverted. Together they were like a 24-hour drag show. I loved hanging out with them because, somehow, they gave me hope that I could express my sexuality one day. I told Mel in confidence that I thought I was bisexual. It was "run of the mill" to him. I felt like I had revealed trade secrets to him.

ॐ नमः शिवाय

One evening, I went to support Mel in his end-of-term show, *Electra*. As the show went on, my eyes became glued to the girl who was playing Clytemnestra; she had phenomenal stage presence with olive skin and a jet-black wig. Afterwards, I grilled Mel to tell me what he knew about her.

Her name was Holly* and, according to Mel, she had expressed bisexual tendencies.

"Mmm, interesting," I thought, and let it go. A few days later, Mel said he had told Holly about me. She had been clocking me from a distance. One night, while drinking in a wine bar off Guilford's high street, Holly came up to me and started chatting. In fact, we were there together until closing time. Mel said he was off home to bed.

Holly walked me to the bus stop back to Merrow, and I felt like I could have carried on talking forever. I got home, fell into bed and lay there, knowing I was smitten. A day passed and I wondered whether Holly would contact me. I had a late rehearsal in the Scout Hall when the phone rang for me – it was Holly! She asked me to join her in a pub up the road. Once again, we talked until closing time. I couldn't face the bus journey home, so I asked if I could kip on her floor. She said I could share her bed, but we should sleep on opposite ends. We lasted about five minutes before something happened. Suddenly, I was in a secret lesbian relationship at drama school for two whole years. The pressure of keeping us secret from the school was immense. We were too scared to come out to everyone. The only people that knew were Mel and Andy.

It was my last year at Guildford when Holly was in her second year and was struggling with the drama training. She had a lot of unresolved issues from being raised in a children's home and having foster parents. She was continuously grieving over her natural mother abandoning her and she had self-destructive tendencies. I tried to save her from herself on numerous occasions. I became a chronic rescuer, with no tools to deal with it at only twenty years old. Holly was, nonetheless, exceptionally talented and was spotted by a director who was opening a new drama studio in Central London. To my dismay, Holly announced that she was leaving. I felt like Romeo being separated from his Juliet.

My grief was apparent to the school during the days and weeks that followed, until it became obvious as to the nature of my relationship with Holly. People were amazingly kind and supportive about it as I sobbed between rehearsals. However, I soon found a new solution from one of my best friends, Freya*. She had begun taking drugs and told me she was bringing a substance up from Bournemouth called speed. She was selling a gram for seven pounds a packet back then. I was curious. I remember snorting my first line in the toilet of an old-fashioned tearoom called the Tudor Rose, which was full of "fuddy duddys" (boring, stuffy people) with blue-rinsed hair-dos. It was a very unlikely venue for drug abuse.

The hit that I experienced was intense. I remember skipping all the way to rehearsals. It felt like I could suddenly walk on the moon. It didn't really occur to me that I was doing something illegal because I felt incredible. When I drank and took drugs, I felt free and youthful. I had always been a very old young person — never daring to be light-hearted and youthful in case something bad happened. I felt like I was carrying a bag of rocks inside. I was serious and depressed most of the time. From the age of twenty to twenty-seven, I used a daily cocktail of alcohol and drugs, when I could get hold of them, to help me cope with my struggle with feelings of inadequacy and being misunderstood. I never drank during the day at college, but as soon as rehearsals were over, I would go with Holly and Mel to the wine bar and spend student money that I didn't have on vodka and lagers. My credit card would soar into more and more debt.

On the weekends, I would always ensure to score a gram of a horrible drug called sulphate, which looked like Ajax powder (probably was) in a magazine wrapper. I would buy the package for fourteen pounds a gram from Freya*, and occasionally I would score some for ten pounds. I used to go up to London at the weekend, and Holly and Mel would join me. So long as we had our drugs, we knew we would definitely have a great time. We used to drink vodkas from mini bottles and then snort the powder up our noses before making our way to a nightclub called the Hippodrome in Leicester Square. I remember buzzing through the club. With the drugs inside me, I felt like I could do anything.

All the addicts would congregate around the toilets. The men would party in the ladies and the ladies would party in the gents. Nobody cared as a parade of androgynous characters dressed like Spandau Ballet, Polystyrene, and Adam Ant mingled, all buzzing together. Deep down on the inside, I knew this scene on the outside wasn't really me, but I went along with it for the escapism it provided for me on the inside. The Sundays after, I felt exhausted — having been speeding all night. Mel and Holly would stay at my place after, and we would eat a large brunch around 1:00 p.m. and fall asleep for most of the afternoon between coffees and cigarettes.

It was the Mondays that were the worst. The coming down effects from the speed would slowly start, and then a slow looming depression would arise from the inner gutters, where I had to face life sober for a whole week ahead. In those moments, I would always say to myself, "Wouldn't it be great if I could feel as expanded as I do on speed naturally? Then surely I could accomplish anything?" I knew that the quest for inner expansion was an intelligent one. However, that said, surely there was a natural way where I wouldn't have to experience the crashing come down afterwards? I just didn't get how people could go through life sober. How on earth did everyone handle the storms of life uncut? Is it possible?

ॐ नमः शिवाय

The news that Holly was leaving Guildford hit me so badly that I decided to leave my Guildford digs and commute back and forth to London so I could still see her. I stayed at home about two nights a week and spent the rest at Holly's. My parents thought I was staying with friends in Guilford after late rehearsals. I didn't tell them where I was because they couldn't stand Holly. They felt that she was unstable and a bad influence on me. I was too smitten with Holly to see their point of view at the time, and this caused horrendous eruptions in my family that spanned the best part of fifteen years – eight years of which I spent drowning my sorrows with booze.

I firmly believe that all addicts are, in truth, asking the most important question of all. Where is inner bliss? Where is inner ecstasy? They then seek it in all the places where it doesn't exist, which ultimately leads to self-destruction. In retrospect, my entire journey with drugs at that time was building a strong desire within me to find my source of inner connection and bliss. My perilous journey with alcohol and drugs took me into promiscuity, and near physical danger, and lasted from fourteen years old to twenty-seven years old. These were the darkest years of my life, apart from the moments when I was on a high where, for a brief moment, I would have a temporary glimpse of freedom. In the main part, addiction was a mental and emotional prison.

I would love to reflect here that if I had been introduced to the mantra OM NAMAH SHIVAYA during those drinking and drugging early years, I am clear that I would have had a much more harmonious experience and a chance of getting sober – and there are no mistakes where destiny strikes.

My last term at The Guilford School of Acting was great. It was then that I auditioned and got my first professional acting break with the Unicorn Children's Theatre in London. My father, meanwhile, was being taken to court by the Richmond conservatives for allegedly running his GLC electoral campaign illegally. He had been newly elected as the first ever Liberal Democrat councillor for Richmond, where he would later represent the Liberal Democrats on the Greater London Council alongside Ken Livingstone of Labour and David Mellor for the Conservative party. The Richmond conservatives were livid that my dad had won by such a narrow victory of just fourteen votes. They demanded several recounts at the ballot station

because they couldn't accept that his victory could possibly be authenti.
They sent a solicitor, who arrived one rainy afternoon on his office doorstep
proceeding to falsely accuse my father of foul play, and presented him with
a court order from the Conservative party for fraud. The impact of this news
was devastating for my family, and my poor father was faced with having to
do something drastic to raise funds for his lawsuit.

My father called upon all his Cambridge Footlights buddies for help, including his cousin Humphrey, a successful TV producer, whom I mentioned
earlier. Humphrey pulled together an extraordinary event entitled An Evening
at Court in the genre of The Secret Policeman's ball. It was a star-studded
event, including Cambridge stars John Cleese, Peter Cook (from the Goodies),
rising stars French and Saunders, and Rowan Atkinson. David Frost was to
be the compere. I was also approached by Humphrey and my dad to see if I
would like to sing in aid of this revolutionary fundraising event. The evening
was to be held on a Sunday night at The Theatre Royale Drury Lane. I was
invited to sing a satirical version of *I'm Singing a Song for My Daddy* from the
movie *What Ever Happened to Baby Jane?*, originally sung by Bette Davis. My
cousin rehashed the lyrics, creating me as a brattish babe who didn't give a
damn about her daddy and who just wanted to be on the stage!

I will never forget the fear and excitement that night. I shared a dressing
room with the distinguished actress Angela Thorne. We had a bottle of cham-
pagne in the room, half of which I slugged down before going on, as well as
sniffing cocaine up my nose. I just couldn't go on without dosing myself. I
was costumed in an obnoxious nightdress in baby pink with my hair in huge
pigtails with red ribbons whilst holding my teddy. I sang in a ghastly nasal
American accent and fake tap-danced to off-stage drum beats. Halfway
through the song, I had a rapid costume change whilst my Uncle Julian, who
was accompanying me, sang a verse of the song at the piano. Meanwhile, I
slipped into a scarlet red outfit that made me look like a vamp!

I had to hold a glass of scotch in the second part. I went to sip it thinking it
was brown sugar and I nearly choked as it had been spiked with neat whisky
by stage management in the wings. The lyrics concluded that, although I was
"singing a song for my daddy," what I really wanted was to steal the limelight
for myself. My performance with Julian brought the house down, with a huge
whoop from a gallery filled with my drama school friends, and the rest of the
theatre was packed out. Afterwards, that week, I received a golden review
in a small column in the *Evening Standard* called, "Slade them in the Aisles."
As a result, an agent named Bill quickly approached me and secured my first

professional audition – before any of the students in my year at Guildford had. I was extremely lucky.

My first engagement was a season with the Unicorn Children's Theatre company. This was a very lucky break for me and earned me my Equity card. I was to play an American eagle in a production called *The Wild Animal Song Contest*, which toured several London primary schools. Ironically, my early career consisted of playing several birds in children's theatre companies. I remember being photographed on the front of *The Independent* portraying a parrot in *Aesop's Fables* at the London Zoo. That company was called the Neti Neti theatre. My landlord was called Boon and my therapist was called Maya. I lived, at that time, in Candahar Road (Little India), Battersea. Later, I realized that these Sanskrit names were synchronicities for my future destiny in chanting. It also occurred to me that the birds I played represented vocal freedom and wings to fly.

ॐ नमः शिवाय

Meanwhile, my relationship with Holly was extremely challenging. I was at the Arts theatre in London for the Unicorn Theatre Company each day and Holly would show up there waiting in the bar for me. I felt pressure as Holly continued to be self-destructive, which included drinking heavily and self-harming. I began to find it extremely stressful to support her as well as remaining present in my job. The show would come down in the afternoon (as it was for children) and I would go home afterwards to drink and drug with Holly. This pattern continued into my next three jobs, including being at the Sheffield Crucible theatre. One week, I missed my train up north because I had overslept due to staying up all night with Holly. Nonetheless, despite this insanity, Holly was my world. I couldn't give her up even though those around me, especially my folks, said she was a bad influence.

When I was twenty-four, after five years together, Holly suddenly withdrew from me, initially by not answering my calls. When I did go to see her, she didn't want me to stay overnight. She was acting cold and out of character, and I began to suspect that she had feelings for someone else. I was shocked to discover that I was right when I learned that she had formed a bond with a young woman who worked in the box office at Watford Palace Theatre. I was soul-destroyed when she eventually chose to leave me for this woman. I began drinking to oblivion to bury my heartache – not caring what anyone thought.

For the following three years, I descended into chaos and rebellion. I sought out friends who enjoyed drinking as much as I did. I would ring my two dear friends, Chad and Kath, who were social drinkers. They opened their doors to me, offering an infinite supply of red wine and brandy. We frequently drank into the early hours of the morning. They would politely hint at one a.m. that it was time for me to step into a cab.

"Oh, let's just have one more drink!" I exclaimed. I figured that if I could stay with them and have just one more drink, I could avoid being on my own, which I hated because it made me think of Holly and that was unbearable.

In 1985, I had been out of work for a whole year, largely due to my drinking and my unhealthy pre-occupation with Holly. I wasn't focussed, and the more months I stayed out of work, the less confident I was that I would get a job. Finally, in 1986, I auditioned to understudy for Felicity Kendal in an edgy play called *Made in Bangkok,* written by the late playwright and director Anthony Minghella. I was twenty-three years old. Michael Blakemore was the director. I was extremely dedicated to rehearsing this part impeccably in case I ever had to go on for Felicity Kendal, an overwhelming prospect for me.

I remember loving the process as the other understudy, Tim, and I would rehearse together every given moment. I never went on for Felicity Kendal, in the end. However, Anthony Minghella spotted my enthusiasm and dedication to the part and discovered on the grapevine that I could also sing. Anthony kindly put me forward to his good friend Harvey Kass, who was the producer of a brand new musical opening in town. It was a musical production of *The Mystery of Edwin Drood*, based on a Dickens novel, for which I was given the opportunity to audition at the last minute. Anthony Minghella was definitely one of my angels, and I will never forget him – may God rest his soul.

So it was, I was auditioned by the writer Rupert Holmes and chosen as an ensemble member and understudy to two of the leads. One, who was the renowned British singer Lulu, totally changed my life. She had poise and energy, which I was attracted to, and a light that drew me. Her generosity was immense.

She said to me one day in rehearsals, "We both have to learn these songs, Nikki. Why don't you come back to my place to learn them? I have a BBC pianist coming this afternoon." I was blown away by her generous approach – a rare quality with famous stars, especially with their understudies.

ॐ नमः शिवाय

Lulu lived in Mayfair in a beautiful apartment. We entered her front room where there was a wall-to-wall stereo system. She asked me whether I had heard the new Anita Baker album *Rapture*. She put on the first track, *Sweet*

Love, and she began to dance and sing to it right there in the living room. The energy emanating from her was all-pervasive. I felt so happy and alive in her presence. It was much later on into the production of the Dickens show that I learned she had a meditation path and that one of the key practices in her path was chanting.

I regarded that afternoon as an enlightening invitation into what turned out to be my future spiritual destiny. I picked up on Lulu's vibrant energy that day and I was curious to know the source of it. One day I received a call from Lulu saying, "You know you never went on stage for Felicity Kendal? I would like you to go on for me for this afternoon's matinee. I have a cold and I am feeling a little rough."

I was gob-smacked! Before I knew it, I was tumbled into her costume and wig, then marched through all the song and dance routines before lunch. My heart shuddered as the two minute curtain call was announced. Once again, I was so nervous that I slugged down a beaker of port under the pretence that it was helping my throat! My opening entrance was in one of the private "ashtray" seats in the gallery of the auditorium. I looked out into the blackness with the lights blaring into my eyes into an auditorium that was full – including several professional actors. It was a pros' matinee performance with all the other actors from other West End shows who were not performing that day.

The moment came for my solo song, *The Wages of Sin*. I sang, and when the final chord played, the house erupted as all the actors acknowledged my debut as the princess Puffer. This character lived a life in a den of iniquity and was descending into self-destruction with opium and booze (which seemed to be a mirror of my soul's condition at that time, and was ironically easy for me to play). Her other solo song was called *The Garden Path to Hell*. These songs were all about the dangers of going astray on your path and turning to opium and other drugs for solace. The other character I understudied, by contrast, was an Indian woman named Helena who, when she danced, shaped her hands into Indian mudras, which I didn't understand or relate to at all. (At that time, I didn't know that this character would be a perfect reflection for my future with devotional Indian chanting.)

After the West End show came off, I had contracted nodules on my vocal chords through the sheer vocal wear and tear of the show. I decided to call Lulu because I was scared that I would need an operation – what if I could never sing again? I wondered if Lulu had ever faced vocal challenges once in her career. She invited me to come and see her in a production of Peter Pan, and she invited me back stage to watch her get ready for the part.

"Nikki," she said as she placed mascara on her lashes, "whether you do or don't have an operation, the woman you need to see is Helena Shenel. She is a wonder cure with voices!"

Helena was her private singing teacher who, by coincidence, was called Helena like the Indian character I had understudied. I noted this and decided to look up the definition of the name. Helena means "shining light." I had certainly spent a lot of time in the dark. Perhaps it was now time to enter the light. I watched Lulu from the wings as she flew as Peter Pan. I felt immensely grateful for her time and for the referral.

I booked my first appointment with Helena Shenel. It was to be in her apartment in leafy Maida Vale. Helena was a master in the technique of singing, and was renowned for working with really big names because of her exceptional results.

She told me in her theatrical voice, "Darling! If you do what I ask you, you will not need an operation; but these steps are essential!"

Hence, I began a four-year journey learning about vowel modification to create the right opening in my mouth. This would enable me to make space to sing the vowels without incurring stress on my vocal chords. I recovered so rapidly that the speech therapist herself was speechless!

This therapist had occurred to me as very judgmental of singers and their singing styles. She had previously diagnosed me as having "two footballs" in my throat, and that there was no hope for me outside of having an operation. I chuckled happily to myself as the fibro scope camera finally revealed no swelling on my vocal chords. The therapist stared in astonishment at the screen of my result. Her righteous thunder was stolen. She could no longer prescribe an operation for me. What for? There was nothing there! Helena had caused a miracle. She was a first class teacher whose father was one of the early day hypnotherapists in Ireland in the early 1900s. Helena had learned much from her father, and she swore by something called the power of suggestion.

As I reflect now, I see that she had installed this positive power of suggestion about my voice into my psyche every time we met for my session. I have a lot to thank that lady for. I spent two years as her accompanist, too, and eventually she invited me to train with her as her student teacher. One day, I asked Helena if she knew anything about the meditation path that Lulu followed. Helena told me that she had attended many of the meditation programmes herself, and that she had even met the spiritual teacher of the path personally. Helena eventually took me to my first ever meditation programme in central London, which was known as satsang.

ॐ नमः शिवाय

The year was 1987. When I first arrived at the meditation centre, I was struck by how weird it all was to me. The main hall had a photograph of a beautiful Indian woman in red with a red dot, or bindi, between her eyebrows. The incense was burning and some live musicians were playing Indian devotional music. I didn't understand what they were saying, and yet, I felt strangely drawn to the sound. Soon, a TV monitor came on overhead. The same Indian lady in the picture, who I realized was the spiritual master and head of the lineage, started sharing an enlightening story.

She told the story of a frog who had been stuck in the bottom of a well, covered in mud with all his relatives. One day, the frog started to climb boldly up the side of the well. After days, he reached the top and looked over the edge.

"Wow!" he said. "A whole ocean of water I have never seen before! Enough for me and my whole family to swim!" He shouted down to the other frogs to come up and join him, but they all declined. They all felt safer stuck together in the mud. "I'm going!" said the frog. He immersed himself in the ocean of bliss. I have never forgotten this story and a seed was powerfully sown for me that day.

Now, once again, chant:

OM NAMAH SHIVAYA

Please continue to enjoy chanting this profound and beautiful mantra. You might like to repeat it silently on the inside as you go through your day. Feel free to return to this recording any time you are inspired!

BOB LAYTON 23   DERYK LAYTON 20   TERRY LAYTON 22.   NICKY LAYTON 28.

काली दुर्गे नमो नमः

Part 2: Kali Durge Namo Namah

Kali is the fierce aspect of the divine feminine principal within us. She is sometimes described as the dark Mother who liberates us from ever-deeper layers of the lower self, which seem to come back more and more powerfully whenever we thought we had already integrated that aspect.

Durga symbolizes the transformative energy within us that dissolves aspects of the personality that we are ready to let go of. She is steadfast and courageous and leads us powerfully through darkness into light.

Whenever I am afraid, I chant the names of **Kali** and **Durga**. We are often in the delusion that we have the power to move through darkness through our own sheer grit and strength. Multiple times the fear inside me has been so completely overwhelming that I feel like I am drowning. It is in those moments that I have to remember "of mine own self I am nothing", let go and chant **Kali Durga Namo Namah**. Peace instantly floods through me again, and I have the courage to move forward.

Whenever you are facing a challenge in your life – or you feel that you cannot see the way clearly – chanting the names of these supremely powerful symbolic goddesses will empower you to move forward with great strength and clarity. Whether you are dealing with a dispute with your boss, a redundancy or a divorce – in fact, whatever you are facing – this chant is pure gold and will see you through every challenge without fail!

It took me years to get over Holly. For several months after she left me, I drowned my sorrows every night. I, invariably, would go to Chad and Kath's house for company and another free round of drinks. One evening, they introduced me to their friend Liz*, who was a responsible midwife teacher ten years my senior who worked for the NHS. She was in a dead-end relationship with her girlfriend. I remember one fateful night I got very drunk and we all went out with a few other women to Madame Jo Jo's, a highly renowned drag bar in Soho. In 1987, I decided through my blurred vision that Liz was a nurse and she was going to be the one who would make it all better. I unashamedly seduced her. It wasn't long before she left her long-standing partner for me.

Our connection developed into a four-year relationship, during which time I was cast in a professional production of *Cabaret* at the Liverpool Everyman Theatre. This time I was not to play Sally Bowles, but rather one of the sleazy Kit Kat club girls from Berlin. This was a perfect role for me, and it accurately mirrored how I felt at the time. I loved this production, as it was both fun and wild. I loved the director, Glen Wolford, too. I was very popular both on- and off-stage during that show, largely due to the copious amounts of alcohol I slugged down my throat, which freed my inhibitions. Liverpool was the perfect paradise for me, where drinking and clubbing were all the rage.

I behaved like my bawdy character Elsa off-set, too, where I managed to end up in the beds of half the company – both male and female – in a state of inebriation. For a short-lived period, I had become very entertaining. The cast used to call me Briggers because I wore an army cap constantly and looked like a brigadier. The magic soon wore off as I realized I had stretched hedonism to the limits. Back at home, Liz knew about my sleazy behaviour and, luckily for me, she chose to write my behaviour off as a temporary phase and give me another chance to be faithful to her.

At the end of 1987, when I completed my season at the Liverpool Everyman Theatre, I knew that I needed to cleanse myself. My parents had come up to Liverpool to see me in *Cabaret* the musical that year. When we went out after the show, I took them to a club where I managed to down about eight bottles of Grolsch lager in front of them. A week later, I received a letter of concern from my dad, warning me of the perils of alcoholism. He reminded me that, if truth be told, alcoholism was a legacy in our family on both sides. I was deeply offended by his concern at the time and I defended my position as, "I am just having fun up here!"

When I returned to London, I reflected upon his letter and decided to return to the yoga meditation meetings (satsangs) where I had felt really peaceful when I went with Helena earlier that year. In 1988, I began to dedicate myself to meditation, which, for a time, became my rock. During that period, the power of attending satsang and meditating regularly kept me off the booze and sober for nine months. In the spring, I was cast as a parrot and a hare in an outdoor portable community production of *Aesop's Fables* for kids at the London Zoo – of all places – continuing my destiny of being cast as a bird that, once again, mirrored my soul's quest for inner freedom. As a cast of six, we used to set up all our props daily. We had a large wheelbarrow filled with costumes and props that we pushed around the zoo shouting out to nearby children, "Roll up! Roll up! Show's about to start in the elephants' exercise enclosure." We were like the pied piper. Kids and parents came from everywhere to follow us. It was a challenging show, as the enclosure we performed in was invariably filled with elephant dung!

We used to change in a porta-cabin inside the zoo car park. I remember arriving early one day and meditating in front of a mirror. I was keen to keep up my practices and not drink. My body suddenly started to contort into different positions. I looked in the mirror and I resembled a frog as my neck jutted forward. I didn't know at the time that I was going through the early stages of a "Kundalini awakening". Since the beginning of time, yogic masters have talked about the power of Kundalini and that, when it is awakened, the seeker recognizes his/her connection to the whole cosmos. Kundalini brings psychic awareness and knowledge of previous births; she refines and enhances the skills that we already have. Kundalini is the latent potential of the Feminine Principle of Creation – the primordial Life Force and life consciousness of every cell of all physical life. When her dormant spiritual energy, that is coiled at the base of the spine, is awakened through meditation, we begin to breathe as one with Universal Consciousness.

काली दुर्गे नमो नमः

Later that summer, the late Eithne Hannigan, who had played Sally Bowles in Liverpool, invited me to the Edinburgh Festival to perform with her in a modern-day production of *Quasimodo* at the Pleasance Theatre. She was playing Esmeralda. I was asked to play Quasimodo's mother, and I decided to portray her as a drunken tramp. Naturally, this was very easy for me and was another of my best performances. The show was successful. In the late nights, I would perform at the festival in a cabaret with Eithne and her husband in their musical duo, *Some Like it Hot*. Eithne was a fantastic violinist.

Quasimodo transferred that autumn, once again, to the Liverpool Everyman. I couldn't believe I was going back to work there again, only this time I was clean and sober – a stark contrast to the previous year of reckless hedonism. This time I would go home early after rehearsals, much to the surprise of Eithne because the previous year we had been great drinking buddies. We had some good laughs in the pubs of Liverpool. Years later, in 2012, I was devastated to hear that Eithne had died so young, in her early fifties, leaving a young family behind. She played hard and worked hard and I loved her. May God rest her soul.

After the Liverpool production of *Quasimodo*, I was then cast in a pantomime for Christmas called *Aladd-in – Liverpool*. This was a classic rock musical show in which we had actor musicians as band members playing all the 'sixties classics. I found it very hard to remain sober, being back in Liverpool for six months. All the theatre staff had looked forward to my return as "the fun-loving lush and good-time girl!" However, I was no longer that person. I wanted to stay clean and sober. Liz and Patsy May, two actresses from the *Cabaret* production the year before, were really surprised at my abstinence. I managed to last without a drink through the *Quasimodo* show. However, as we moved into the Christmas pantomime season, I couldn't resist the temptation to drink again. The peer pressure within the Liverpool drinking culture was too much for me.

The pantomime performances began and we had our first night party. After almost six months of sobriety, the pressure from everyone else drinking in the cast affected me. It was Christmas and the cast was in party mode. It was then that I picked up my first bottle of Grolsh. This was disastrous for me, as one bottle led to another. I managed to stay sober before the show, but as soon as the curtain came down, I was off to pub and club land again. This time my experience wasn't fun. I felt maudlin and sad that I had started again. I had been so proud of my short-lived sobriety. The season in Liverpool finished – and I was finished, too. Even Eithne, my drinking buddy's last comments to me were, "Nikki, you are drinking too much. You are pressing a self-destruct button." This was the last straw, to hear that from a friend. I went back to London feeling like a failure.

On New Year's Eve of 1988, I went to a drag party hosted by my dear friends Chad and Kath. I was dressed in a wild wig, false lashes and heels. I lasted about one hour before I was blind drunk, ending up on my hands and knees vomiting all over the pavement. The ground was covered in ice and freezing cold that Christmas. There I was on the pavement in cat pose watching my vomit freeze over – feeling a level of desperation that I had never felt before. I awoke the following morning feeling depressed and ashamed about my state the night before. I knew that I needed to drastically transform my alcoholic behaviour. I didn't know what to do; I was desperate. I decided to attend the meditation satsangs (spiritual meetings) again that had previously brought me so much peace. This time, I was determined to give myself fully to the practices – and especially the chanting.

It was January 1989, and I attended satsang on a weekly basis. This time, in my resolve to commit to the practice of chanting, I thought I would buy myself a couple of the chanting cassettes that they sang during the evening programmes. During that time, I was between acting jobs and I was working in a delicatessen to earn extra cash. I was bored and felt lost. I was still living with Liz in Wandsworth. On the outside I was secure, but inside I knew that this relationship wasn't right for me. Liz was a lovely woman. She did everything for me, including dealing with my dyspraxia and latent alcoholism, which had not officially been identified. Sadly, we had nothing in common and we were rivers apart.

One day, things felt so bleak that I decided to find solace in the chanting cassettes that I had bought. I would go home to my flat during my lunch hour every day and start chanting along with the tapes. For the first couple of days, I didn't notice anything in particular changing. It wasn't until the third day when I noticed a tingling sensation after I had finished. I was in a much lighter state of being. To my amazement, for the first time, I actually felt connected without the use of alcohol or drugs. After one week of chanting during every lunch hour, and cutting out all alcohol and narcotics, I started to feel happier and happier. I didn't realize that my Kundalini energy was being activated again, following on from my experiences after meditating in the changing hut in London Zoo. An awakened Kundalini energy manifests in a multitude of ways, from heat in the body, physical spasms, tingling and waves of love arising from within.

The next week, I continued my practice. I experienced a blissful feeling of belonging to everyone and everything around me. I would go to my job at the delicatessen, making sandwiches with a spring in my step. I felt an over-whelming desire to be of service wherever I was. I was fortunate and grateful to serve customers each day. For one month, I felt fearless, with an expansive feeling inside of life opening up. Suddenly, the finer details of my life were sharpened as though they had been brought into strong, clear focus. For example, one day at work I was folding pink pieces of tissue paper. I arranged them between the Granny Smith apples for my boss, Anthony. I looked at a basket of potatoes and decided that they needed brightening up, too! I felt intoxicated inside and, in that moment, this felt completely natural.

काली दुर्गे नमो नमः

My boss, Anthony, tapped me on the shoulder and said, "You're not serious are you? Nikki! Look at the way you've done those potatoes!"

I looked at them all, decorated with pink papers and said, "Why not cheer them up with the apples?" I felt so much joy celebrating the colours of life, I failed to remember in that moment that Anthony had not been chanting. He was not in the same state as me and couldn't actually see the wonder of what I was seeing.

"You've got to be kidding," he said, "they look bloody ridiculous!" That exchange was a metaphor for my life.

I had lived with that mantra forever. "Shut up and just do it like we've always done it, and don't rock the boat." It was habit for me to be spoken to in this way. Any new thought or ideas I had were, in my experience, invariably demeaned.

However, I was in such an incredible state of bliss that nothing could affect me. I felt free for the first time in my life! As I walked down the hill to my apartment in Wandsworth, I stopped at the top of the high street to witness the most magnificent sunset. My heart burst open and I felt my whole being become one with the radiant colours of the sunset. I spontaneously began chanting whilst walking along. I acknowledged to myself how cosmic it was to be experiencing total liberation in an urban high street. It was the weekend and my vibrational state started soaring higher and higher. I was super sen-sitive in this state to everything, particularly to my cat. I had a tortoise-shell cat called Bluesy. In my heightened states, I could suddenly communicate with her in cat language. I absolutely knew that she understood. I was oper-ating from a totally different realm inside. I would say things to her and she would meow at me and blink in a way I hadn't seen before. It was as though, somehow, we were both vibrating on the same frequency.

On one level, I was living in this present material existence. Simultaneously, I saw that I was also existing in other dimensions, too. These were all deepening symptoms of a Kundalini awakening, of which I was still unaware at this point. As I shared earlier, Kundalini is a spontaneous and natural journey where the dormant spiritual energy that is coiled at the base of the spine is awakened and becomes a classic experience for spiritual seekers. It has been recorded for centuries, according to the tradition of the seeker. The mystical saints of the Christian tradition, such as St. John of the Cross and Frances of Assisi, for example, would describe it as awakening to the Holy Spirit.

A scientific explanation of the bliss of Kundalini is as follows:

"During and forever after a Kundalini awakening, there is constant bliss to varying degrees. Some of the chemicals involved in bliss include the endorphins, endogenous cannaboids, sex hormones, nitric oxide, oxytocin, ionized cerebrospinal fluid, dopamine, phenyl ethylamine and possibly the ATP molecule itself. The concentrations of these various bliss agents change with the different Kundalini events, the stages and the seasonal and lunar variations in the flux of Kundalini. One can be blissed out and simultaneously be in ennui and depression due to cortisol burnout and hyper-parasympathetic activity.

"Kundalini can leave one both less functional and with a reduction in spiritual faculty, while at the same time being blissed out of our tree. So the whole thing is very complex, and to navigate such waters we need to stay focused on the creation and integration of the Whole Human. Although there may be a deepening or change of flavor of the bliss and a rounding out of other functions to rise above the dysfunction of being blissed out, I don't think one could classify bliss in stages and lines of consciousness, other than to say that bliss affects all states, lines and stages. The good news is that when we are well into our substantiation phase, we can have our bliss and our high cognitive function, too.

"Bliss appears to be Kundalini phenomena especially related to heart expansion, and is a consequence of increased energy flow in the nerves. One of the functions of spiritual bliss is to incapacitate the higher cortical functions rendering the individual childlike, soft, malleable, changeable, and open to conserve energy and internal resources for the metamorphosis of the physical body that occurs."

** [This excerpt is quoted from Biology of Kundalini by Jana Dixon, available on Amazon.]

My experience connecting with cats continued into the next day. I went to meet my friend, Deb, about a fashion show she had invited me to present in Cardiff. Deb lived close to Battersea Park, so I decided to take a walk. While en route to her house, I cut through the park. I walked past the Pagoda memorial statue of Buddha. That day, I felt a continuous pulsation of vital vibrant energy coursing through me. I stopped and marvelled at Buddha. I will never forget how absolutely connected to everyone in the park I felt. I was wearing a flat cap and I doffed it to everyone I passed. I suddenly saw the world around me as being my limbs and a complete extension of my divine Self.

काली दुर्गे नमो नमः

I arrived at Deb's house and her boyfriend, Leon, answered the door. He had jet-black hair and a beautiful face. As I stood before him, a voice arose from inside of me informing me that Leon and I had been connected in Egypt. It was apparently in a previous life, when Egyptian cats were a big part of our spiritual journey. It must have been curious for Leon because I started speaking to him as if we were back in the lifetime we had shared in Egypt. For me it felt like it was happening right then! My experience was that I was co-existing in that time as well as now.

"Cats are incredible," I said. "They know, don't they?"

Leon looked a little confused as he stood there in his modern gothic clothes and smiling at me with a puzzled expression. "Yeah! They are incredible," he quizzically replied.

Communicating from an altered dimension was a curious experience. It was like speaking to someone who was deaf without a hearing aid or lip reading skills. You know they want to understand, and they give you warm vibes, but the experience of not being understood can be awkward. It was almost like I was trying to communicate with Leon through a goldfish bowl. I was speaking, but he just couldn't hear me. There was a veil – a time warp – between us.

In retrospect, it occurred to me if we all really have been reincarnated, then it definitely makes sense to only concentrate on one lifetime at a time. If we didn't, then we would all end up in a psych ward with the stress of trying to work out which dimension we were in (famous last words for me moving forward). Back with Leon, I soon realized that I had come to see Deb on the wrong day. I was finding living within linear time very challenging, to say the least.

"When is Sunday?" I asked.

"Tomorrow!" said Leon.

"Oh! Okay, I will come back tomorrow then," I said, feeling ridiculous that I didn't know what day it was. I proceeded to walk home to Wandsworth.

That evening, I was invited to a gathering at someone's house in Clapham. I got in the car and tried to read the A-Z for directions. As I stared at the page, I found the whole idea of a map both comical and confusing, only this time it was different to my struggle with dyspraxia. I was actually having trouble staying in my body. I was driving in the car, and yet, at the same time, I was having an out-of-body experience. It was a miracle I didn't cause an accident. I tried to make sense of the map, which was quite impossible in that heightened state of vibrational expansion.

I finally found the address, goodness knows how. When I arrived, the hosts had a beautiful blond-haired, blue-eyed baby. I remember the baby intently staring at me, similar to the connection I felt with Bluesy, my cat. I felt a pulsation of energy moving through me. In India, they call this energy divine Shakti. My hand spontaneously reached out to touch his forehead just between his eyebrows. His little face lit up and he beamed at me.

His parents said, "We have never seen him respond this way to a stranger. This is extraordinary." I didn't realize until a year later that I was having experiences of unity consciousness – or, simply put, oneness.

The following day was Sunday. Liz and I were due to go to dinner with good friends locally. I told Liz that first I had to go and see Deb. Liz said she would be out for the day and she would be back by five p.m. That morning, I remember sitting in the front room contemplating. As I looked up, I noticed a copy of Shirley MacLaine's well-known book *Out on a Limb* on the top bookshelf just somehow waiting to be read. The book suddenly fell off the shelf onto the sofa beside me. This was a spooky moment for me. My ability to see inner worlds suddenly playing right out in in front of me was really pronounced. Suddenly, to my utter astonishment, a three-eyed goat manifested in front of me.

I know this sounds far-fetched, but it really was there, and right next to it, coiled up on our front carpet, was a snake.

I froze in terror and said out loud, "I am not comfortable seeing you. Please go away!" Within seconds, they both vanished.

In many books on consciousness, including Swaamii Muktananda's book *The Play of Consciousness*, he describes many of the different realms a seeker connects with during a Kundalini awakening, some of which are the dark realms, which are sometimes fearful to behold.

Back on the sofa, I opened the *Out on a Limb* book to a random page. There, inside, was a full description of Shirley MacLaine's awakening into the inner world through meditation. She was guided by a man named David in the mountains of Peru. David guided her to write that book to help people like me to awaken. Well, here I was, awakening!

My inner voice began whispering inside me again, "You have just begun your inner journey, Nikki! You will never be the same again. All is well, just listen and follow. I will guide you!" I began to think I was going mad.

"Which world is real, the inner or the outer world?" I asked.

"Don't worry! If you follow my guidance, you will come to no harm!" said the inner voice.

काली दुर्गे नमो नमः

I went to the phone and called Deb. I apologized for coming on the wrong day and asked if we could have our meeting over the phone, as my state was fluctuating a lot. I picked up the receiver and there was this alien growling sound. It was like demons coming out of the telephone receiver into my ear.

"Be not afraid," said the inner voice, "these are the lower realms and they are disturbed right now. Trust me, all will be well!" I began to feel concerned. I felt that I was losing my connection to the third dimension as these other realms became more vivid and louder to me.

Normally, our conditioned "I" is kept so busy, hyper vigilant and preoccupied by the tasks of daily life and obligations, that this "fall" into the spiritually receptive state doesn't occur. Hence, the preponderance of humans populating the planet, all vigilantly remembering who they are.

**[Note: This extract is taken from *The Biology of Kundalini* by Jana Dixon.]

At that point, Liz arrived home. "Are you okay? You look shocked!"

I tried to explain what had happened, and Liz looked bemused. I suddenly felt isolated in my experience. She didn't understand. She was on the other side of the goldfish-bowl dimension. We started to get ready to go out to dinner. As we arrived outside Chad and Kath's house, I looked at Liz. She sat in the driver's seat. I couldn't help but stare at her face because it had started to shape-shift. Suddenly, her face split like a lightening crack. The particles of her face were like rocks parting.

In that moment, my inner voice said, "Nikki, I want you to understand that everything in this world is temporary. Let go and you will know peace!" My small self was fearful. I didn't want to let go of Liz. I relied on Liz in this dimension. You might say I was co-dependent towards her.

The experience stopped. Liz's face came back to normal and she said, "What's the matter, sweetheart? You look all shocked again?"

"It's nothing, I just…" I realized it was best not to speak. I knew she wouldn't be able to truly hear me.

We got out of the car and walked into Chad and Kath's house. Their good friends, Paul and Vicky, were at the house, too. They were all there, but I was definitely somewhere else. As we sat down to dinner, I couldn't believe my eyes. They were all suddenly wearing Egyptian costumes.

"Would you like some salad?" asked Vicky. I became fixated with the crown that she was wearing on her head. Naturally, she wasn't aware that she was wearing it. It was a coiled golden snake. Vicky had West Indian colouring and looked amazing. She wore this rare crown and a glimmering jewel at her navel. I looked across the dinner table at Paul, who was dressed like a Roman eunuch. He had a posy of flowers around his head. He was naturally pale, blond-haired and blue-eyed. But that night, I had never seen him look so innocent.

Chad was at the head of the table dressed like Cleopatra. In real time, she was inhaling smoke in circles through her modern cigarette holder. Kath was serving a casserole, oblivious to the fact that she was dressed as a Roman centurion. This was all massively entertaining for me. It was similar to watching a good movie in 3D.

"It's so great seeing everybody dressed like this!" I suddenly exclaimed.

There was a big pause. They all looked at me rather puzzled. One by one, they looked down to examine their actual attire of t-shirts and jeans.

I took a deep breath and realized, "Oh dear, they're not seeing what I am seeing!"

"You are having a past life recall, Nikki," said my inner voice. "You have been with all these people before. They are not in the same stage of awakening as you are. They will not understand what is happening to you right now. You will find later that Chad will be the most sceptical."

I looked at Chad as she inhaled another full draw of smoke. She looked like a chimney. It was surreal to watch. I snapped out of reflection mode in that instant. They brushed off my comment as some weird kind of compliment. I changed gear swiftly, finding myself slipping into a more modern, comedic lifetime of the 1930s to the 1950s. I felt the spirit of a Max Wall type of character enter into me. I sat bolt upright at the table. I started channelling some priceless comic patter. It came rushing through me in the same fashion as Mozart probably channelled inspirational classical music. I wished I had recorded it, as I can't remember any of the jokes. However, they must have been good because Paul, who was a comedy writer by profession, practically fell off his chair laughing. I realized that they all thought I was just in good form that night. They didn't realize I had journeyed through Egypt and a Victorian comedy hall all in one evening!

At 11:00 p.m., we adjourned to the sitting room, and I felt profoundly connected to a blissful vibration of love. The feeling became more and more extreme, so much so that I managed to persuade four relatively cynical people to hold hands and sing! My inner voice told me that innocence was coming back. It might take 100 years, but nonetheless, it was coming. Liz, however, elected to sit this one out. She began to wonder who she was in a relationship with as my behaviour became more and more whacky. She became frustrated with me. After all, Liz was a down-to-earth, conventional woman who had worked as a midwife and teacher for many years with the NHS.

काली दुर्गे नमो नमः

Liz was the perfect rock for me. She offered me practical care and grounded normality. It was unfortunate for her that I was unable to appreciate it at the time. I was often stifled by her presence, through no fault of her own. She stood by me as much as she could. I didn't realize what was happening to me at the time. However, months later, I realized I had undergone a radical mystical awakening – the experience of which had no bounds. The spiritual energy could not be repressed by the constraints of social conditioning. I, therefore, ignored Liz's grumpy expression. I stood in the circle, singing (arm-in-arm) with the other four guests like something out of Woodstock. We left that night with everyone in a swinging mood – everyone, that is, apart from poor Liz. She became increasingly disturbed by my unpredictable and out-there state.

The following evening, Liz and I went for a family meal with my parents and my brother Rupert. I had never experienced a night with my family with no barriers before. There was a strong love vibration present. My dad played the piano and I sang beside him, just like the old days. As my Shakti got higher, I noticed everyone in the room getting jollier.

"This is the nicest evening I've had in years," said my mum. It was as though we were like children, all giggling and laughing together.

That night, Liz and I went home to bed early, as it was a Sunday night and we had work the next day. I had to get up super early to travel all the way to Cardiff to present a fashion show.

My friend, Mark, was due to arrive at my Wandsworth flat at 7:00 a.m. to travel with me as he was to be one of the makeup artists for the models in the show. That night, I was awakened by tapping on the window.

"Nikki, Nikki let me in."

"Who is it?" I asked.

"It's Holly!" said the voice.

I went to the window and no one was there. This triggered a strong memory for me of when Holly and I were at drama school together and she had sleep-walked onto a window ledge. I had managed to coax her safely back inside after an hour of heart-thumping suspense being totally afraid that she would fall! Back in my room in Wandsworth, I anxiously thought this event was happening all over again.

As I lay in bed, I felt this tremendous juddering at the base of my spine. I didn't know what was happening to me (another symptom of Kundalini awakening). In that moment, my intuitive eye, or third eye as it is sometimes described, opened. I saw, as real as day, a very clear scene in Egypt, centuries ago, where Holly was dressed in Egyptian costume and was being tied to a pole and lashed to death by a soldier with chained straps. She was then set alight, like a brutal sacrifice. As I watched this ancient scene playing out before me, I flashed forward to this lifetime and the horrible memories of Holly's arm, which had knife scars on it from her own self-harming. In that moment, I saw the parallel connection between the two lifetimes.

My inner voice told me that this torture had happened under the instructions of my father, who, in that life, was an Egyptian leader (in another, he was a Roman emperor). My inner guidance told me that Holly and I were lovers at that time, too, only then I was male and she was female. At that time, my father had regarded her as a witch. The guidance said that his ferocious anger towards Holly had been a left-over from this previous Egyptian incarnation when we had all shared karma together. This made total sense to me as to why my dad couldn't tolerate Holly's presence in our house this lifetime. He had always considered her to be a bad influence on me. I had never seen my father quite so averse to anyone before. The degree of animosity he held towards Holly was always incredible to me. I had always felt there was a much stronger root cause to his reaction to her, and this powerful vision gave me clarity and understanding that his connection with Holly went back much further than this lifetime.

Back in my bed – in present time – the force of the pulsating energy inside me was so strong that it felt like an electric shock moving through me. I stood up and couldn't straighten my spine, so I walked, hobbling, along the corridor to the kitchen. I opened the back door and right above me I saw a bolt of lightning crack in the sky, the sight of which was of biblical proportions. It was like something out of the book of Genesis: "In the beginning was the word..." Two of our dustbins were rolling around furiously in the yard. I was terrified that I was in the middle of a hurricane. I was petrified. How could I possibly be experiencing this? I was in the middle of my back garden in Wandsworth, London. It seemed impossible to me, as I had not taken any drugs or alcohol for two months for that to have affected my judgement.

काली दुर्गे नमो नमः

The force of the gale was so strong that I had to force the door shut. (I have no idea to this day whether anyone else was experiencing this weather condition in current time.) I managed to slam the door shut when something extraordinary happened. I heard an intense, snake-like hissing noise. I looked down at my ankles and Bluesy, my cat, started to circle, coiling around me faster and faster like a snake. The energy inside me shot up through the back of my neck and into the front of my forehead. I clearly saw a snake shooting out of the front of my head, like one of those Egyptian god heads. I rushed into the bathroom and looked in the mirror. My eyes looked wired and my hair was standing up on end like Shakespeare's King Lear in his madness scene.

Suddenly, my apartment doorbell rang. It was Mark, the make-up artist. Mark had arrived to accompany me to Cardiff for the fashion show.

My inner guidance spoke: "Mark is your guardian angel for today. Do not permit him to leave your side; he will protect you!"

Mark really did look like an angel that day. He had long curly hair that he had dyed purple, a bit like that children's programme on TV called *Chrystal Tips and Alastair* where the main character had wild frizzy purple hair. I asked Mark to wait while I got dressed. At this point, he had no idea that I was in a strange state of mind. Liz was still fast asleep. I looked at her knowing that I was about to go on a huge journey. It felt like I really didn't know whether I would ever come home again. After all, I had already travelled between so many lifetimes – who could tell where I would end up next?

I leant over Liz's shoulder and whispered in her ear, "I am going now, and I may be some time!" I kissed her on the head, then Mark and I left the flat. We proceeded to walk towards East Putney station.

As we walked along the street together, I encountered an extraordinary experience. It felt as though we were the only two people who were fully alive. Everyone else around us appeared to be walking but dead – and they didn't realize it. As we arrived on the platform, the train pulled in. On the front of the train I saw plain as day "HEAVEN-BOUND."

"Wow! Do you see that Mark? It says heaven-bound!"

"No it doesn't!" he replied. "It says Dagenham East!"

I realized, once again, that Mark was not in the same realm as me, which was so confusing to keep remembering. I looked up and down the carriage at all the people on their journey to work. For the first time, I saw them as souls instead of bodies with attributes. I could see clearly one continuous pulsating energy, threading everybody together. I could see there was a governing energy operating equally in everybody. However, the people did not seem to realize it.

Mark and I arrived in High Street, Kensington, where our coach was waiting for us. We stood outside the tube waiting for this special private coach to Cardiff that was transporting all the models onboard for the fashion show. I looked at my watch to check the time. This object strapped to my wrist was supposed to measure all time? I started to laugh. It seemed comical to me. Having a man-made clock to represent all time was a ridiculous concept. My awareness was NOW, infinitely expanding. It would have been more realistic if the watch face had said, "Now! Now! Now!"

The coach arrived and I sat in a double seat next to Mark. The coach pulled out of London and passed a parade of West End theatres. I had the most surreal *Back to the Future* experience for that brief moment. We had a long trip ahead of us on the coach, but I was immersed in a time warp as I gazed out of the window. The year we were in was actually 1989. However, it was occurring for me as though we were living as far back as the 1940s. As I looked out of the coach window as we drove through the West End, it was like looking out at London from a completely different perspective.

"I remember playing in a musical based on a book by Charles Dickens at the Savoy Theatre," I thought to myself as we drove past. This was where I had performed in 1987. Although it seemed decades ago, not just two years. "I wonder what was playing at the Savoy then," I said out loud. It was as though I was taking a ride through history, like something out of H.G. Wells' *The Time Machine*. I glanced down at a newspaper, on the seat next to me on the bus. I didn't need to read it because it looked like old news from ancient press cuttings. I read a section of an article and, although it was today's news, I knew it already – like revising historical events. In my eyes, I was in infinite time. The bus left the West End and drove along the embankment where we passed Battersea Park. I saw the Pagoda of the Buddha where I had walked the previous weekend. In that moment, I realized that I was back in current time, February 1989.

My inner voice starting speaking again. "Look, look, Nikki, look at the Buddha; see this symbol of peace. Do you see the East is meeting the West? This is the way of the future; the qualities of both worlds are uniting. They tried it in the 1960s," the voice said, "but everyone got lost in the drugs and flower power. The state of self-realization has to be attained naturally. We are in a new era, a transformational era. Watch and see."

I tried to share what I was hearing from inside me with Mark. He just looked at me confused, but nodded politely anyway.

He said, "Are you all right, Nikki?" It was frustrating that he wasn't on the same page as me, as everything the voice was saying sounded so plausible.

काली दुर्गे नमो नमः

As we journeyed out of London, my state of mind heightened even further. I started to look at the TV monitor at the front of the bus. Right there, staring at me from the screen, I could vividly see the form of my spiritual master.

She appeared to me in that moment like a newsreader, at which point my inner voice said to me, "Listen carefully, Nikki! No one else on the bus can see her form on that screen, only you. Watch closely and I will show you something. Now, I want you to look closely at her hands." My teacher was Indian and her hands were long and slender. Her thumb was notably curved in a beautiful arc shape. She had the hands of a healer. Her appearance made me think of Holly. I suddenly recognized that Holly actually resembled my spiritual teacher. She also had the same shaped hands and arched thumb. I realized that Holly had come into my life for a reason. It was no accident that these visions were now appearing. Holly and my spiritual teacher definitely shared similar characteristics. How surreal it was for me to see the visual connections between my spiritual master and Holly.

I then had a massive a-ha moment. Holly's surname was similarly spelt to the term given to a potent fertility symbol of spiritual awakening in Hinduism. In that moment, I knew with certainty that our relationship had not been a mistake and, indeed, that no relationship in my life was merely incidental. As I looked back at the TV screen, my inner voice pointed my attention to my spiritual teacher's root chakra – the centre at the base of the spine. I saw, inside this centre, a tiny form of Holly seated there.

My inner voice began to instruct me again. "For every chakra that you pass through, Nikki, on your inner journey, there will be a significant relationship for you to learn your lessons with. This will last until you merge into oneness at the sahasra, or crown chakra, where I dwell eternally. At this point, you will become established in your inner Self and you will transcend the need for an attachment to an outer relationship."

This download was overwhelming to take in and, although it occurred as far-fetched, there was an inner comprehension for me that it was true. At the moment this teaching had been given to me, the vision of my spiritual master disappeared from the screen just like the good witch of the north in her bubble from *The Wizard of Oz*.

The bus then made its first stop at a service station as we crossed the border of Wales. The sun-scape in the sky was of glorious pinks, oranges and lemon-yellows, and I felt myself drop inwardly into a state of absolute oneness with everyone and everything in the universe.

Fearlessly, I stood up in the coach and started to address the models. "Do you see all this beauty, everyone? Isn't it incredible? Do you see the connection between all of us, and our connection to the sky?"

The models looked puzzled by me, but strangely allured as there was very strong Shakti (conscious divine energy) emanating through me. It made them smile happily back at me.

They all looked at me with so much love. I felt like I could have said anything to anyone in the world at that moment. The power that came through me felt like I could stop wars. Even the darkest of souls couldn't have disturbed my ecstatic state in that moment. This was the freedom I had been looking for all my life in drink, drugs, fantasies and outer relationships. I was experiencing my own inner bliss and, what is more, I was communicating with other people whilst remaining connected to that delicious space. I will remember that moment as long as I live.

We drove on into Cardiff. Outside in the traffic, someone's car radio was playing a Paul McCartney track. It was *Magical Mystery Tour*. I felt that I, myself, was onboard the *Magical Mystery Tour* in this bus. I had an inherent knowing that the Beatles, especially John Lennon and George Harrison, had experienced this type of spiritual connection in their initiation from Maharishi Mahesh Yogi and George's later journey with the Hare Krishna movement.

Our host on the bus was called John. He was the manager, taking care of all the fashion show models. He piped up on the loud speaker: "Okay, everyone! We have arrived at the Cardiff conference centre! Please file off the bus and we will all meet in the reception area."

I felt like I had walked into a futuristic dream – and in many ways I had. The building was neon and modern. All the models were directed to side rooms to iron their clothes for the fashion parade. This event was one of the early heats for the well-known eighties TV programme *The Clothes Show* and was to be filmed by the BBC. I saw everyone ironing, and it reminded me of seva – or selfless service. This was service performed every Thursday evening at the centre where we have our weekly meetings or satsangs. The seva could be, for example, ironing clothes, making tea, setting up the audio or welcoming people.

I immediately wanted to offer seva. "What can I do to help?" I asked.

"I'm going to buy sandwiches for the models. Do you want to come with me?" asked a helper named Karen.

"Great, I'll come with you," I said.

As we left the building, it began to rain. I was looking down at grey pavements when suddenly I felt that pulsating expansive feeling again, where my inner eye opened once again. Whereupon a vast red carpet appeared before me and a golden Roman palace with chariots parked in front. I was dressed in armour, like a warrior soldier in a scene with Charlton Heston from the classic *Ben Hur*!

Suddenly, I was actually walking up the carpet as my inner voice said, "When you reach the top of the steps," – which looked miles away – "you must bow to your master like the ancient tradition of heraldry."

I could see the golden throne in the distance with an emperor figure sitting there. I took my first step towards him, and as I looked down at my feet, to my dismay, I saw rain splattering on a concrete grey pavement. The red carpet had vanished and I was back in Cardiff.

काली दुर्गे नमो नमः

Meanwhile, Karen had been chattering away to me all that time, but I hadn't actually heard a word she said. She was oblivious that I had been to ancient Rome and back all in the space of ten minutes! We arrived at the sandwich kiosk and picked fifty sandwiches, at which point I said to Karen that I wanted to take a walk.

"Don't be long," Karen exclaimed as she headed back to the conference centre.

In truth, I wanted to find the red carpet again. Where would I look? Perhaps the nearest church would know, I thought.

I stopped a local Welsh man. I asked him, "Where do I go for the nearest church?"

"Straight ahead, love," he said.

I kept walking, about a mile, until I reached the church. I walked inside and looked at all the pictures of Christ, St. Frances, Mother Mary and various saints on the walls. I was willing them all to take me back to the blissful red carpet. Sadly, they all stared back motionless out of their stained glass faces, giving me no clue as to how to get back to my mystical dimension.

Despondently, I started crying and turned to walk back to the conference centre. Suddenly, I panicked as I had lost all track of time; in fact, I was out of time. I stopped off at a phone box, not knowing what was happening to me. Prophetic images were coming into my mind thick and fast. I was losing all sense of this current time reality. I thought I was fifty years or more into the future. My stomach leapt into a somersault of shock. If that is the case, my mother would surely be dead? I started to panic. I needed to check. I fled into a phone box to dial my best friend, Melvyn, from drama school.

"Hey, Mel! Please don't ask me questions, but I am in Cardiff, somewhere in the future. I need you to call my mum to ask if she is still alive."

"Nicola, are you all right?" asked Mel.

"Just do it!" I said. "I will call you back in an hour." I hung up the phone.

I arrived back at the conference centre, apparently two hours later, everyone had been searching for me. I was really late for the technical rehearsal.

Deb looked livid when I arrived and said, "Where have you been, Nikki? Quickly get changed and come to the stage."

Mark accompanied me to the dressing room, and I promptly slapped some makeup on my face. I felt strangely surreal, but also extremely powerful beyond the confines of conditioning and rules which just couldn't constrain me. I walked to the stage feeling as expanded as the ocean itself when suddenly this incredible rumbling sound of a volcano bubbled up from within me. Its immense force propelled me onto the stage like a Greek muse. As I opened my mouth, it felt as though the whole universe was speaking through me.

"MOTHER EARTH IS WEEPING! WE MUST ACT NOW!" boomed my voice throughout the auditorium. My voice echoed like the wizard in *The Wizard of Oz*. The microphones in the auditorium were switched on and were amplifying my voice a thousand-fold from the stage!

In 2014, as I reflected back on that extraordinary time, I recognized that back then, in 1989, I was actually receiving Nostradamus-type prophecies of many of the natural disasters that were about to rock the world: the Tsunami, Pakistan, New Orleans, Florida, Granada, etc. Back in the conference centre, as my words echoed through the auditorium, I noticed the stunned faces of the cameramen in the conference hall. My outburst visibly shocked everyone, as naturally I was not scripted to say this in the fashion show tech dress rehearsal! Even the models in costumes couldn't understand what had just happened. I stared intensely at the models. In the midst of a Kundalini awakening, it is possible to see events in the future before they happen; supreme consciousness is beyond time and has no future. It is always now.

My inner voice was saying, "The East is meeting the West, Nikki!" The energy within me was so liberated that I began rejoicing by singing freely on the stage. I was totally free from all inhibition. It felt absolutely incredible. I also noticed at that point that there were large TV cameras filming me. I later discovered that the BBC crew thought that my spectacular interruption had been a deliberately staged disruption to be used in training as a method for the conference centre to practice what to do in a crisis!

Deb came rushing over and said, "Nikki, you must stop singing. This is a dress rehearsal. Go over and see John. He has the script. You are on in a moment." John was the show manager with the bald head (from the bus journey) I spoke of earlier.

"John is your Buddha for the day," said the inner voice. "He will understand your state of consciousness. He gets who you are. You can trust him."

John gave me the script. He told me that I would be the host introducing each section. The first section was entitled *Chasing the Dragon*. This title seriously reactivated me. I had images of addicts inhaling liquid heroine on tin foil. I was particularly sensitive as I had seen Holly's roommate do it some years back. This habit had slowly destroyed him.

"You cannot call it that name, John!" I said. "It doesn't feel right!" I explained to him why. I recalled, once again, the inner guidance that I had received on the bus about us now all being in a progressive movement of consciousness that would leave behind the drug abusing culture of the sixties and seventies.

John looked at me with gentle care and said, "Okay, then what would you like to call it, Nikki?"

"Err, how about *Chasing the Flower*?" I said.

काली दुर्गे नमो नमः

"Okay, no problem," he said softy. "I will let Deb know we are editing the script for you." He was the first person I felt truly heard me, and who didn't think I was mad in my wavering state. He went away for a few minutes, and I immediately started singing again. I didn't care what all the cameramen and models thought of me. I was in a reality where there were no boundaries and no limits to what was possible. In fact, in that transcendental state of consciousness, all structures and social conditioning seem utterly futile. It felt like trying to stop a tsunami with a little finger! I realized that when the Divine Mother Nature moves through you, you just have to flow with her or you feel like you are pushing a seven-story block of apartments uphill. I didn't intend to be deliberately aggressive or rebellious. It just felt completely natural to me to express every spontaneous movement of the Shakti inside me to the outside world. Therefore, when I felt like singing, I just did. The times of secretly singing alone as a child in the woods were now but a distant memory. I was totally free.

Deb came onto the stage once again, and this time she was furious. In that moment, she became the force of order. It was her job to make sure the show ran smoothly without any fuss.

"Nikki, you've got to stop this. I'm going to give you thirty minutes to calm down in your dressing room! Then we will start the full dress technical rehearsal again!" she said sharply. She was panicking because the rehearsal had lost time. She had a show to put on. Deb sent me to the dressing room and instructed Mark to stay with me.

Mark and I sat together in a small side room with a dressing table, long mirror and toilet. I implored Mark to never leave my side. My inner guidance had told me since we left early that morning that Mark was my angel and that I must not be on my own for the rest of the day, as it would be unsafe for me. Mark definitely was my guardian angel that day, and my inner guidance was so right. I sat closely by his side in the dressing room. It was in that moment that I experienced a miracle. I saw his ear transform right before me! It changed before my very eyes into the ear of a god. In fact, his whole body then transformed. He looked just like TARA, the female form of Buddha.

"Listen," said the inner voice, "the gods are listening to you. We want you to know that Mark is a very high soul. He doesn't realize it now because he is in the delusion of this dimension. He is too sensitive to live free from the drink and drug scene in this realm."

I kept asking Mark if he could relate to me seeing him as a god – if he could at least understand what I was experiencing. Mark said he couldn't exactly understand, however, he could appreciate that I was having this experience. He was so kind to me, and extremely patient. Sadly, Mark never got to be the makeup artist that he had been hired for that day; instead, he was to be my guardian angel. I knew he had been divinely assigned that role in service to me that day, and I am eternally grateful to him for being there.

The inner eruptions continued in the dressing room. It was traumatic for me. I could see into the future and I was having bad future experiences, projecting the time when my mother would inevitably die. I stood up in front of the long mirror. I saw myself shape shifting back and forth in the mirror between being me and being my mother.

I cried uncontrollably out loud, "Mummy!" I couldn't believe she had died without me having the chance to say goodbye. I begged Mark to get me a phone. I just had to call her to make sure she really was dead.

Mark knew not to leave me, so he beckoned to someone to get a manager from the conference centre. A lovely lady called Liz appeared. I knew her name because of her badge. I connected to her because of my Liz at home.

My inner voice said, "My Liz was sent to me in this life to nurse me into recovery from my shaky past. You won't be with her for long this life, as she lives in a different vibrational realm from you. However, you will be together in your next life. You will owe her one. The next time you will be a man and she will be a woman – all is well."

Liz, the manager, took me into a room with a phone. We didn't have mobiles then. I dialled the number. There were a few rings, when, to my utter relief, my mother answered.

"Hello? Hello, darling, is that you?" she asked. I actually seriously wondered if I was communicating with her spirit only and that it was trapped in the telephone line.

"I'm so happy you are alive!" I exclaimed.

"Are you all right? Mel called me earlier. Yes, of course I am alive. Where are you?" Mum replied.

"I am in Cardiff somewhere," I said, "is there anyone with you? You don't sound all right."

I passed the phone to Liz, who explained to my mother there was a lot of concern about my behaviour at the conference centre. She asked my mother if there was any chance my parents could come and fetch me. At that point, I didn't realize my parents were on their way to Cardiff.

काली दुर्गे नमो नमः

Mark escorted me back to the dressing room. Deb came to the room and said that a decision had been made not to include me in the show. Deb said that Mark would be staying with me and someone else would cover his make-up role. We must have both stayed in the dressing room for another five hours whilst my folks drove across to Cardiff from London. As I sat there, I kept receiving these insane downloads about the mass control that the British government had. My inner voice revealed that the human race was being brainwashed through food additives as a way to sedate us from our power and authority. Recent research has discovered that more and more evidence points towards the negative effects of food additives, so there was some rational truth to what I heard.

In fact, the guidance was so strong that day that I told Mark not to drink his bottled water because it had been programmed to make us addicted. I refused to drink anything out of a bottle all day – only from the sink. Suddenly, there was a knock at the door. It was Liz, the conference manager. She had brought a doctor with her.

He had on a tweed jacket and glasses, and he began quizzing me with a barrage of questions: What's your name? Where do you live? What do you do? Where are you now? I answered all his questions accurately. He had a very intimidating stare and a very judgmental attitude.

"Are you on drugs?" he said.

"NO AND NO AND NO!" I replied.

Still not contented with my answers, he asked me the entire sequence of questions again!

My inner voice said, "No one will hear you or understand you in this space. They can only judge you by what they already know. What they see now is a person who appears to be nuts. They are ignorant and cannot help it. Release your judgement, Nikki."

My parents finally arrived after five hours. They were exhausted, having travelled all the way from East Sheen in London. My mother was shaking and inhaling cigarette smoke very fast and furiously. Once more, my intuitive eye opened and I saw an incredible sight, where I was staring right into her lungs like I had x-ray vision. I could specifically see the destructive effect the smoke was having on her lungs in graphic detail, like a David Attenborough film in close up.

I screamed out, "STOP SMOKING, IT'S KILLING YOU!"

She never smoked again after that. There must have been something in my tone of voice.

It was now time to finally leave Cardiff. I said goodbye to Mark. I remember feeling sad letting him go. The conference staff were mightily relieved to see me go, and Deb dropped her anger momentarily and wished me well. The drive back to London was perilous – my poor parents. As I sat in the back of the car, I started receiving constant downloads through my crown chakra or top energy centre. It was my spirit family talking to me – or at least, that's who they said they were. They felt enormous – like gods watching over me. In fact, they showed me a vision of how tiny the earth was in comparison to the other realms. It felt like we were driving a Tonka toy car with these huge King-Kong-sized beings, pushing us down the M4 like in the old black-and-white King Kong movies.

They said to me, "Hey! How's our Nik? Are you ready to come home yet? You can if you want to. You signed up for this, so you can stop it." As I heard their voices, I was suddenly transported back to very early childhood, when I had wondered why I had felt like such an oddball, and how I had wondered whether an alien would one day come down to earth to take me back home. Well, perhaps now the moment had arrived when they had finally come! That said, I knew it wasn't my time to leave Planet Earth. However, it was somehow really comforting to know that I had the option. It was such a relief to me that there was a bigger picture behind this vacuous earth-walk that I had been engaged in.

We pulled over into a petrol station, and my mum got out of the car to use the bathroom. I started to madly panic that if she left the car she would die. I was obsessed with her dying that day. I began shouting out very loudly, several times with my father trying to supress me.

"Through Jesus Christ our Lord! Through Jesus Christ our Lord!" came loudly out of my mouth. I was surprised that Jesus's name came that clearly as I had never been remotely religious. I watched my mother walk into the garage toward the loo, terrified she would never come back. As I now reflect, I was going through a fast-track experience of non-attachment that day, even though, physically, my mother is still very much alive all these years later. The grief I felt in that period of her possibly dying was unbearable. I saw so clearly that my mother was my soul ally in this life. Our bond is precious and eternal and whatever challenges our relationship has had in this life, I see now what a perfect set-up for my soul's journey our relationship has been. My mother selflessly gave her life for me and, when I saw that fact when the veil was taken from my eyes, I wept in recognition of her eternal love and service to me. This traumatic experience has profoundly prepared me for her inevitable future passing.

काली दुर्गे नमो नमः

After a very turbulent five-hour journey, we finally arrived back at my parents' home in East Sheen. I was sitting on their sofa in their front room when my spirit family started speaking to me again. They made me laugh as they were communicating in a tapping language like Martians. I started laughing as I tapped my head in response to them, and then they would tap me back through my subtle body awareness. My dad was, understandably, really concerned watching my outward madness and went to call the family GP, Dr. Hazel, who had known me since childhood.

Dr. Hazel arrived and started questioning me in a much more gentle fashion than the Cardiff doctor. I was extremely lucid in my responses and, in a very down to earth manner, I told her that I had been speaking with Martians!

"Ah ah," said Hazel. She managed to stay professional and detached. "Look, I think it's important that you sleep, Nicola, so I am going to give you some sleeping tablets to take. See how you go and I will pop by in the morning." I eventually went up to bed, with pills inside me, when I had another rush of energy through my spine. I started speaking very fast and jumped up and down on the bed in my nightdress.

My dad started shouting and told me to lie down, to which I roared, "No! I won't lie down! You can't tell me what to do now! You are not in control!" That was the first time I had ever stood up to my father from a space of internal power. It felt extraordinary to be in that space, and he knew he was powerless over me in that moment. I ran down the stairs to the kitchen, by which time my partner Liz had arrived. At that point, I heard the spirit voice of my parents' deceased neighbour, Mrs. Hall, channelling into me. I felt like a trance medium for the dead. My parents never got on with this woman. I started channelling her voice very loudly, shouting, "MR. SLADE. How dare you?"

My father looked helpless at this point, and Liz (who had done psychiatric nursing in her time) said, "Adrian, it's not safe for Nikki to be here. I'm afraid we need to admit her into hospital!"

Years later, I met with Dr. Andrew Powell from the Royal College of Psychiatry for a business lunch. He said that, in his view, there is a crossover between those rare individuals who have the gift of being a trance medium and those who are being diagnosed with schizophrenia. He said the challenge is, even if the truth is that some people are mediums, if they cannot ground themselves and are identifying with destructive voices which are negatively impacting those around them, then that is when medical intervention becomes essential for the sake of everyone concerned.

Dr. Hazel returned and, before I knew it, an ambulance arrived. I was dressed in a red spotted dressing gown. The ambulance men came to our front door and I had an immediate (past life) recall of some hideous rape I had experienced with two men. I was fearful. I thought I would be dragged into the woods and it would happen all over again. I started hissing furiously and pointed to one of the ambulance men's genitals. I can't imagine how this poor man must have felt, innocently standing on the doorstep of a smart house in East Sheen. I swooned into a faint on the top step outside my parents' front door. In that moment, I saw a vision of Jesus Christ's crucifixion as I looked down at my own feet. The sandals I was wearing suddenly occurred like something out of Nazareth. I was soon sitting with Liz inside the ambulance. I looked down at my left hand, in particular at the ring she had given me to acknowledge our relationship. I looked at it with sadness because I knew our relationship was going to end. I took it off and dropped it carelessly onto the floor.

Liz looked hurt, yet managed to remain in her nursing mode. I didn't know where the ambulance was taking me. The voice in my head told me that I was going to a place run by the government, where you go for knowing too much and for speaking uncomfortable truths. Instead, we arrived at a vast Victorian mental institution in Epsom, Surrey.

As we drove through the grounds, I shook as I saw all the trees and prayed in my heart that I wasn't going to be raped in a forest again. I was driven to A Block, which apparently was where they section people who are diagnosed insane and unsafe to themselves and the outside world. I remember standing in an office with at least three people in white coats. My father was there with them, deciding what treatment should be prescribed to me. As I stood there inside the psychiatrist's office, I had an instant past life recall experience. I saw flames coming up from the ground and I started shaking my head with fright from side to side. I thought I was being burnt at the stake for speaking out loud.

काली दुर्गे नमो नमः

I stood against the wall in the office of the A Block hospital wing when my inner guidance revealed to me that my father had sentenced me to death in a past life. He was squaring his debt by giving me life this time. It suddenly all made sense. He adored me and had always expressed his love by being incredibly generous materially. Yet we never saw eye to eye on our view of life. Our fundamental clash has always been our differing values. My father's values have been to change the world through politics, and mine have been to transform the world by each individual turning within and connecting to the inner self.

The great irony and paradox is that, in truth, we have both shared the same value of wanting a better world – one that works – but we have approached it from opposite sides. My vision soared. I saw that we were in Rome, where I was a mystical Christian and he was like Caesar with enormous political power. He had the power that could have me killed for my inner conviction. He objected to my mystical truths and for speaking out. In that moment of immense revelation in the hospital office, I suddenly saw again the mythical flames of my past life torture around me.

My dad was taken to a room adjunct to the office and the doctor left the door open. I could hear dad being asked whether, if necessary, he would agree to me having electric shock treatment. My father flatly declined.

My inner guidance spoke again. "Your father is reversing his karma for the better with you this time around. He may not understand you, but all will be well between you two in the end!"

However, in that moment, the impact of my father's debt to me was incredibly real and painful to behold.

The doctors came towards me with liquid largactil (an archaic sedation drug) to drink.

"Shit," I thought, "not more drugs!" Only this time, they were legal ones. I chucked the medication beaker onto the ground and glared defiantly at the faces of all three white-coated psychiatrists in the room, at which point I was pulled into a wheelchair and strapped in. I remember being wheeled to the other side of the glass window of this office with my parents standing on the other side of the glass looking at me with dismay.

The inner voice said, "You have entered a new dimension, Nikki. You will never dwell in the same realm as your parents again."

For a moment, I felt sad as I left my mum and dad forever on the other side of the glass. I felt a little like Alice through the looking glass. How could I ever explain coherently which dimension I was in? The two nurses who wheeled me were very small and reminded me of two hobbits. They wheeled me into Ross Ward in the basement, which was apparently where all the insane people go.

The hobbits came towards me with a syringe. I leapt up with athleticism due to the Kundalini energy that was coursing through me. I jumped and started climbing along the curtain rails of the beds like a little monkey. The two hobbits were chasing me from the ground and, suddenly, I saw a flashback of me in that same previous life running through Rome in a white robe and sandals. Roman soldiers in leather tunics were chasing me with whips and mastiff dogs. They caught up with me and hauled me to the ground. I was taken back to the ward. As the nurses twisted my arm back, I had a flashback of my arm being twisted behind my back and me being crippled. The nurses injected me with this horrific medicine, largactil, and I conked out like a light.

Approximately forty-eight hours later, I woke up in a straitjacket inside a padded cell with a blue nightgown that stank of urine – probably my own. I barely remember it because the drugs were so intense. Apparently, Liz came with my family to visit. I didn't recognize them. I eventually came around when a tall Jamaican nurse called Fred let me out of the cell. I will never forget him; he was the kindest man and treated me with so much dignity. He showed me to my bed, which was crisply waiting for me in a long ward of beds. That night, the energy in my spine started surging once again as I lay in bed. I had an inner vision of a huge army tank coming up the driveway. It had a canon on the front, ready to fire!

As I lay there, I knew I was simultaneously living in two realities. At any minute I felt I would be taken out of my bed to the front of the building and shot by the army tank. I was breathing heavily. I must have been sighing loudly, too, as my neighbour in the bed next door came to the side of my bed. She was a tall African woman called Julie.

"Are you okay, dear?" she said.

"I'm going to die soon," I said.

"Don't speak that way, there's no way you're going to die now," she said. Her face abruptly morphed into a male face that I had seen before.

"You won't rape me will you?" I said.

"Are you kidding me? Mind your tongue!" she said. "I am Julie, and I am no lesbian!"

काली दुर्गे नमो नमः

The next moment, again like Alice's experiences of walking through the looking glass, I found myself, once again, in an altered dimension that was as real an experience for me as people who declare that they see ghosts. It also reminded me of the episode I wrote about earlier in Cardiff, of one moment walking in an actual ordinary high street and the next moment being propelled into another dimension where I was walking on a red carpet in a *Ben Hur* epic-like film. I was now in an altered dimension once again – which was as real to me as the hospital bed I was lying in. I walked out of the front door of the hospital main entrance in my red spotted dressing gown, whereupon I saw a huge tank advancing towards me that promptly blew me into tiny pieces. Years later, as I progressed further on my meditation path, I realized that I had gone through a classic death of the ego, symbolized by the graphic appearance of the tank.

The following day, to my astonishment, I woke up in crisp, pristine sheets in a pale blue new nightdress to the potent smell of flowers. I felt that I must have died and gone to heaven. I looked at my bedside table where there was a vase made of white china in the shape of a cat with pink carnations in it. This had not been there before. The perfume from the flowers was overpowering. I stepped out of my bed and looked into my bedside table mirror. My eyes were the most royal blue I had ever seen.

"Am I in heaven?" I asked my inner voice.

"No, but you have been through a rebirth," the voice replied. "Your old self died last night. The Nicola as you knew her is no more. We want you to know that the only 'real' thing in life is your spirit, which is eternally free."

As I listened to this voice, I felt crystal clear inside. I felt as if I was sitting serenely in an English country garden. It was an incredible feeling – so innocent, like a newborn baby.

In that moment, a very friendly, matronly nurse appeared at the foot of my bed. She had piercing blue eyes and a round face with her hair neatly set.

"Now then, dear, we just need to do a little routine check-up. Please kindly roll up your sleeves." As she spoke, she began to tap my body all over with a medical instrument. It felt to me like she was seeing if I was cooked or not. "Ummmm," she said to her junior assistant, "she's not ready yet!"

"Ready for what?" I wondered. She magically disappeared from my view with a sweet smell of roses around her. Shortly after, the duty nurse came by my bed and I asked her, "Who was the matron that smelled of roses who has just visited me?"

The duty nurse looked puzzled and said, "Nikki, I am the only nurse on duty this morning. There must be some mistake."

As the duty nurse left my bedside, my inner guidance revealed to me that the matron was not a physical being (an earth-bound soul); she was, in truth, a spirit doctor from the spirit realm. Her mission with me was apparently to determine whether my time here on Earth was up yet. It clearly was not my time as I never saw her again during my stay in Epsom hospital.

From that day forth at the hospital, I was living in a state of grace. It felt like an exquisite reprieve from the burdens of this world. One afternoon, I was inspired to take a walk and explore the breadth of the hospital. I had never ventured beyond my own ward before, so I walked what felt like a long way into one of the lower ground wards, where the elderly indefinite long-term patients lived. There were rows and rows of beds with white-haired patients in them. These men and women had been institutionalized for years and lay in their beds, gazing into space.

I saw a very old woman with her hair scraped back in a bun and pimples on her face. I was guided to approach her and I felt this soft energy coming through me that wanted to bring light to her. I kissed her on her forehead and said, "It's okay. There is peace waiting for you!" I will never forget her face. It must have been previously frozen for goodness knows how long. She suddenly cracked into half a smile, making a strange gurgling sound in appreciation that someone had made time for her. I was grateful for those words that came through me. It felt like an honour to be a messenger for her.

I decided to go for an amble outside the ward door, where there was an enclosed garden. Nobody saw me, so I slipped out through the door and a most extraordinary thing happened. I stood by a large oak tree when three wild rabbits came straight over to me as if they were tame house pets. They sat at my feet – one even sat on my shoe. The grace that poured through me in that moment was extraordinary. My inner voice told me that this was the state that Francis of Assisi had experienced. He had always had unique relationships with animals. The ecstasy that was moving through me seemed to magnetize all the creatures around who came so close that one felt safe enough to perch on the edge of my shoe. I wished, in that moment, I had a camera to capture the scene. However, I understood that this was a divine blessing.

The next day was a bright morning, and I decided that it would be nice day for me to begin a daily chanting practice routine on the ward. One night I couldn't sleep, and neither could Sue who was three beds up from me. Sue was a cockney woman about forty years old. She was pale with blue eyes and spikey bleach-blonde hair. I leant over and said to her, "I am going to ask the night nurse if we can sing in the dining room! Are you up for it?"

Sue looked puzzled at first, then she got really excited at the idea. She said she'd been bored all day and had ended up cutting her hair.

काली दुर्गे नमो नमः

I could see that by looking at her slanted and crooked fringe. We started giggling as we walked towards the nurses' office. We were in luck as the friendly Filipino was the nurse on duty that night. She was always warm and friendly.

"We want to sing," we said, "in the dining room. Will you unlock the door for us?"

She smiled and said in her strong Filipino accent, "So, you want sing?"

A broad smile stretched her face as she led us into the dining room. I could feel that she had a soft spot for us, which was nice. She locked the door behind her and she could see us through her office window.

I stood up on the table and began singing my favourite all time tunes, ranging from Judy Garland to Tina Turner and then went on to a devotional chant. Suddenly, before my very eyes, the most beautiful thing happened. A perfect trail of rose petals manifested on the ground, making its journey all the way to the dining room door.

"Wow! Do you see that, Sue?"

My inner voice whispered, "Nikki, this path of roses is the path to the great SELF. Follow it and it will take you home!"

Sue replied, "Yeah, I can see it!" in her broad cockney accent (whether she really did I will never know).

"We're going to get out of here!" I said. "We're going to get out of this ward and into the garden of freedom! Are you ready, Sue?"

The hospital rules were very clear about where you were allowed to walk when on a section. We were only allowed to visit the gardens if we were accompanied at all times. We both started following the rose petals in a mindfulness trance, like Pooh and Piglet following footprints in the snow. I remember the excitement I felt as I stepped onto the petals. I felt like I was about to step into a great light like Gandalf from *Lord of The Rings*. At that point, we were disturbed as the nurse's keys jangled outside. We had only just reached the dining room exit when the nurse abruptly entered. Sadly, all the petals vanished instantly. My inner voice revealed that because this nurse was not living in this subtle dimension, the petals couldn't remain.

"Okay, ladies, singing time is over, time for bed!" she said again in her strong Filipino accent.

Over the next few days, I felt very perky on the ward. I had a spring in my step. I felt connected to the whole universe. I was longing to be let out into the garden for a walk. The garden always represented freedom to me, and getting better. All the "sick" people, like Sid, were permanently on a section and never allowed out. I had been asking for days but the hospital staff kept saying, "You can go out when you get better, Nikki." The man on duty that day was called Andy. He used to call me David Bowie because I had ginger streaks in my hair and a spiky haircut. I liked Andy and decided to pluck up the courage to ask him if I could go out.

I had been looking at the bunches of keys the staff always had on cords around their necks or belts, thinking to myself, "These people have the keys to my freedom; one day they will open the door for me." Andy was sitting at his desk doing the football pools. I remember having a surreal conversation with him about football. I seemed to know a lot more than I thought, or was it spirits giving me inside information?

Andy looked up from his desk, intrigued at my chatter and said, "Okay, David, you can go for a walk, but I am going to ask one of the staff members to go with you." He took me downstairs to the garden entrance. I will never forget the Chinese man in a uniform greeting me at the door. He was to escort me as I walked through the grounds.

My heart started thumping as I saw his uniform. I immediately thought that he was a policeman. I was obsessed with the thought that he had come from the "thought police!" I thought I had been set up to be interrogated as to my journey with drugs and that I was going to be tortured, or that my loved ones would be, if I didn't grass someone up as a dealer. He kept asking me questions about my past. My head told me that it was critically important that I mustn't think of the word drugs. Otherwise, he would surely arrest me. This was a tall order to never think of drugs, so I would keep shouting out "bananas" every time I was in danger of saying, or even thinking, the word "drugs". I was convinced he was a policeman. The police could be corrupt sometimes, too, I thought.

Upon reflection, this stage of my journey was the Kundalini energy expelling the paranoia and fears around drug abuse from my past. The divine energy was giving me powerful warnings to never go down that path again, otherwise the future that was shown me would be full of danger, with life threats to loved ones and, ultimately, death. The fear was so intense, I swore in that moment I would do anything to be free of that bondage.

My inner voice whispered, "Remember, your granny died a miserable death through alcoholism. You do not have to follow that path. You have a choice, Nikki. You can either take a spiritual recovery path, or you can remain in terror. Which do you choose? You have free will."

काली दुर्गे नमो नमः

To deflect the paranoia I was experiencing at the very thought of being arrested for my hedonistic past by this policeman who, in fact, was an unassuming hospital security guard, I shifted into another brilliant and spontaneous comedy routine. It was very similar to when I had dinner with Paul and Vicky when they were all in Egyptian costume and I became like the great comedian Max Wall. The routine was that I had to get ahead of the thought police. The comedy routine was to outwit the thought police in case they heard the word drugs in my head. Instead, I used the word "bananas" for drugs, spoken ten to the dozen and very fast, every time drugs entered my head. It was a massive achievement to keep up! The security guy in uniform thought I was hilarious. In fact, at one point, he rolled around on the ground in front of me in hysterics. I must have been funny. However, I couldn't actually remember a single word of what I said, but I do know that it felt like a virtual reality performance with the essence of a Richard Prior solo show.

When we arrived back, I was standing outside the ward. I could hear the applause in my head of my outstanding performance in the gardens. I honestly thought I was about to be on a stage in front of hundreds of people – I was so eager to be discovered. I walked into the ward with maximum anticipation and expectation of cheering from a room packed full with crowds, which I swore that I could hear when I was downstairs. To my dismay, there was nobody there apart from big Julie. I stood there stunned and disappointed that nobody apart from security had heard the performance of my lifetime.

I realized that the sound of applause I had heard was actually the drying sound of big Julie's hair dryer! Years later I was to understand that I had undergone some very painful ego deaths during my period in Epsom hospital, particularly the severance of my attachment to fame prior to my time in the hospital. My spiritual journey had caused my soul to put me through virtual realities that felt dangerously real to expel and purify behaviours and attitudes that were not in my highest good. They were necessary for my evolution. I could see that, from early childhood, I had been deluded by fame as the only destiny and THE answer to happiness. How mistaken I was.

Back in the ward, I said, "Hi Julie."

"Hey Nikki. You made it to the garden finally!"

"Yes, I did! You've been going a long time out there, haven't you?" I said to Julie. "What do you do out there?"

"Oh, I like to go to pottery class, and sometimes I go shopping!" "What!" "Pottery and shopping."

That sounded like the most magical thing to me. I wondered where the secret pottery buildings were outside. If there was a shop, where was it? It all looked so institutional to me, out there in the grounds. I couldn't believe you could shop there.

"How come you get to shop?" I asked.

"Oh, you will, honey, you just have to ask. It's all a matter of when you are ready!"

That phrase, "when I am ready," and "when I am well," came up a lot. I didn't know what anybody really meant by it. Liz said it every time she came to visit and so did my parents and the nurses. I felt free and better than I had ever felt. What on earth did I have to do to prove that I was well? I asked Julie how long she had been in the hospital, and she said three years on and off.

"Three years!" I gasped. "That's a long time!"

"Some folks have been here ten years or more," said Julie. I realized right then and there how few people actually make it through mental illness.

"You will not stay here more than a month," my guidance told me. "You are not ill, but rather, you are going through a transformation." I began to question Julie more about her life. I learned that Julie was divorced. She also told me that she had been in the interior design trade. However, now she was being treated for manic depression.

My inner voice piped up again. "If you want to get out of here, Nikki, you must act 'normal.'"

"What do you mean?"

"For a start, stop giving your gifts away!" This was bizarre to me. I had regular visits from my family, who came armed with chocolates, flowers and brand new pairs of pyjamas. I gave my new pyjamas to Sid, who I mentioned earlier. He was on an indefinite section. He was a scrawny guy in his fifties and he had been there for years with no visitors or gifts. I began to realize that one third of the inmates of Longrove hospital were long forgotten and lost souls. It, therefore, seemed to me to be loving and kind to give my things away to other patients.

My inner voice piped up again. "If you give your gifts away, the doctors feel that you are regressing. I know, spiritually, that doesn't make sense to you, Nikki, but I tell you now, don't cast your pearls before swine! They can't appreciate what you are doing. It is not their fault they don't understand." At this point, I realized that life was based upon playing the game of betraying yourself to fit social appearances. What a twisted world we all live in!

काली दुर्गे नमो नमः

That afternoon, I had another visitor, my friend James. I was thrilled to see him. He looked just like the actor Hugh Grant with straight hair, and he dressed like Hugh Grant, too. James was a dear friend, and a wonderful pianist and accompanist. We used to do *Cabaret* gigs together in local South London venues. Every time I had a visitor, Sid and others would all stare as though this was a novelty to them (they never had visitors). There happened to be an upright piano on the ward with some keys missing. James walked straight over to it.

"Come on, Niks, surely you can't be that ill?" he chortled in his posh public school voice. "Why don't we have a song?" James was magical that way, always bringing humour to everything. James started to play our most popular number from our gig list, *Honey Suckle Rose* by Fats Waller. It worked. I started to sing out loudly until everyone on the ward, including the nurses, was clapping. As the song ended, I felt this deep love for James. I had a revelation that we were married in a previous life, or that we would be in a future life. Singing that day had a purity to it that wasn't about recognition. It was simply sharing the joy with others. It felt fabulous and freeing.

Fred (the nurse I loved) said, "You sing well, Nikki." I thanked him and then promptly asked him if I could go with him one afternoon to the place where big Julie shopped.

"Maybe," said Fred.

James gave me a hug and said, "Well done, Niks. I told you that you are perfectly fine. I reckon you'll be out of here by the weekend." I watched James leave and drive away from the dining room window.

Eighteen months after my eventual release from Longrove, I was invited to sing for the twenty-five-year anniversary of SPA supermarkets at The Royal Albert Hall in London, courtesy of the boss who had seen me sing at The Drury Lane theatre six years previously. It was a concert that completed the cosmic circle where James accompanied me on piano, and, by pure grace, Lulu from the Dickens show was miraculously the star turn that night! And by incredible divine coincidence, John, the stage manager from the fashion show in Cardiff who had been the only person who actually heard me that day, astonishingly was the stage manager for that event, too, at The Royal Albert Hall. John came up to me after the dress rehearsal and said, "I am so happy to see you, Nikki. I knew all along you were well. I am so happy for you, and great performance, by the way."

Back in Longrove a few days later, Fred said he would take me out for the afternoon with Julie and a few others to the shopping centre. We boarded a mini bus and headed out of the building. This was my first time out of captivity in three weeks. I wasn't sure at this point at all which reality was real. Was it the hospital where I thought I was being kept for knowing top-secret information? I now realize that when the Kundalini energy opens up your crown chakra, you become wide open like a radio mast and can literally pick up countless downloads of information as you tap into the source vibration behind all forms. Was this large, neon-lit shopping centre in Epsom reality? I experienced the shopping precinct as a real treasure trove that day. We walked into Sainsbury's and Fred went into the frozen food and bought himself some chicken.

"You buy chicken?" I asked.

"Hmmm," said Fred.

"Where do you eat it?" I said.

"At home!" he replied.

"You mean people actually eat outside of the hospital?" I asked.

Fred looked at me with compassion in his eyes at how disconnected I had become from the real world. He felt like my special friend. I felt that he had a unique respect for my soul – that he saw that I was somehow rational in my madness. I noticed next to Sainsbury's a large pair of white trainers in a sport shop window. I fell in love with them and, fortunately, I had some cash with me from one of Liz's visits. I instantly blew all my money on these trainers – which turned out to be much too big for me in the end. I just liked the look of them in the window, all shiny and white. I think I only ever wore them a few times. That afternoon I was proud to wear them though, and I sported them like slippers on the ward.

I used to hate night time at the hospital. That was always the time when my lower mind would start talking to me. It was very frightening. I would go through immense mental waves of Kundalini energy. The energy would expel latent samskaras, or trapped memories, from my psyche. (Naturally, I didn't know that this was occurring at the time.) One night was the worst example of this. I got up to go to the bathroom and I could hear trapped voices coming up from the plughole in the bath. They were dark and sinister, like lost souls were speaking through the plughole. That night, I just couldn't sleep, so I went to the night nurse, who was called Rosemary. She had a horrible way about her, not like my favourite Filipino nurse. She had a patronizing manner and was also very homophobic. She would react with horrible judgement whenever Liz came to visit me. She would try and prevent Liz from speaking with me anywhere near my bed! She was probably a closet lesbian herself, trapped in religious rites.

काली दुर्गे नमो नमः

"Can I have a sleeping tablet?" I asked. "At two a.m.! A ssssssleeping tablet?" she said with a lisp. Her 's' sounded really prominent and then I knew why.

My inner voice said, "Watch this karma, Nikki!" My intuitive eye opened again and I saw clearly a life that Rosemary and I were previously together in. In this vision, I had my tongue slit at the front diagonally (for speaking out truths). I was a mystical Christian, and apparently I was one of the Cathars the inner voice revealed. I had never heard of the Cathars before. Rosemary had been my enemy in that life. Here we were again, only this time she was the one who was lisping. She gave me the tablet contemptuously. Looking back on it, Rosemary got away with "blue murder" on that ward. She could get away with unmerciful behaviour on night duty because we were all "insane" and she knew that we wouldn't report her. Even if we did, the doctors would never believe us anyway.

The following morning eventually came and it was, once again, time for the medication run. I ignored the bell they used to ring. I reached for my copy of Erica Jong's book, *How to Save Your Own Life*. I read the part in the book about this alcoholic friend of hers who had been sober for some time, with several relapses and brave attempts to recover, saying that she could no longer keep the demons down, and how, days later, she was found dead in her room. I cried as I read those paragraphs in recognition, and I swore loudly in my heart that I would never go down with her. I lay on the bed when this very irritating girl called Melanie, who was on duty, came to the side of my bed. I was always confused as to whether Melanie was a patient or staff as she always behaved so annoyingly around me. She made me get up for my medication. I staggered out of bed — disturbed from my rough night of no sleep — and pretended to swallow the pills, but later spat them right out.

That night, I decided that I was ready to leave this prison of a place. People kept telling me, "You'll leave when you are well." I felt perfectly well. What did I have to do to prove that I was well? I knew the drugs made me walk like a yeti (stooped over, zombie-like) and I always felt much worse after taking the medication. I felt dead inside and dull. That lunchtime, something extraordinary happened. I went into the dining room and stood by the window. I felt the Shakti, or divine energy, moving very powerfully and expansively through me. Right out of my third eye appeared a shimmering blue being. It had jet-black hair, coal eyebrows and tears (like dew) that crystallized under its eyes.

The blue colour that he or she (I couldn't tell what gender) was wearing was the most translucent blue that I had ever seen! The light, love and compassion that poured out of its face were heavenly. The feeling of ecstasy that I experienced in its presence was beyond anything I had ever seen or felt before. The blue being started to pour forth tears of compassion, at which point I felt my heart open. Tears were flowing from my eyes simultaneously.

"Oh, Nikki," the being said. "Why do you fear? All THERE IS and all THERE EVER WAS is LOVE." This feeling of love that I was tapping into was exquisite, ecstatic, transcendent and eternal. I knew in that moment what John Lennon had tapped into when he wrote *All You Need is Love* and, also, John Denver in his song *You Fill Up My Senses*! The eternal question of life for me, thus far, had just been answered. It was so simple, but the exquisite vibration behind these words had me know that this was true.

Suddenly, the being disappeared from in front of me. I said, "Where are you?"

The being replied, "I am inside you! I am you and you are me! We are both one!"

This was a pivotal moment for me – one that has sustained me for the past twenty-three years in whatever challenges have tested me in the past since that experience. I have pushed forward, even when I have wanted to give up. I go back to that moment over and over again. I remind myself of the wisdom of the blue being and that, ultimately, this earth plain is NOT real. It is a temporary existence, where each soul has the opportunity to make new choices and create a wonderful life of contribution that reflects the power of that divine love within us.

The next few days in the hospital were surreal. My mind was on overload, like it was a constant TV channel with thirty-two different programs with virtual reality movies playing over and over, one after the other. They would flick from fictitious movies with Elizabeth Taylor and Richard Burton to real-life dramas of birth, death, and war. These were more like news reels, where not only would I see the news as reported, but I would be shown behind the walls of parliament where I witnessed corruption. I saw ministers having affairs and political informers being quietly bumped off and put into the trunks of cars in deserted woodlands with no trace left behind.

काली दुर्गे नमो नमः

Although I had no actual evidence for all of this, I somehow knew in my bones it was true. On this day, my fear of knowing too much and being locked up for it felt justified. I saw that if the scandals that probably go on behind the scenes in government were ever exposed, the nation would be in serious trouble. Right then, in 1989, I received prophecy that there was corruption and cover-up in the UK government concerning paedophilia during the seventies and eighties. This prophecy turned out to be right. In 2012-2014, it was exposed there was a paedophilia ring in the seventies and eighties that involved ministers and celebrities, not least with the horrific exposure of Jimmy Saville.

I then switched over to a vision of Elizabeth Taylor and realized that her life had been a prime example of living life on the edge. She was a great movie star. I saw how the screen movies we watch for leisure captivate us. We get caught up in them – even the dark ones. Then, I remembered the words of the blue being who had appeared in my previous vision and had spoken. "It does not matter how serious the drama is, whether reality or fiction, it is ALL, in the end, still drama and 'NOT REAL' (whatever the appearance). Only the consciousness behind all events is real. In that reality, you will only ever be present to love, Nikki."

Today, I have realized through inner revelations that this Earth plane is a temporary reality. It is but a phase of our souls' journey – and an essential one for our evolution. We have many incarnations and, in each incarnation, our soul has the chance to make new choices that will either develop or hinder its growth from one incarnation to the next. Through the multitude of sufferings we go through each lifetime, when we identify with the drama that we are all in as being true, we eventually awaken to our true identity. We then experience ourselves as being our soul rather than our body. We come to realize that we have the pure light of consciousness within us and that our true purpose here on Earth is to reflect that divine love; to create a wonderful life of contribution and service that uplifts others in their journey to enlightenment.

काली दुर्गे नमो नमः

Back in Epsom hospital the following evening, the Kundalini energy intensified and took me through another massive expansion of consciousness. I was sitting in the dining room, with the tables and chairs cleared to one side. It was before our evening meal when I began to feel the Shakti pulsing through me really strongly.

The inner voice said, "You come from the Aryan race. We don't mean Hitler, but the Aryan race from a thousand years ago in India. You were one of the first beings to deliver the Vedas."

I had never heard of the Aryans or the Vedas, and 'and was amazed to research later that the Aryans were the race that originally preserved the early Indo- European language of sanskrit as Deva-Vani the language of the

Gods and the sacred stories told by the Aryans were preserved in the sanskrit syllables in the Vedas approximately 3500 years ago. I suddenly realized my past lives link to chanting and why chanting had such an extraordinary effect on me. In that moment, I had an unforgettable experience of the Absolute and felt liberation for a few split seconds. My small self (my ego state) panicked. I realized that this was an expansive state – a state where there was no duality – and my small self panicked, realizing I would be lonely on my own. Once more, my ego was in peril.

A powerful force arose up from deep within and bellowed into the dining hall, crying, "It's the end of the world!" The voice was so powerful, just like the voice that came out of me when I was in the auditorium in Cardiff. The other patients on the ward who were settling into their normal routines of watching TV, or just staring into space, started to panic and freak out at the sound of my voice. They clung to each other and to the walls of the dining hall, scared at the sheer force of the message behind my voice.

"We are all about to be blown up!" I shrieked. My inner vision saw an aeroplane, a Boeing 707, coming to meet me. I was told in revelations that it was to take me to another dimension where there is complete joy. I heard the songs of Phil Collins and Dusty Springfield beckoning me and playing from this joyful place.

Looking back, I see how the aeroplane was symbolic. It represented a place on a vibrational frequency where I could exist, where I could be more like my true Self. I idolized Dusty Springfield at that time, so it did not surprise me at all that she would be there waiting for me. This plane was presented to me as per the fable of Noah's Ark, where the animals boarded two by two. I remember vividly walking up the gangplank towards the cabin and longing for Liz to come with me; then the two of us could be together on our continued journey.

To my dismay, my inner voice said, "You will only be allowed onto this plane if you go with the partner who is your truth."

I shuddered because I knew in my heart that I cared for Liz, but that she wasn't my truth going forward. I just couldn't let go of her, though, as I was too dependent on her emotionally.

"The plane will be leaving in two minutes," said the voice. I started to panic. I was panicking so badly that the other patients could feel it. My energy was so forceful that they started kicking up a huge commotion in the dining hall. They were shouting so much that several nurses had to come in to calm them down!

"Go!" said the scrawny-looking patient Sid. "You have to go!"

I felt he was urging me not to miss my plane. He suddenly pulled a religious souvenir card out of his pyjamas that said, "There but by the grace of God go I." I knew that he was my divine messenger in that moment who had come to remind me to follow my truth and there was still just enough time. However, the seconds were ticking and running out for me to catch the plane. What should I do? I was seriously torn. Should I go for my truth, which felt scary but exciting and expansive, or stay behind with Liz? I began to sweat with fear and stood there frozen in panic on the spot. I just couldn't take my freedom and fly. Suddenly, all those bird parts I had been cast in as an actor now made perfect sense. This constriction felt like the space I had been in all my life – always following what was expected of me and what wouldn't emotionally rock the boat for others.

I see now that the root of all my drinking and using had always been motivated by the terror of being judged and rejected by others. As I looked at the cabin doors of the aeroplane that was to take me to this plane of joy, music, Dusty Springfield and all that was metaphorically precious to me, my heart pumped faster! I felt like my heart had turned into a huge tribal drum that was being beaten by natives. As it got louder, I witnessed the patients put their hands over their ears to deaden the noise of the drum beats. Louder and louder, faster and faster as Sid circled around me holding up the "There but by the grace of God go I" card.

"NIKKI, you have to choose now!" screamed the inner voice. My whole body shook and then... I flunked it. I just couldn't do it!

The gravity of my dependency on Liz was pulling me back to the drama plane, to that which was familiar and safe and, before I knew it, the symbolic aeroplane had departed without me. I heard in my head the sound you hear on quiz shows when you get the wrong answer and the whole audience goes "AWWWWW!" All the patients looked at me like I was a loser.

"Is it really the end of the world?" they asked me nervously.

"No," I said. "You can go to bed now. Sorry. It's all over now."

I felt I had let everyone down really badly – especially my inner voice. I felt frustrated with myself, but then I thought of Liz, and my inner guidance was now disturbing about her. It was shown to me that Liz and big Julie were going to be in a wrestling match the next day. Liz would be knocked out by Julie and she would seriously hurt her back! I was terrified and knew that I had to stop this contest from going ahead. (I realized much later, on looking back, that these were early symbolic premonitions of the future inevitable breakdown of my relationship with Liz.)

The next afternoon, Liz came in to visit me. She always looked calm and responsible with her big doleful eyes and Barbour coat.

"How are you, love?" she asked.

"I don't want you to have the match with Julie!" I said.

"What match?" said Liz, bemused. "Listen, love," she said, changing the subject, "you have accrued quite a nice sum of money from your sickness benefit whilst you have been away."

"Yes, and I will be coming home soon," I responded.

"Indeed, when you are better, yes, you certainly will!" Liz replied.

Here we go, I thought to myself and sighed out loud. I knew she didn't get where I was but, then again, neither did anyone else. Why would they, though? They hadn't been travelling between inner dimensions like I had been – not really a common occurrence in the "real" world. Liz stayed for an hour and then left.

That afternoon I felt despondent, until I saw an American comedy show on TV. It was *The Cosby Show*. The Shakti (spiritual energy) was dancing inside me wildly, trying to get my attention to look at the screen. I felt extreme joy watching this show.

"Watch the actors carefully," my inner voice said. One of the actors in that show, it later turned out, was on the same meditation path as myself. I discovered this years later when I met the very same actor in London at a business networking function where she was the guest speaker whilst appearing live on stage at night in the West End. I approached her afterwards and we shared fond memories together of times we had spent in the ashram.

The next day, I was determined to get out of the hospital. After twenty-one days of incarceration, I had definitely had enough of being an inmate. However, how was I going to prove that I was well? What did they all think was well? What did they think was sick? That afternoon, my friend Sue and I got into one of our inter-dimensional playing journeys. I would suddenly get past life flashes and enter into them like they were happening in the present. That afternoon, I remember vividly being transported to a life when I was a German soldier.

I would inspire Sue to enter into these realms with me. She would reenact being a prisoner of war on the run whilst I was the soldier who was chasing her back into captivity. We were both crawling beneath the undergrowth until, at one point, we found ourselves back in reality again and under a melamine dining table! The nurses watched on as we continued playing like carefree children. I felt them suddenly staring, at which point it suddenly dawned on me for only a split second that my behaviour was occurring to them as super strange and insane! My mother appeared in the doorway to visit me as tea was being served that day. It felt just like when she used to come and collect me from kindergarten when I was four years old.

काली दुर्गे नमो नमः

I was so immersed in reenacting my German past life that I was oblivious to her as Sue and I crawled under the tea trolley.

As we stood up again, I said, "Oh, hello, Mummy. Come and see our adventure playground." Like a toddler, I took my mother's hand and led her around the dining room and showed her all the different scenes of my previous incarnations located in different parts of the room. "This is Rome, here by the piano, and here's Egypt by the window, and this is Colditz by the TV!" I said with great conviction.

My mother looked at me and said, "You know darling, I think you are actually 'rationally' mad. It all makes curious sense, somehow, but I don't quite know why." On reflection, this was an amazing moment of recognizing the innate ability of all mothers to read their children and know instinctively whether the child is imagining things or telling the truth. Only a mother has this kind of antenna.

My experience of my behaviour was that it was authentic and free. However, part of me was, for the first time, acutely aware that if I seriously wanted to get out of the hospital environment, I would have to play the game of life as it is designed and act NORMAL. So, this was exactly what I did. The next day, I began to do "normal" acts, like locking all my chocolates, gifts and pyjamas in my dormitory cupboard rather than immediately giving them away to Sid and others. I would also, whenever possible, volunteer to mop the dining floor and lay the tables. This felt like selfless service to me, such as a yoga devotee performs in the ashram. I was happy as a whistle doing this, and very close to being released as my behaviour was noted by the staff nurse as me "getting better."

However, one evening at dinner time I was unable to sustain acting "normal" and I offered to help the ladies serve dinner, whereupon my hand started to shake. I cast the ladle into the beef stew and, as I looked down at the plate where I had put the beef, I froze. There on the plate was a golden retriever dog that looked just like Liz's dog at home. It wasn't even cooked; it had all its fur still on, only it was dead.

I was horrified when the dinner lady said, "Are you all right? Come on, this lot is hungry – serve up!"

"I can't," I said. "It's a... it's a... DOG!"

"There ain't no dog there, girl, look. Go sit down. You're probably hallucinating," said the cockney lady with the round face.

I did sit down, whereupon I received an inner download about the importance of vegetarianism and being kind to animals. The shakti was showing me that eating beef was just like eating my dog. I started shouting at the patients not to eat their dinner. I was more worried at that point that they were actually about to eat my dog! This outburst had me sent back again to the medicine run that evening. For the next few days, I knew I would have to toe the line if I wanted to escape, so I remained quiet and in constant service. After one week of this reformed behaviour, I was allowed out for my very first weekend out of the ward. Thank God my plan had worked, and at last I was out!

Coming home to Wandsworth with Liz felt like Dorothy waking up from her dream in the *Wizard of Oz*. Just like Dorothy, I knew that I had visited somewhere extremely powerful. However, nobody in my everyday reality had been there to share my experience. I felt sad that I couldn't wholeheartedly share what had happened to me with anyone. I walked through the flat, despondently touching the objects around me. I was present but, at the same time, I felt imprisoned again by this limited place called my life.

I felt more alive in the hospital, I thought.

By this time, however, the medication had started to dull my senses. They had, unfortunately, given me a stronger dose for going home.

I felt barren and alone in Wandsworth, even though Liz was with me. It was like I was walking through an alien stage set that was called my home, when inside I knew this wasn't really my home at all. The realm I had visited in Cardiff had felt ecstatic. I reminisced about speaking to the models on the bus when I had been in such an exquisite state that truly felt like home. Now I felt depressed, and I was somewhat relieved to go back to the hospital on Sunday night. I, naively, hoped that there I could connect back into the bliss. However, when I got back there, my experience was just as barren. I began to realize that home is on the inside. I stayed in Epsom for just one more week, when the doctors formally confirmed that I was behaving normally and I was "ready" for normality.

काली दुर्गे नमो नमः

It was the end of March 1989, and I had just turned twenty-seven years old. I left Epsom Hospital for good. My state of elation began to decline rapidly. The expansions that I had been experiencing stopped. I was becoming more and more deadened by the medication that I had been prescribed. When I arrived home, I was assigned an outpatient psychiatrist called Elizabeth. Each time she came to visit, I longed to share my authentic experience to someone who could hear me. Elizabeth, nice as she was, just couldn't understand me except through a medical lens. I felt at a loss – lost as to where and with whom I could share this extraordinary inner voyage I had been on.

One day, Elizabeth sat down in the armchair of our front room. She always sat there when she came to visit me. She asked me if I would like to be an experimental patient for the junior psychiatrists at her hospital. They were undertaking their exams at Springfield Hospital. "Your case would be very interesting for the juniors to diagnose," she said. "This might be an opportunity for you to express your experience!" I naively thought that perhaps I could sway the minds of doctors to believe in mystical realms – realms I knew were beyond insanity. I wanted them to recognize and acknowledge my experience as valid.

"Yes, I would like to do that," I said.

The next week I went to Springfield. I sat in an examination room with a junior doctor called Vicky. She asked me twenty questions in order to gain details about what had happened to me. I was debriefed not to tell her (in advance of her exam) the prognosis of "psychotic episode" by the Epsom doctors. She then had fifty minutes to write a dissertation on what I had said, after which we were both escorted into the senior consultant psychiatrist's office. He was an icy looking man with slicked-back white hair with a grey double-breasted suit, pink tie and a white medical coat. He really reminded me of Charles Gray in the James Bond movie *Diamonds Are Forever*.

"So, Vicky, what has the patient said to you?" the senior psychiatrist asked in a smooth and smarmy voice.

"Nicola claims to have heard voices over a period of a month," replied Vicky.

"Mmm," said the consultant in a most patronizing tone. "So, Nicola! Where do you suppose these voices come from, hmm?" he asked, glaring into my eyes.

"I don't know!" I said.

"Well, they don't come from the bathroom cupboard, now do they?" The cynicism in his voice was caustic. It was very abrasive to my heart. "Naturally, Nicola, they come from your imagination!" he sniggered. "So, what is your diagnosis, Vicky?"

Vicky replied, "Psychotic episodes, sir."

"Well done, Vicky! Undoubtedly correct."

"Thank you, Nicola. That will be all!"

My heart wilted as I knew I had definitely cast more pearls before swine. I knew that trying to get my message into the world would be like trying to cry for attention from inside a goldfish bowl.

I would love to acknowledge, at this point, the works of progressive psychiatrists Dr. Andrew Powell and Dr. Larry Culliford, founders of The Special Interest Group at the Royal College of Psychiatry, who have taken on the explorative debate as to the difference between a spiritual emergence or mystical awakening and psychosis. In other words, what is divine madness and what is genuine mental illness?

You are invited to chant once again!

KALI DURGE NAMO NAMAH assists us to break
through the challenges we face in our lives.

जय जय प्रेमानंदा/जय जय मुक्तानंदा

Part 3: Jay Jay Premananda/ Jay Jay Muktananda

This chant invokes divine love and the bliss of inner freedom.

Prem is the Sanskrit word for **love** and **Ananda = bliss** and **Mukta = inner freedom**.

For centuries, seekers of truth have written about inner ecstacy (quote Tukaram or Kabir).

Mirabai (16th century saint) talks about the supreme ecstasy she felt within whenever she chanted Lord Krishna's name. Her devotion to chanting set her free in the face of her own family who tried to poison her. This mystical tale is symbolic of how, as human beings, we can drown in the poisonous negativity of those around us unless we keep our own inner vibration vibrant, expanded and free.

Chanting the Sanskrit words **premananda/muktananda** has always uplifted me whenever my spirits have been low. This is my favourite chant, as it instantly uplifts my soul and sets me free from the chains of negative reaction.

If ever you are disconnected and seek instant upliftment, this chant is perfect. It also has a magnificent energy for celebrations and mass community gatherings.

**DOWNLOAD "JAY JAY PREMANANDA/JAY JAY
MUKTANANDA" AND CHANT ALONG!**

I would love to invite you to join me in chanting as
you journey through the next part of my story.

You can download this chant for free by logging on to
the following website and entering your details:

www.nikkislade.com/freechants

Let's Chant!

I left the hospital feeling disheartened and low. The next three months were horrible. The drugs were depressing me and I longed for the spiritual connection that I had previously felt during my awakening. In that initial period after leaving the hospital, not even my chanting practice could pierce the brick wall of the anti-depressants. I then went on vacation with Liz to Greece. I was so low there that I started drinking heavily again. Liz kept trying to control me by refusing to buy me any more beers. She nagged constantly that I'd had two beers already, so why did I want another one? I ignored her and carried on drinking.

At this point, we had a terrible row on the beach one night which resulted in me lashing out at her. I accidentally smacked her lip as my arms were waving around in protest. The shame of this unfortunate episode was written on her bruised lip the next day. This was the beginning of a downward slope in our relationship. After two weeks of a fraught holiday, we returned to London. I managed to white-knuckle my sobriety for a few days, when one night, we went to an Irish pub with some friends. I got absolutely smashed and starting socialising with the Irish contingent – the real drinkers who were sitting in the corner of the pub. When I had a drink inside me, I could talk to anyone. Liz was furious as I became more and more raucous and oblivious to what anyone thought of me. Eventually, Liz dragged me away and drove me home. The next day, Liz said that I must control my drinking or she would have to throw me out of her flat. This was the beginning of the end of our relationship.

In that same month of August 1989, I was called to an audition at the Royal National Theatre. It was by one of the musical directors I had worked with from the Liverpool Everyman Theatre. He asked me if I would like to play ensemble in a new production of Ibsen's *Peer Gynt*. They were looking for actor musicians to play trolls and all manner of parts. Once again, my French horn, trumpeting and piano skills got me the job. I couldn't believe it. I had been released from a psychiatric hospital at the end of March 1989 and then cast in a leading production at The Royal National Theatre in September of that same year. We began rehearsals on September 4th, which was the same day that I made a conscious decision to recover from alcohol and drug dependency. One day at a time. Happily, I have now been clean and sober for twenty-five years.

The National Theatre offered me parts in two different productions. The other production was *The Good Person of Sichuan* (about three Gods who come to earth seeking a human channel through which they can carry out their work). There was a synchronicity around both productions in that both texts featured the main character and his/her spiritual journey.

At the end of the summer 1989, I came off the prescribed medication. I felt it was counterproductive, and I let go of these drugs before rehearsals began. Immediately, I began to feel the Shakti or spiritual energy flowing through me again. I began chanting consistently again, as I knew this daily practice would now be my inner rock. After coming off medication, I began to feel radically better. A friend gave me a present after her travels to Egypt. It was an Egyptian ankh (which is the fertility symbol for eternal life and looks like a cross only with a round head with an oval hole in it). The moment I opened it, I felt goose bumps; it was a sign. It integrated my visions of those Egyptian lives I had visited before being in hospital. I wore it on a chain around my neck, and I felt a powerful protective energy around it whilst wearing it.

Throughout 1989-1992, I was continuing to train my voice with Helena Shenel, who was referred to me by Lulu from the West End show. At that time, she was also training a famous feminist lesbian singer from the 1970s. This singer, who was also following the same yogic meditation path and had a love of chanting, was called Mira* Mira recommended a book for me to read as I recounted to her my experiences of Egypt – *Initiation* by Elizabeth Haich. It was a powerful book, channelling truths from pharaohs of ancient Egypt. I then began a practice of meditating regularly whilst wearing the ankh. One day, I felt the metal of the ankh ping. I glanced down and the left arm had snapped off during meditation! How could this happen? I was perturbed and decided to go instantly to a market store in Wandsworth to purchase another one. I put it on again and the very same thing happened. It was during my meditation that the bottom stem snapped off. I decided that, if this happened a third time, this was definitely not an accident!

जय जय प्रेमानंदा/जय जय मुक्तानंदा

A few days later, I was sitting by the swimming pool of some acquaintances in Henley. I had been invited to sing at the Henley Music Festival. It was the summer of 1990. James, who had visited me in hospital and who was also a recovering alcoholic, accompanied me. It was dear James, my pianist, who led me to the path of recovery from addiction through his own example of giving up alcohol. I owe my life to him to this day; he doesn't know just how much.

As we walked away from the pool, I felt a sharp chain whip my leg. I looked down and a hole had appeared in my plastic swim bag. It was the chain, but this time of the third ankh I had worn, which was swinging like a pendulum back and forth against my flesh. It had burst out of the bag. This felt like a miracle happening right there. I saw during my Kundalini awakening that I had experienced a strong lifetime in Egypt exploring the occult or hidden realms. It was surreal to have the interruption of this ankh momentarily remind me of this vision. These miracles continued until one day, which was my day off at the National Theatre, I came in to find my dressing room up-turned! My French horn and trumpet had been moved from my cupboard. All the drawers had been pulled out and dumped. There, on the floor, was my *Initiation* book, which I had carelessly left in my dressing room cubicle over the weekend.

Inside, I heard the voice of the book saying to me, "Don't leave me here! I am only to be read by those who are ready."

My heart was beating fast. This book had occult power, for sure, and I felt scared in that moment that I was being warned to respect its power. Later that year, I recommended *Initiation* to James and my friend Roz. Roz told me that her copy broke out of her desk one day, and James's wedding car went missing when he and his wife got back from their honeymoon. They felt it was because they had spoken irreverently about the name of the pharaoh whom they had nicknamed Pha–hot tap for fun whilst on honeymoon!

From that day forth, my inner guidance grew stronger. My inner voice gave me clarity about my path going forward. I was, at that time, very focused on my journey as an actor. My inner guidance revealed to me that I would now be cast in parts that would bring a peaceful completion to my past. It started with *Peer Gynt*, the story of one man's journey to know his inner Self.

He is tempted by the lower nature of the trolls (for me, this represented my addictions). His time in the desert pursuing Arabian women (this reflected the lust of my past). His preoccupation with ambition and success to become a revered business man (symbolized my attachment to fame). But most importantly for me, his time in the asylum where he goes temporarily mad to know himself.

Rehearsals began for the asylum scene, and I will never forget that day. Our director started by saying, "This scene presents our biggest challenge yet! This is something the majority of us will never experience! So, where do I start?" He cleared his throat awkwardly.

I felt this pulsating energy to speak. My psychiatric experience was so fresh in my mind that it felt natural for me to offer it up. I felt a fearless urge to share my experience with the cast of twenty actors. In my case, I wasn't mad or psychotic. I was clear I had experienced a spiritual awakening or spiritual emergence, and I was perfectly sane. In my immediate enthusiasm to speak, I forgot to check in with my inner voice.

"Remember not to cast pearls before swine," it always told me. I failed to listen and I raised my hand to speak.

"Yes, Nicola!" the director said. "What do you have to say on this subject?"

I paused for a moment, my heart beating loudly. The entire cast of *Peer Gynt* gazed at me. I looked around the circle at their eyes staring back at me. I put faith in my mouth and spoke. Slowly, I began to recall my encounter with madness to the whole company. I shared with them that little is understood about mental illness. In my case, and other cases, mental illness can relate to a higher channelling. This type of channelling, when not integrated, is frequently diagnosed as psychosis. I watched as the whole cast stared at me with their mouths open. You could hear a pin drop. Fifteen minutes later, I finished, feeling expanded and empowered that I had offered my unedited truth.

I glanced over at the director and immediately felt his vibe towards me. He seemed very uncomfortable. Once again, my inner voice whispered, "You should not have cast your pearls before swine. They cannot hear you!" I felt a sinking sensation in my stomach, and I knew something was wrong.

As we all stood up to go to lunch, several of the actors came up to me and said, "Thanks, Nikki, for sharing what you did."

"What an amazing experience!"

"You're so brave to share it!"

As I was about to leave the studio, the director called me over to him. My heart thumped as I felt his vibration doubting me. My worst fear was that he was mentally calculating my release date from hospital six months prior to production. If this were on paper, it could potentially be an embarrassing situation for him.

"Nicola! Ermm," he said, trying to be tactful, "thank you for your sensitive sharing this morning! Ermmm. I just wanted to mention that, we have the *Guardian* newspaper in this afternoon. They will be reviewing our rehearsal process for the asylum scene." He nervously bit his nails. "You see, Nikki, we wouldn't want the journalist to think we had based the asylum scene on a real life, actual experience, would we? It might be rather awkward... so, errmm... the thing is... would you mind not repeating your experience to the journalist when she arrives?"

Outwardly, I found myself saying, "Of course not." But inwardly, my heart sank; again, I was in the world where, to fit in, you have to suppress your authentic truth. My inner voice advised that the world of theatre is really only comfortable creating when it doesn't have to face actual reality. Therefore, it was much safer to play at reality. From that moment forth, I learned not to share my awakening experiences with anyone who I felt would judge me for it.

जय जय प्रेमानंदा/जय जय मुक्तानंदा

For the first two years after the awakening, I longed for people I could share it with. I tried to share with Chad and Kath, as they had been so much a part of my *Wizard of Oz* experience. They were like the Scarecrow and the Tinman to me, as I remembered them in their Egyptian costumes at that dinner. Liz and I went to dinner with them shortly after I was released from Epsom Hospital. Their friend, Alex, was there; she was an older lesbian with a monocle and was also a retired nurse. As drinks were served, I stupidly went straight into recounting the whole story of my hospital experience.

Chad looked at me sceptically (as my inner voice had warned she would several months previously) throughout my descriptions of snakes coming out of my head and said, "That's what comes of people who meditate too long, Nikki, really!" The tone of her voice floored me.

Alex added, as she drew a lug of her cigar, "You'll be better soon, Nikki."

There was that familiar phrase again that I thought I had left behind safely in the hospital. As I look back, could I blame them really? My experience did sound crazy, but I knew, just like Dorothy did, that I had *been* there. I must add that Chad and Kath are still my great friends today. We did, however, have a few years when we lost touch just because so much had changed between us after that episode. Nowadays, we get along even better than ever, and they respect my path even if they don't totally understand it. I also no longer try and force spiritual exotica on them or others as, after a while, I learned a difficult lesson – this was not my place, unless authentically guided, hence this narrative.

The worst example of this was when I bought my parents a book called *The Road Less Travelled* by M. Scott Peck for Christmas. This book is a profound and in-depth insight as to how "mental breakdown" cannot be solely attributed to one single member of a family. That, in fact, it is the dysfunctional family system that is the main component in breakdowns; if a family system heals, then so do the individuals within it. I found it fascinating and I naively thought my parents would find it interesting, too. I went over for tea one afternoon with them, and they sat on the sofa absolutely furious and barely spoke to me, and it lasted for days.

"What have I done?" I asked nervously.

"You should know," my mother said icily. "That book you gave us for Christmas. How could you?"

As I look back now, of course, they both naturally thought that, through the book, I was implying that everything was their fault. It was also during that period that I went into psychotherapy, and part of the process was releasing anger towards your family of origin. They, understandably, felt this hostility from me and were rightly extremely defensive at that time. It was a very painful part of our journey as a family on both sides.

One person who really did hear my awakening experience was my friend, Mike T. We went for lunch one day and I recounted the whole story, including singing in the hospital ward with Sue, and I shared with him all my divine visions. As I was talking at our table in a little café in Notting Hill, Mike's eyes welled up with tears. I paused.

"Are you okay?"

Mike took my hand and said, "You are extraordinary, Nikki. You are very special. Don't let anybody ever harm you. Thank you for sharing your very sacred story with me."

After that day, I learned to tune in with who was safe to hear me. I could sense this by feeling the energetic vibration, which was either a contraction in my solar plexus, which signalled "no," or an expansion, which meant "yes." Two people I did deeply trust were my friends Bobby and Anne from Colorado.

One day, when I was thirty-two years old, I decided to call Anne, who is a highly evolved soul. As I spoke to her, she said, "Stop one moment, Nikki. As you are speaking and I am listening, do you realize that you are a shaman?"

"What exactly is a shaman?" I asked.

"A shaman is one who travels through different dimensions and realms, some of which are ecstatic and some are frightening realms of hell, but the purpose of a true shaman is to lead other souls through these dark realms into the light. Why can shamans do this? Because they have already been there," said Anne with great wisdom.

I listened to what Anne said with deep curiosity. It has taken me over twenty years of working with hundreds of souls for me to understand that perhaps her instinct was right, based on the feedback I have received from several clients.

It was in the winter of 1990 that saw the birth of my new career as founder of my company, Free the Inner Voice. That same year that Free the Inner Voice was in its infancy, I opened as an ensemble actor in *Peer Gynt* and the *Good Person of Sichuan* on the Olivier stage. This marked a seven-year period where I had two careers running in parallel.

Free the Inner Voice was a destiny that revealed itself to me. In meditation, I saw that thousands of people throughout the world were seeking a safe and non-judgemental space where they could connect and express their authentic voice. My intuition revealed that it would be a sacred environment where people could safely express their core voice in a non-judgemental space, free from criticism. I was acutely aware of the terror that human beings have of their voices being exposed and judged. In the 1970-90s, in the area of singing, only those who made it onto *Top of the Pops* were praised for their voices. These days, only five percent of the nation who are in the finals of *The X-Factor* have the loyal listening of the public at large without abject criticism, which is shocking to me. Free the Inner Voice was to be a space where people could be held and risk going outside their vocal comfort zones. It was to be an unconditionally loving space, where they could free their inner voice!

जय जय प्रेमानंदा/जय जय मुक्तानंदा

I didn't know, initially, how to develop this idea until, one day, I was sitting in St. James Church in Piccadilly. It was in spring of 1990, at an evening called Alternatives, which was held on a Monday night. The night focussed on hosting a platform for transformational speakers and facilitators from all over the world. The location is one of the most beautiful churches in central London.

On the night that I attended, there was a voice facilitator from Australia. His name was Chris James. He led us all in an inspiring evening of sound and harmonic overtone chanting. I had been recommended to him by a friend called Lisa, who was from my yoga meditation path.

She told me, "This man is reaching people in the world through sound, and he is not from an ashram."

I went to his talk and watched him with great interest that night as he inspired us to make releasing sounds and overtones. He taught us overtone chanting and invited us all to sculpt our lips into a specific shape. He then encouraged us to sing beautiful spiritual ballads and to open our hearts to our authentic sound.

As I observed him, I saw a strong future mirror of myself being a leader in this field of natural voice. However, as I sat on the church pew, I also felt very uncomfortable as an acute fear arose within me as to whether I would have the courage to start a group myself, let alone what that would actually involve. I happened to be sitting in the church pew next to a lady called Cathy. Chris James then invited us all to sound with each other in pairs.

After the concert ended, Cathy and I started talking and I told her of my dream of starting my own voice-toning group.

She said, "I don't believe this, Nikki, but I have the perfect venue for you to start! I am opening a health centre in Brixton! When do you want to start? It would be so great if you would come and offer something there."

My heart shuddered. I felt way too scared to start a group. However, I said that I would come back to her in a few weeks. This fearful pattern has been a constant battle over the years since being sober between the inner voice that says, "GO FOR IT," and the sabotaging terrorist voice in my head that says, "Don't even emerge from under your duvet, Nikki!"

जय जय प्रेमानंदा/जय जय मुक्तानंदा

During the next few months, I attended some further workshops with Chris James. In fact, I went to some of the earliest overtone chanting secret soirees he held. These were hosted by a lady called Melanie at her beautiful home in Holland Park. About ten of us would meet there and chant harmonic overtones together. It was, at that time, the most eccentric way to spend the evening, but the experience was always so great. We would all feel cleansed and tingling afterwards, and much more connected to ourselves and others. Melanie and her husband said that they did voice toning together as a couple and that toning together, for them, was the antidote to arguments and promoted harmony in their marriage. They said that vibration was the key to everything and that peace existed in vibration alone. Melanie was also one of the earliest new consciousness leaders in the field of affirmation and neural linguistic programming. I didn't understand what she meant at the time when she said, "Affirmations are extremely powerful," and, "they are not to be played around with!" I felt all these new people I was encountering at that time were all manifesting as important guides in my new unfolding destiny.

As we all made these incredible sounds together, I realized we were all experiencing the bliss of chanting that Tibetan and Mongolian monks had savoured for centuries. Afterwards, we would all be ravenously hungry due to the raising and expansion of our vibration. We would then eat copious amounts of crisps, peanuts and dips. There were two brothers that used to attend these meetings called Marc and Sean. I got on really well with both of them, especially Marc. He was newly trained as a hypnotherapist, but he was also a qualified dentist.

Marc loved toning, and I told him one night that I was thinking of starting my own voice-toning group. He was really excited and actively encouraged me to start a group, and he began to let other interested folk know my plans. I realized that, initially, it would be easier for me to start a practice group in something that already had a following, like voice overtone chanting, even though I knew, eventually, I wanted to explore with others a deeper connection to the inner voice. This way I could build confidence and then, over time, develop my own thing. Chris James gave me his blessing to start a practice vocal toning group.

"The main thing is that people everywhere just start vocal toning groups," he exclaimed.

I made up my mind that same night to go ahead. I decided to call Cathy the following day to see if her space in Brixton was still available.

"Oh, Nikki! Great to hear from you! Yes, Wednesday nights are free. When do you want to start?"

My heart shuddered as I said, "September?"

"That's fine," said Cathy. "Will you want food after? I could make some snacks, falafel and nibbles."

I thought back to Melanie's house and how hungry we all got after. "Oh, that would be great," I replied. As I put the phone down, I just couldn't believe I was going ahead despite the fear I felt.

And so, it was in September 1990 that I started my first ever voice circle in Brixton. The centre was a residential space right opposite Brixton prison. It was to run weekly alongside my three nights of performance in *Peer Gynt* at the Royal National Theatre.

I arrived in my car at the venue with Marc, who said he would be there to support me at the opening of my first ever voice group. We parked outside Cathy's house, and we both looked up at the ominous walls of Brixton prison right opposite. I took my harmonium out of the trunk (which is a beautiful classical Indian instrument for accompanying chanting), my Egyptian drum, a Tibetan bowl and an electric keyboard. My hands shook as I turned the keys in the lock of the centre door.

Marc smiled at me and said, "You can do it!"

This was a symbolic moment, and there was no turning back now! Cathy had said she would be arriving later and to let ourselves in. The space was cosy and friendly inside. The room could hold thirty people at a squeeze. It had a grey carpet with a couple of rugs and Native American pictures on the wall. Cathy had put out food for us all in the neighbouring kitchen.

I was extremely nervous, as I hadn't a clue how many people would actually turn up. I set up my instruments in one corner and then lit a candle. I burned some incense, which I wafted around the room and then promptly placed in the entrance for the aroma to welcome people. I then recited some opening mantras to invoke blessings for the evening. I sat in the corner with my harmonium, trying to meditate and deal with my fears that no one would show. To my amazement, the doorbell rang and it was lovely Anna Ziman who arrived first, with some flowers, her warm smile and oodles of enthusiasm. I immediately felt much better.

Then Sean, Marc's brother, arrived, some fellow recovering alcoholics called Katrina, Carol and Vince, a lovely young woman called Joanna (a drama therapist who I had met at Melanie's house), two ladies who were both called Heather, and a Liverpudlian called Paul (who came on his bicycle). There was also another wonderful lady whose name I have now forgotten. Cathy finally arrived.

"Gosh, that's twelve people," I thought. What was I going to do with them all, and where would I start? I took a deep breath and invited them to sit in a circle around the candle. As I welcomed everyone and thanked them all for coming, I felt like it wasn't me talking and that an energy was speaking through me that flowed naturally and easily.

I took a deep breath and guided them all into some vocal overtoning exercises as inspired by Chris James. I then slowly guided everyone into partner work, where they would all sit closely together and send the tone of the sound into one another's chins and feel the vibration moving back and forth. This caused huge hilarity, especially when Katrina and Vince were paired together – as they were rebellious like me and they couldn't stop laughing at the eccentricity of putting their heads together and making strange sounds. I loved to witness the participants letting go. I would affirm whatever experience they had as being the perfect expression for them as a result of the practice. I was vigilant that there should be no deliberate sabotage in the group, as non-judgemental listening of each other was imperative.

I then invited everybody to divide into groups. One person would lie in the middle whilst everyone else crouched around like angel helpers and harmonically toned different areas of the body. People felt like they were being bathed in a heavenly choir. I chose to conclude the evening with a Native American chant, which I had learned from a book. I began to beat the drum and I also had a bag of shakers, rattles and tambourines which people could play along with. The energy in the room was buzzing by the end, and everyone had huge smiles on their faces and said they felt immense joy.

Afterwards, we all moved into the kitchen to enjoy a lovely buffet, courtesy of Cathy. Everybody was on a high. They said they were excited to have this oasis to come to each week and that they were all definitely coming back for more overtoning. They promised they would even bring more people. I couldn't believe the feedback.

Marc gave me a big hug and said, "Well done, Stormer!" as he affectionately used to call me.

जय जय प्रेमानंदा/जय जय मुक्तानंदा

As I drove home, I felt completely uplifted and peaceful, trusting that, somehow, I was on my journey to fulfilling a greater purpose. This was beyond anything I had ever experienced before in my life. I reflected upon the gathering in Cathy's kitchen and how people had said they felt like they were in a brand new and exciting secret society doing something out of the ordinary. They said the voice circle was certainly better than going to any pub or other social settings. They had all felt enriched inside as a result. I knew in my heart that this voice group needed to be a regular event. I looked at my performance calendar at the National Theatre and noted that *Peer Gynt* played mainly at the Olivier on Tuesday, Thursday and Saturday. The performances were alternating with *Sunday in the Park with George*. This meant that Wednesdays were mainly free.

I made an arrangement with Cathy for Wednesday nights, and rang round to every one of the keen chanters to declare that the voice group was officially underway! In the early days, it was known as "Nikki's voice toning group" in Brixton. There was no fee then, only donations placed into my colourful flat cloth cap which was left by the front door as people made their way home. Each week, the class got stronger, and the word of mouth spread, until some weeks we had as many as thirty people show up. It was a long walk from Brixton station up the hill, but they were keen and there was a real buzz about the group and a lovely sense of community.

Nine months into facilitating my group, I seriously began to wonder whether voice work was actually more my calling now than being an actor. I went through a major conflict about this because I knew that, although I loved the group, I still needed to earn a living. My income came from being a professional actor, and even that wasn't a reliable source of income as I was generally out of work for half the year and would have to wait tables. I would consistently ask my inner voice, "Where am I going? Where is my destiny leading me?"

Meanwhile, my workshops continued to blossom and develop hugely throughout the 1990s. I would sometimes bring an electric keyboard to my group and inspire people to collectively write songs where everyone would contribute their own lyric.

Within minutes, everyone's combined effort would magically unfold into a beautiful song. It was an incredible night where several men happened to attend, and one called Andy was moved to tears as he touched the song in his heart. That night, Damien, who worked in the veggie café next door, came into the group at the end of our session to listen. He was inspired by what he heard. He said he ran the kitchen for a great residential venue in Glastonbury. He said that, if I chose, I could have it at a really good price as a space for a vocal retreat. My heart thumped. The thought of running a voice residential weekend was both scary and exciting at the same time.

Whenever I felt that sensation, my inner voice would push me to go for it. Hence, my first ever voice residential was born. One client, the other Paul, worked in a mental health day centre and lent me the centre's mini-bus. I took a mini-bus driving test to be safe. I then drove my eight residential participants to Glastonbury. This was a very special retreat, as it was my first experiment and, luckily, everyone's feedback was amazing. We chanted late at night on Glastonbury Tor, a famous church ruin set on a hill in AD 1184. Each day, I was filled with floods of inspiration for the course. The exercises and improvisations that channelled through had a transformative effect on the participants. I felt excited and on purpose with my destiny. I was the most fulfilled I had ever felt to date. The voice residential has since become an annual event over some twenty-one years, and has definitely been where I have facilitated some of my best work.

जय जय प्रेमानंदा/जय जय मुक्तानंदा

In 1995, a friend of mine called Tess, from my yoga path, showed me a flier she came across called *The Naked Voice* offering voice workshops and private sessions with a teacher called Chloe Goodchild. My intuition told me strongly that I should contact her. I booked a private appointment with Chloe, which took place in a large house near Notting Hill in London. I didn't know what to expect but, as soon as Chloe opened the door, I fell in love with her essence. She was tall, blonde, and radiated light and warmth. I was about to be guided by the most monumental influence on my new destiny as a facilitator of the natural voice.

She recognized my destiny much before I did, and I knew as we commenced our first session that I had come home. She was so free in her approach. She sat at a grand piano in the corner of the room. She invited me to just vocally improvise and advised me that she would follow. She gave me a vast space for vocal exploration. I touched a creative vocal depth that I had never experienced before. We spoke together afterwards as we sat on the comfy white sofa in this prosperous house.

Chloe turned to me and said, "I am embarking on a new venture to facilitate my first ever Naked Voice training, a space where participants can explore the depths of their voices in different modes and traditions – Indian chant, Taize, Gregorian chant, etc."

I was so inspired by Chloe's being that I signed up immediately for a whole year. It was a Naked Voice Facilitator training program with Chloe Goodchild. The course was magical, ground breaking and beyond convention. There were about forty of us on the course. We all met alternately in Bath and London over six weekends. I loved the process, and I made friends that resonated with me on a very different level.

The participants were unlike anyone that I had closely connected with before. I realized it was because they weren't addicts or luvvies from the theatre. They were all focused and interested in conscious creativity, and they all followed a spiritual path. They were also committed to developing heart-centred connections. I felt strangely punky amongst them, and I suppose I was with my peroxide blonde hair, Dusty Springfield black mascara and colourful cap. Most of the participants had been to university and ranged from twenty-five to sixty-five years old.

One woman had her own business, but she said that she had gone beyond money because, where she lived in Bath, everyone bartered their skills, just like the old days, to the extent that you could have your plumbing fixed without money exchanging hands. I found this concept fascinating and somewhat whacky, as I hadn't encountered it before. In the dark world of addiction, where I had come from, everyone lusted after money.

There was also a lovely woman called Annie on the course who loved to hug trees. Now this really was new to me.

"What happens, Annie, when you hug a tree?"

"You feel deeply connected to the natural world," she replied.

I nodded and gave her the benefit of the doubt. Years later, Annie became an interfaith minister and spiritual teacher. We have since happily worked together.

I remember on the first weekend of the Naked Voice training, we were all asked to share a song that was important to us — ideally one we had composed. I chose to sing my *Believing* song. Everyone listened without judgement. Chloe seemed to love my rawness and the authenticity of the lyrics. Chloe was also clear that my voice wasn't yet completely free. She said that she could hear that my vocal chords were wrapped around emotions from the past. She provided a non-judgemental environment that gave me the space to explore unlocking my hidden trapped octave.

The day came when I expressed in sound my pain voice, as Chloe referred to it. Chloe's work included free movement as well, and I remember rolling around on the floor following my natural voice and letting its sound penetrate the walls of my conditioned personality. My voice spiralled into the depths of the unknown. It was the most liberating experience, and one that Chloe held with so much love. Chloe was like my big sister. She was even an Aries sun sign, just like me. For the next decade, she championed my career in voice. She simply got who I was. I felt truly seen and heard by her for the first time in my life, and I loved her deeply.

Chloe gave me many generous opportunities to sing or chant solo in her Naked Voice concerts. These were big events, where we would have The Naked Voice Choir performing at St. James church in Brighton or at St. James church in Piccadilly It was in Brighton that my old teacher, Chris James, came to our concert for one performance. I was nervous that Chris was in the audience because, in the past, he had once given me harsh feedback about my vocal toning after one of his workshops. I had approached him at that time to thank him for his inspiration and for encouraging me to start my first ever harmonic vocal overtoning group. I shared with him that the group had been going well, with many people attending regularly. I was hurt and somewhat surprised — because he had initially encouraged me — that he didn't appear to celebrate this news. Instead, he harshly criticized my vocal tone. It felt to me that perhaps there was professional rivalry in the space, as many people had mentioned to him that day how much they had enjoyed my group. Who knows?

That night, I had a gig fronting a soul cover band in London Covent Garden for which I needed to be bold to perform in the Rock Garden, but I had allowed my confidence to be knocked by Chris's feedback. I remember walking across Waterloo Bridge amidst a student protest march to the venue with my friend, Kamali. I was clad in my band gear of patterned top hat, black leather trousers, electric silver shirt and Dusty Springfield mascara.

We pushed through the crowds and, as we did, a strong voice arose within me: "Keep going, Nikki. You will rise above this. Chris is in your life to bring you trials of strength, not defeat!" Suddenly, I felt this rush of adrenalin as I boldly walked towards my future path.

"Never give up; keep on going," whispered my inner voice. I deeply trusted that all was well.

जय जय प्रेमानंदा/जय जय मुक्तानंदा

At the end of that concert in St. James church, Brighton, five years later, my whole journey with Chris James came full circle. I hadn't seen him in that period. He came up to me with so much love and gave me the most beautiful compliment about my performance. I looked into his eyes and I felt my heart open to him and, in that moment, I felt that we were like two old soul-mates winking at each other who knew exactly our soul contract together. I recognized through revelations that Chris was my teacher for developing belief in myself and letting go of reliance on outer approval. That night, I knew that my performance had gone well, and Chris mirrored that back to me. I thank Chris James on a deep soul level for inspiring me to start my own group and, ironically, for the tough feedback he gave me which gave me the determination to persevere beyond what I thought I was capable of.

I completed the Naked Voice training in 1996-97. It was a very progressive time for me. I started to facilitate many more Free the Inner Voice groups, including one-day workshops in all sorts of varied venues UK-wide. I particularly enjoyed leading at the Life Times Festival in Reading, which was run by a lovely woman called Chrissie Waters, who always championed my work.

In July 1991, my time at the National Theatre was coming to an end, and so was my relationship with Liz. I was changing rapidly, and Liz just couldn't relate to me in my new way of life. I was weird as far as she was concerned – doing all this meditating and chanting with strange pictures of Indian saints in our flat. We had a terrible row one night when she demanded that I take the pictures down.

"You give your mediation teacher more attention than you give me!"

From where she was standing, I guess she was right; I had drifted from our relationship. The truth was that I was unfulfilled and I did want to meditate more than spend time with her. I felt bad and guilty for this, as I always did whenever I chose to honour my inner voice at the risk of upsetting others.

In the summer of 1991, I moved into James's house. James was my rock and, as you may recall, he was the man who introduced me to the path of recovery from alcoholism. We performed really well together. Before my hospital episode in the late 1980s, we were an excellent local cabaret duo, with me singing and James on the piano. We played nights at several wine bars in Battersea. However, our best gigs came later, between 1991-95, at the Jazz Room's Pizza on the Park. We had an exceptional musical rapport, perhaps because we had done our serious drinking together and gotten sober together. We had a mutual understanding that was very evident in our music. Therefore, I felt I could turn to James in my hour of need whilst adjusting to my break up with Liz. I remember one evening at James's house, Liz turning up literally begging me to come home.

She yelled at James, "You are brainwashing Nikki. She wasn't like this before!"

James very calmly talked her down and gently showed her to the door.

Liz had progressively felt that I was being brainwashed, both by recovery groups and my yoga meditation path. We were no longer a match as we had very different values. As I look back, Liz had given me a tremendous amount of nurturing and support at a time when I really needed it. She had been my saviour, supporting me both emotionally and financially, in the most vulnerable (yet emotional) time of my life. To this day, I am eternally grateful to Liz. I would also like to think that, perhaps, I was a catalyst for her to move on, too, from the stagnancy of her previous relationship. Liz did move on in the end, into a very happy and compatible long term relationship. My beloved cat, Bluesy, who I left behind with Liz, spent the rest of her contented life with them both, and she passed away gracefully at the grand old age of twenty-one years.

I eventually found myself a new place in South London. It was in Streatham with a landlord named Boon, which had a divine resonance for me. The sacred text I chanted every morning talked about boons as blessings in life. Boon was a retired member of a renowned pop group. He had a large house, which he laid out in Japanese-style design with hardly any furniture. I had a huge bedroom above his downstairs studio with one futon, a chest of drawers and my keyboard. I remember when I first wrote *Believing,* which was one of my most expressive songs, in that room. It was a good song. In fact, so good that Boon thought I had inadvertently copied some of his improvised guitar melodies from his studio downstairs that must have somehow wafted into my room. I didn't even connect with his riffs, let alone copy them. He was very paranoid, as I could be at times. The song had a chorus that repeated:

"What do we do with the anger inside us?

What do we do with the pain?

What do we do with those angry thoughts and feelings?

What do we do with the people all around us
who continue to lay all their blame?

On the way they grew up and the problems they had BELIEVING."

It was very much an anthem about my early emotional struggles, which were coming up for transformation now that I was sober. It was a song that I performed at various events, and it was always well received as people could identify with the lyrics. As I continued my writing, I continued to train with Helena Shenel to develop my singing technique. It was in 1991, that same year, that my old friend Freya from drama school days called and asked me if I ever gave private singing lessons. I shared with her about the success of my voice group. She said she had a friend who was a self-made millionaire who had a passion for singing karaoke. I felt nervous when she asked me, and immediately doubted whether I could teach someone to sing conventionally.

My intuition, however, said, "Just say yes. You will discover how to do it by doing it!"

जय जय प्रेमानंदा/जय जय मुक्तानंदा

And so it was that my first private student, named Mike C., arrived at my flat for his first lesson. He was a sunny character, dressed in a suit and tie. He worked in the IT industry. I shook his hand and immediately apologized that his lesson would be in my bedroom with him seated on the edge of my bed, due to a lack of space to put the keyboard.

"Ah, don't worry," said Mike cheerfully. Clearly, nothing seemed to bother him. He was a very keen student and, once again, by just experimenting in teaching him, I realized that I actually knew much more than I thought I did. I began to teach him some helpful techniques that Helena had showed me, and he was a fast learner. Each week he reported that his Bruce Springsteen impersonation was improving and how free he felt doing it.

I was only charging him the bare minimum per hour back then, when one day Mike said, "Listen, these lessons are excellent. I'm going to give you more."

Vicky, my friend from earlier in my story, also called me for lessons. She was about to star in a musical about Josephine Baker. After her first lesson, I asked if she would like to listen to my new song, *Believing*. I always felt in awe of Vicky, as she was an Oxford graduate and wrote articles for the *Guardian* and did all these clever things that were out of my comfort zone. She was always very frank in her feedback.

As I sang the last phrase, she said, "It's good, Nicola. You know, you should write a musical."

I was pleased she liked it, but I wanted her to view it more as a soul song than a musical. However, musicals had been my childhood routes, and so, inevitably, these memories impacted my writing style. Meanwhile, my voice toning groups were starting to develop into my own unique style. I found myself beginning to take more risks than simply leading people into overtone chanting.

As I tuned into the Shakti (sacred vibration), I could see people's stuck energy fields, and I was continually guided to give the clients exercises that would free them from their former rigid blocks to self-expression. My intuition would reveal inspiring pictures of me putting three people together, where one person would lead one of the others in movement and sound whilst the third person would witness. This would free both parties, for by serving one another to let go, they would simultaneously release, too. At the same time, I would give them specific sounds or mantras to chant to shift their vibration whilst moving. It was thrilling to watch people opening up and laughing whole-heartedly as they dared to go beyond their comfort zones. My private sessions, on the other hand, at that time, had a more conventional and technical approach.

One of my devoted Brixton group members, a lovely man called Nigel, asked me if he could see me privately for voice toning. This was my first glimpse that private work could be more varied. He was passionate about my work. So much so that he offered to design a flier so that I could promote my voice work more visibly.

"We need a catchy name for your product," he said. "Voice toning isn't catchy enough."

"How about 'Free the Voice Within?'" I said. Nigel and I played with the words until "FREE THE INNER VOICE" was born. It was printed on the front of 500 pink fliers, and thus began a five-year journey with Nigel. Each season I would collect the next bundle of fliers that were orange, pink, blue, and apple green.

It was a blessing to have something manifest to give to people. Nigel also set me up with my first email account. We got on well because he was a geek and I was an airhead, and somehow it worked. At this point, one of the Heathers from the group came forward, offering to help me promote my work. Over twenty-five years, I have experienced a constant flow of the perfect person always showing up at the perfect time to professionally help me with administration and referrals. This always affirmed for me that I was on the right track. Through chanting, I developed a strong intuition that has guided me all the way through my career. I would always listen closely to my inner guidance as to whom the universe had chosen for a particular role. Each time, I just needed to surrender and accept their help. I have felt very blessed in this way.

The Free the Inner Voice group continued to thrive, with more people joining. People were reporting that it was the highlight of their week. They felt free and released. They said that they felt a deepening connection with other members of the group. For some, they would share that those two hours spent connected chanting in the group were more beneficial to their lives than anything else they did in their week. The actors in the group were discovering that, through the chanting and voice work, they were feeling more connected to their creativity and performance work.

I went to see three of these women who put on a performance together in a local theatre. It was so rewarding to witness the fruits of the voice work manifesting in their performances. The more self-conscious and studious men in the group returned weekly, gaining more confidence in their self-expression through voice and movement as they allowed their bodies to move and make sounds you were more likely to witness at a carnival in Brazil. They also seemed to get better looking as their bodies opened out. I remember Vince sharing that he felt so happy in the voice toning work, it made him laugh and take life less seriously. Many of the women reported that they were gaining confidence in the workplace, whether it be when they went for interviews or when they gave presentations in their field. The reports from the majority of the groups in the early years reflected this change.

"Why would we go to a pub or a wine bar when we can do this?"

They loved the social element of connecting with others without the blah blah!

जय जय प्रेमानंदा/जय जय मुक्तानंदा

After I left the National Theatre in 1991, I continued to deepen my devotional chanting practice each day, which helped me to connect to a higher vibration. Chanting daily helped me to be clear, focussed and open, whilst, at the same time, my practice inspired a momentum with my career. My life felt like it was flowing, which was a notable contrast from my twenties – where everything occurred as largely stagnant with occasional successes, largely relative to the amount I was drinking. This was now a totally different experience, and I could sense that my acting career was finally moving forward. Indian saints have written that once the Kundalini Shakti is awakened through mantra, whatever you do in life refines for the better because you are then consciously connected to the source of your life.

At that time, I was cast in a production called *In the Midnight Hour* at the Young Vic Theatre, which turned out to be my favourite show of my career to date. It was set in a nightclub in Liverpool during the 1960s, when all the great Motown (soul) classics came out. They wanted actor musicians who could sing, act and play. As I played trumpet and keyboards, I fitted the bill. I was cast as Mcagey. She was a young Liverpudlian girl dressed exactly like Dusty Springfield – which was perfect considering my aforementioned love of Dusty, which was particularly potent during my time in hospital. I loved seeing all the synchronicities unfold through the fruits of my chanting practice. I was asked to play lead trumpet in the show, playing all the classic riffs in tracks like *Dancing in the Street* and *River Deep, Mountain High*. My solo song was the famous soul track *Rescue Me*. I sang it whilst dancing around my handbag in a northern nightclub with my best friend Duffy in the show.

Two other actresses played saxophone, and one of them (Charlie) also played my best friend, Duffy. We definitely were a red-hot horn section! My physique suited the Dusty look really well. I enjoyed slapping on the false eyelashes every night. I also got to play the Hammond organ for the number, *Stop! In The Name Of Love*. The company had some truly wonderful and talented people. Every actor in the cast played an instrument or they were great singers, and we had an awesome musical director. I adored this new experience of being clean, sober and confident with the sense of belonging to the cast in this show and being a part of a group, which was extremely healing after my bullying memories in the school playground. Here I was fulfilling my creative gifts and able to connect with the cast socially without alcohol in the bar after. I even plucked up the courage to run a vocal warm-up session for the cast, which was to sow the seeds of many future offers to facilitate my work in drama schools and team building in companies.

During that successful run of *In the Midnight Hour*, I wanted to earn some extra cash. So, in addition, during the day I would serve pizzas at Pizza on the Park at Hyde Park Corner. They had a jazz room downstairs. This was generally where I would work between acting jobs. Peter Boiseau, whom I had met when I sang at Kettners when I was eighteen years old, owned the restaurant and gave me a job there as a waitress – mainly because he loved my singing.

"Why don't you serve pizzas and sing? That would be novel, wouldn't it? Quite a gimmick!"

So it was I began to serve pizzas in the evenings in the jazz room and day shifts upstairs according to my acting schedule. In the evenings, between serving pizza pepperoni and dough balls, I would sing Irving Berlin songs. Here I was, once again, singing in a jazz room. Only this time I wasn't running to the bathroom to drink red wine for Dutch courage. Instead, I would lock the bathroom door and chant mantras to plug me into the Shakti before singing live.

It was amazing to be performing solo and sober. I was accompanied by the resident pianist, Simon Becker. Some nights, I would have a hideous confrontation with the Miss Trunchbull-type Manchurian manager, Lisa. She would sneer at me to get off the "bleeping" stage and serve flippin' tut pizzas! Despite Lisa's protests, I rose above it and found this to be a fun period. Some nights, after singing my set with the resident pianist, I would receive compliments about my singing from people who were all well-known in the jazz world.

I would serve their pizzas afterwards at their tables, and they would say, "Well done. Great voice you have there."

Simon Becker, the pianist, would say, "You know who that person is over there, don't you?"

I didn't have a clue who anybody was. I just loved singing.

One night, all the staff who weren't on duty serving at the restaurant came to see me perform *In the Midnight Hour* at the Young Vic theatre. They absolutely loved the show. The downside of that show was that I had a very brief romance with one of the girls who played saxophone. We were a great duo onstage. Unfortunately, the candle soon burnt out quickly between us as she started seeing the girl in the box office. This had a spooky similarity to the end of my time with Holly, who left me for the girl in the box office at Watford Palace theatre. I remember bursting into a fit of jealousy one night after the show. We would all have a drink in the pub after the performance next door to the Young Vic. I would drink ginger beer.

One night, I walked in and there she was with the girl from the box office, who had a k. d. lang-type haircut. They were in the corner, clearly connecting. I totally lost it and I remember throwing my metallic briefcase across the floor in a fit of jealousy. This scene also reactivated painful memories of my first boyfriend, Simon, who replaced me for another girl. I felt I had a Vesuvius boiling inside me. I realized, as I chanted daily, that I had a deeper journey ahead of me to heal my relationship to myself – especially if I wanted to attract more nourishing and lasting relationships.

जय जय प्रेमानंदा/जय जय मुक्तानंदा

One unfortunate evening, on my way in to the theatre, a woman pulled out of a side street and crashed into my car. It happened right outside the theatre. I was stationery in a red light queue when her car collided into my driver's door. Fortunately, no one was hurt, but my car was written off. I received my insurance money and decided against buying a new car straight away.

One morning, it dawned on me that I could use the insurance money to finally fulfil my dream to stay in the ashram of my yoga path. So it was I booked my stay for two weeks, right after *In the Midnight Hour* finished its run. I strategically timed my trip for when my parents were away on holiday. I suspected they would wholly disapprove of this trip, and I definitely didn't want to have to explain myself.

The ashram was in America, and I was both super excited and appre-hensive. I had no idea what to expect, other than that I was to spend two weeks immersing myself in the blissful practices of chanting and meditation. I will never forget landing in the USA, where I was greeted by some yoga meditation devotees who met me and a few others in a mini-bus called The White Dove. The minute I looked into their eyes, I immediately felt that I was connecting to another dimension. The Shakti (divine energy) coming from the driver and his assistant was scintillating. I felt I had come home, and I began to feel my heart racing with excitement that – at long last – I would soon be in the ashram! I found myself bubbling up with questions. I was so intrigued that people actually gave up years of their life in the world to live in an ashram. I felt much too conditioned by my British middle-class upbringing to dare take such a risk.

Just before we left the airport, I asked the driver what value he got from living in the ashram. I was fascinated that he had been a long-term resident for ten years.

He looked me directly in the eyes and replied, "Freedom!"

The energy behind his words was so strong that I felt the vibration piercing my heart and, in that moment, I felt an excitement that one day I, too, might be liberated. All the way in the bus I felt the cells of my body tingling with joy and anticipation for what my experience might be, especially the prospect of actually meeting my meditation master.

We eventually arrived and my heart began beating even faster. I checked in at reception, which had the appearance of a quality hotel lobby, yet, with the vibration of a temple. I noticed there were four glowing women all serving behind reception. The one who served me was from Brazil. Like an angel, she had sparkling eyes and a beautiful smile. As she handed me the keys to my room, I felt like I was being given the keys to a heavenly kingdom. I just couldn't wait to look around!

The ashram environment was magnificent, with glorious expansive grounds, including a spectacular lake that you could walk around in silent contemplation. In the main building, there was a glorious hexagonal temple that was the hub of the building. The energy inside was like velvet. The silence settled on me like snowflakes as I walked in. There were statues of deities all around and a murti (sacred statue) of a great Avadhut (enlightened being) in the centre made of gold, dressed in radiant colours and a turban. He had a permanent and peaceful smile on his face. The whole environment inside the temple was designed to take you deeper into meditation. For the first few days, I was in paradise, as there was chanting every hour, on the hour. There were also shuttle buses that ran between the buildings, and the chants were always playing on the bus with everyone chanting all the way to their destination. This really did feel like the train that had "heaven-bound" on the front from my experience earlier at East Putney station.

On certain days, it was announced that our meditation master would be giving powerful and uplifting discourses in the assembly temple in the main building. This was a phenomenal building made entirely of glass all the way around so that you could view the gardens. I had never been in such a full-on experience before. I looked around in awe. There must have been around 700 devotees, all squeezing in on cushions on the floor, waiting for her to enter the hall. The minute she stood at the entrance door, you could feel her electrifying presence. All heads turned as she glided like a peacock into the room in her pale pink robes. She gracefully walked to her elegant, pale-blue armchair at the front and arranged herself in a cross-legged position with her robes flowing to the floor.

I watched her with my jaw dropped. Here she was, in the flesh and form I had seen in visions, and whose grace had blessed my life. She began to give her discourse about Sadhana (or the spiritual path of yoga); her words resonated so deeply in my heart that I felt like she was speaking only to me. It seemed that everyone had that experience around her. The challenge was that, although our teacher was in the physical form of a female, what was really important was our own connection to our inner Self – the experience of divine consciousness. This emanated constantly from our teacher whenever we were in her presence. She was established in the highest state of consciousness all day long. We were highly encouraged to focus on our own Self and not to get caught up in her physical form, which was ultimately transient.

जय जय प्रेमानंदा/जय जय मुक्तानंदा

That first summer, I found this paradox really hard to understand. I just didn't get that the focus of devotion should not be on her physical form but, rather, on the supreme principal she embodied as the inner Self. I found myself, as did hundreds of new devotees, actively looking for her in the ashram hoping to bump into her. I would then go through unbelievable reactions of anger and rejection that I had come all the way from England and she still hadn't made time for me. Who was I anyway? I soon came to realize that this was my ego flaring up, needing validation and attention. The whole point of this yoga meditation path was to surrender to my inner SELF; our teacher was purely a guide.

Many days proved to be a real burn-up for my ego that summer. One day, it was announced that there was to be a European music festival. All the various countries were invited to perform a traditional song from their country in the main dining hall. I was invited to join with two British devotees who were a father and son and both played guitar. We arduously practised three Beatles songs to represent England. We were going on stage after a Spanish group did a classic number in bright red costumes with fans and castanets. My meditation master stood there transfixed, watching the Spanish with full appreciation. Then it was our turn. My heart was pounding. We had microphones on the stage ready to roll.

We came to the mics filled with hopeful expectation. I started to sing the Beatles *Can't Buy Me Love* pretty loudly, when suddenly my meditation master turned around sharply and abruptly left the room. Suddenly, all the electricity cut whilst we three were left mouthing the song!

A young Asian boy rushed through the room saying, "Shhh, the Shakti doesn't want this. This is why this has happened. Pay attention!"

I could feel my ego melting like the witch's hat in *The Wizard of Oz* when she had water poured over her. I began to realize that the Shakti was working on purifying all my attachments to praise and my insecurities about failure. Of course, it is nice to have recognition and applause. However, if you are attached, it will never set you free. I felt like I was in some kind of harsh detox from praise.

This practice of seva (or selfless service) was profound. The Shakti was really strong and, in offering selfless seva, we were all put with other personalities, generally people who seemed to ingeniously know how to press all our buttons. Selfless service included anything from gardening, chopping vegetables, cleaning toilets, and helping in administration, the music department and multiple other options. Of all the yoga practices, seva works on the ego the most effectively. As I began to work with others, I got to see where and how stuck I was in certain patterns of approval-seeking and the attachment to recognition.

My main seva was in the young people's department. We would coordinate creative yoga programmes for children whilst their parents meditated. I got along very well with everyone in the department and, in particular, I made a lifelong friend with a music therapist named Shelley, who was living in the ashram. We both clicked immediately and became soul support for one another in our challenging times of Sadhana (spiritual journey). We had hours of fun together song writing, creating plays and coordinating art projects for the kids. I realized in this seva that I was reclaiming a piece of my own creative childhood and that it was perfect that I ended up in that department.

Every time, a fear of mine was transformed through meditation, chanting or seva, I felt free, spacious and blissful afterwards. I felt an inner flow of grace from within. This was a very different experience to the intensity of my spiritual awakening. The time spent in hospital had crippled my energy. In the ashram, I experienced permission to expand a steady flow of Kundalini energy, which connected me deeper each time to my inner voice. Each day, I began to have clarity through revelations on where I was going in my life. It was as though I had suddenly been given a new inner satnav that I could wholly rely upon. During that time, I experienced a lot of questions about my future. Acting was beginning to lose its appeal now. Yet, I didn't know what else to do, and I certainly wasn't ready to do voice work full-time.

I wanted to ask for advice for my future from my spiritual teacher. You could rarely speak to her directly. However, as I was new to the ashram, my friend Josie from Wales, who was an old-timer there, managed to make me a special introduction. I will never forget that moment. It was extraordinary to finally meet my meditation master who, for five years, I had only seen in photographs and in visions on that fateful bus to Cardiff.

Josie led me to what was known as the private darshan area (to receive blessings from a realized being). My master stood radiant – like an exotic creature – and her vibration felt other-worldly. She was exquisitely beautiful – even more so in person than in my visions.

I began to shiver as I opened my mouth to ask her, "Where am I going?"

She looked at me and tilted her head in deep thought with a wry smile on her face, as if she knew something I didn't, and said, "Talk to Mira*."

This was not what I had expected. I wanted to ask more detail, but with a lift of her hand, she turned around and disappeared behind a door. I thanked her silently for her advice and set about to finding Mira.

जय जय प्रेमानंदा/जय जय मुक्तानंदा

Mira had been a student with Helena, my singing teacher back home. I had met her a couple of times when she had travelled from the USA to London for singing lessons for her seva at the ashram. I contemplated why Mira could be helpful to me. Mira had, once upon a time, been a well-known feminist lesbian singer/songwriter in the USA. She had also, at one time, been an active alcoholic. Now, she had given up the outside world to follow her yoga mediation path in the ashram. I could see lesbianism, singer-songwriting and alcoholism were connected with us.

I finally met Mira in the dining hall. She was very helpful and friendly and much warmer than she had been in London when Helena had introduced her to me.

"So, how can I help?" she asked me.

"I'm stuck with my career path. I don't know whether to stick to acting, singer/songwriting, and I now have this natural voice group that I run. Should I focus on that now? Or maybe I should be like you and give up the world and live here?" I exclaimed.

"Nikki, the main thing is to trust what is unfolding for you. Whatever is in front of you is what you are supposed to be doing. Do that with great love and your main work will reveal itself," Mira replied.

"Is that how it was for you?" I asked her curiously.

Mira smiled and said, "Of course. You'll see!"

I returned from the ashram after two weeks feeling totally different inside. I had been chanting every day there and I came back to England with renewed energy and zest for life. I was immediately offered a season at Salisbury Repertory Theatre and The Cheltenham Everyman for two years between 1992 and 1994. At the Salisbury Playhouse, I was cast in a production of *A Midsummer Night's Dream* playing Peter Quince (Pat Quince in this case). This was an exciting professional breakthrough for me, being cast in a Shakespeare play, and was pivotal for me to dispel all the doubts I had after the critical feedback I had received about my acting when I was growing up.

During the rehearsal period, I worked so hard to get it right. I was still in early sobriety, doing my best to stay away from the bars and pubs. As a result, I felt somewhat isolated from the cast. Everyone went drinking after the show. I was determined to remain sober. Back then, I felt very vulnerable in drinking environments. Instead, I would go back to my digs and meditate or chant in the evenings. Chanting kept me sane and connected and was my sanctuary each day. I noticed that I was changing rapidly. The people and environments that I was previously attracted to no longer had the same appeal to me. I, unfortunately, had a painful journey with one of the actors in the cast called Andrew*. He played Bottom, the weaver. Andrew and I clashed badly. He then deliberately played games with me to throw me off while onstage during the performance. He would make moves and gestures that we hadn't actually rehearsed which, in turn, caused me to feel anxious in our scenes together.

During rehearsals, I was glowing, connected, enthusiastic and bubbling with ideas. I proposed to all the actors who were playing the mechanicals the bright plan that we could have a Pat Quince and Bottom the Weaver rehearsal dinner. I suggested that it would help us to develop our characters by exploring our relationships in the play. All the other actors loved the idea, except Andrew. He was somehow threatened by the idea, probably because he hadn't thought of it, and he did everything to wreck it. He refused to stay in character throughout the special dinner. The other three men fully embraced the exercise and had fun with it. I looked at Andrew's glum face at the head of the table and began to allow his sour presence to undermine my confidence. Back in rehearsals, our working relationship got worse and worse until, eventually, Andrew said he just couldn't work with me.

He ignored all my suggestions for our scenes until I had a crisis of confidence, and duly gave up on my performance. This apart from on the first night which, by fluke, went really well for me. There was lots of warmth and encouragement from the audience and I got several laughs as Pat Quince. However, I couldn't maintain confidence in my performance. I had allowed my enthusiasm to be crushed. I had completely given my power to Andrew. It was so painful that I remember making a desperate phone call to my therapist who told me that I was going through growing pains and to stay strong, which didn't help much.

At that time, I didn't know how to cope. All I knew was that I certainly couldn't drink on it. I realize, reflecting back, that I had manifested Andrew at the time of my acting breakthrough to mirror for me that I had still not forgiven my father's early criticism of my acting. I see in life that unforgiveness brings those experiences back to you over and over again. Andrew was mirroring my worst fear that I just wasn't a good enough actor.

However, despite being in a crisis of confidence, I now had a major tool I could turn to. I had a bigger voice within to connect to, beyond the cries of my wounded ego. I began to increase my chanting practice to twice a day until the end of the run. Every day I got stronger and stronger inside. Andrew behaved the same. However, I was less affected by him the more I chanted. As I write about such episodes in my life, I once again see how my apparent enemies and critics have been dark angels aiding me forward towards my destiny with natural voice and sound. As the curtain of the last night performance of *A Mid-Summer Night's Dream* came down, I breathed a huge sigh of relief that this production was finally over.

जय जय प्रेमानंदा/जय जय मुक्तानंदा

My season at Salisbury Playhouse, nonetheless, continued, this time with a brand new cast in the pantomime production of *Mother Goose*. I was to play the bad fairy called The Demoness of Discontent. This was a light relief after *A Midsummer Night's Dream*. I used to sit on a green throne every night after entering stage-left with my bright green tongue. The kids would boo and hiss at me as I made my entrance. It was great fun frightening them in every performance!

It was during the pantomime that the renowned choreographer, Bill Deamer, spotted me at the Salisbury Playhouse. He spoke to me after and said, "I don't suppose you play the trumpet do you?"

"Yes!" I replied, thinking, *What are the chances?* "As a matter of fact, I do."

The production he was casting for was to be at the Cheltenham Everyman theatre. It was a Broadway musical called *Gypsy*. I was cast as the trumpet-playing stripper, Miss Mazeppa. I then went on to play Mrs. Rochester in *Jane Eyre*, then Miss Hannigan in *Annie* and Constanza Weber in *Amadeus*. I thoroughly enjoyed my time in Cheltenham.

My performance (as the stripper Miss Mazeppa) in *Gypsy*, playing the trumpet through my legs, got me rapturous applause as this part is usually mimed. I chanted before moving to Cheltenham for the best accommodation to come to me. We were sent a long list of local numbers to select from. I closed my eyes and pointed to one that said Carol White. I couldn't believe the coincidence that her daughter had played Miss Mazeppa in an amateur dramatic production – the poster of that show was still on my bedroom wardrobe door.

The household cat was a ginger cat who, by extraordinary coincidence, happened to be called Mazeppa! Carol also had a grown up son called Simon who had spent some time living with a family in Kuwait. He, incredibly, had practiced the same meditation yoga path as me and had since come to love chanting. Were these coincidences? I think not. As I meditated, it became clear that the universe was looking after my life. There is a saying that "coincidences are God's way of remaining anonymous."

These coincidences were kindred to my journey at the Royal National Theatre. The parts I was cast in all resonated with previous parts of my real life that I still needed to integrate. It suddenly dawned on me that the theatre where I was performing in Cheltenham was close to all the ancient roman villas and ruins in areas like Cirencester. During my Kundalini awakening, when I had experienced my past lives recall, I had seen a vision of a Roman life I had lived with my father when he was a Caesar and I was a mystical Christian. In this lifetime, he grew up in Painswick Gloucestershire, nearby to the Roman ruins. I was performing only a few miles from Painswick as a stripper named Miss Mazeppa dressed as a Roman centurion with a helmet and a spear. In my meditations, I had an inner revelation that something karmic was somehow being resolved here.

Jane Eyre was also a great production, and I excelled at playing Mrs. Rochester (who was the mad wife known as Bertha locked in the attic). Having been in an asylum myself, I could totally relate to Bertha. I received rave reviews for my performance, with quotes including "vulnerable, moving and heart-wrenching." Each night, as my character, Mrs Rochester, appeared at the top of the spiral staircase, I experienced a direct catharsis that enabled me to leave my hospital episode securely in the past. My last performance of the season was as Miss Hannigan in *Annie*. This felt like my swansong of playing eccentric alcoholics.

I got on well with most of the Cheltenham cast. However, I still went home in the evenings to chant and meditate. I was fed up with being single, though. So, one night, a gay actor called Graham said that there was a gay nightclub at the Cheltenham racecourse. He asked if I wanted to go. I felt excited by his invitation. The moment I walked through the door, there was a stunning black woman standing in the doorway. I fell for her like a magnet and made the mistake of expressing my feelings to Graham, who promptly went and asked her if she was single. He came back and told me her name was Donna* and that, unfortunately, she had a boyfriend, but that she was curious when she glanced over to check me out. I was disappointed. What was a straight girl doing in a gay club? Surely she was lying!

The following week, by chance, I went to a regular club in town where she was again, sitting in a corner with a couple of guys. I walked past her on the way to the toilet with my heart thumping. On the way back, I plucked up the courage to approach her.

"Hey, you're Donna, right? I saw you at the racecourse the other night. My friend Graham spoke to you."

Donna had a beautiful smile and said, "Yeah, that's right," in her broad Gloucester accent. We exchanged numbers and, within a week, we began a hazardous and extremely physical relationship. Donna was bisexual and she chose to leave her violent boyfriend for me. She had been involved in the Gloucester drug scene and had been a wheeler-dealer; she was also on the edge of crime. I was extremely attracted to her because, although I had kicked the drink habit, I wasn't ready to give up flirting with darkness and excitement. As with many dark characters, she was both magnetic and charming – and our physical relationship was electric.

जय जय प्रेमानंद/जय जय मुक्तानंद

In autumn of 1993, I was in the veggie café in Cheltenham High Street when another cosmic coincidence occurred. A lovely couple called Angie and Bob walked in. They were on the same yoga meditation path as me. They told me that sixty cheap flights were being sold for British devotees to go to the main ashram in India. I felt a rush of Shakti suddenly race through me. I just knew that I had to go. Graham (my actor friend) was with me and said he would like to come, too (even though he had never been to a meditation programme before). The flight was for the month of February, 1994. We booked it together. Our meditation master was going to be there, so I was full of expectation and excitement. I had never been to India before, and I had heard so much about the ashram there. However, I thought it would be years before I would go. There is something about divine timing — when destiny strikes, wherever you are, the Shakti will find you. Bob and Angie were my messengers that day in Cheltenham. My time had come to fly to India and I was excited!

In February, 1994, sixty British yoga devotees landed in Mumbai. My first impression was the horrific poverty on the streets. It was shocking to behold. As we looked out from the bus, there were children begging and there were people with horrific deformities. This somehow made me feel obscene to be a privileged Westerner. After two hours of driving on decrepit roads, the bus eventually pulled up outside the main gates of the ashram. The building was beautiful and majestic. It felt like we were arriving at a mini Taj Mahal; from the outside it had such a royal vibration. There were security guards in brown uniforms and caps guarding all the main gates.

We all descended from the bus in single file. As we walked in through the gates, it was like entering a Garden of Eden — it felt like heaven on Earth. The gardens were absolutely breathtaking. We arrived on a balmy evening in time to register and pick up our nametags. Once again, there were around ten people serving, all smiling and ready to serve us all in any way they could. We were each led to our accommodations which, because of the sheer volume of people arriving, were in huge outdoor dormitory tents, housing about 100 women in each, from all over the world.

I slept next to a lovely English lady called Lisa who had the vibe and beauty of Julia Roberts. On my other side was an Australian woman who told me a grim tale one night of how she had nearly been murdered by a crazed patient of her husband, who was a doctor. She told me the patient had gotten a crush on her husband and came to destroy her in her home with a kitchen knife one afternoon. She confided in me that if it hadn't been for our meditation path, she would have given up all hope in this life. I listened to this story, stunned, as I took in my new alien environment, and how soon after my arrival I was hearing this radical story.

This was only my second ever visit to an ashram. However, this time it was to the mother ashram in India. This sacred environment was an absolute pressure cooker for the ego. The ashram schedule was incredibly intense. We were up at four a.m. for chanting and meditation, then followed seva. Here the practice of selfless service was even more intense for me than in the USA. My personality traits became amplified – especially the undesirable ones. It was impossible to hide any inauthenticities. I spent much of my stay feeling jealous about what gifts and compliments other people were receiving from our spiritual teacher. I soon learned that in the ashram, things flowed much more easily when I was able to surrender to the Shakti and follow my inner voice. I realized how needy I was for outer validation and recognition throughout my stay there. This would happen particularly when, each day, our meditation master would offer darshan (a personal blessing) every lunchtime for three hours.

We would all queue in anticipation, with flowers in hand, to offer what we had purchased from the market outside. As each person came forward to her chair, they would be touched on the head by peacock feathers as a blessing. Sometimes people would be given gifts, like a shawl, or a quill pen in my dear friend Debra's case. Her love was writing and she was thrilled when she told me that our teacher had somehow read her soul.

When I walked to the front each day, hoping my teacher would address me, she would look the other way. I felt like every day I was undergoing a thousand deaths inside as her penetrating energy pierced my ego. At first, I thought perhaps she was punishing me for being gay and the fact that I was thinking constantly of Donna. India, after all, was such a heterosexual, marriage-focussed culture. I felt like a black sheep out there. These were all my crazy projections. Upon reflection, I realized her outer negligence was actually perfect for me as she forced me to learn very quickly that the answers I was looking for were all inside me anyway. The purpose of a living master, I learned, was solely as a guide to encourage me to turn within.

It was in India where I realized that my relationship with Donna was not going to work due my journey going in a different direction. However, despite this revelation, I chose to ignore it and stay with her. Our relationship continued for another six months. However, upon my return, we started rowing badly. I invited Donna to the ashram back in England to take a one-day intensive meditation programme. The Shakti of the course was strong, and sometimes the energy would work so deeply that it felt as though you were sleeping rather than meditating. The meditation energy could purify blockages without you even being conscious of the process. Donna was one of those who fell asleep throughout. When she awoke, she was livid. She felt, because she had slept, that she had wasted her money.

जय जय प्रेमानंदा/जय जय मुक्तानंदा

Donna began shrieking in the car afterwards on our way home, which felt extremely jarring as I was feeling expanded and light.

She became extremely aggressive and started yelling, "I could have paid for a flippin' gas bill with that money. What a waste. You lied to me, Nikki. I didn't get anything from it!"

I got so scared that I slammed my hand down on the dashboard and bellowed in my loudest voice, "Stop shouting!"

Donna was shocked at how loud my voice was when, to my amazement, she stopped! It took a lot for me to be that bold. We spent the rest of the journey in silence. Unfortunately, Donna smoked a lot of dope, which made her paranoid and prone to violent mood swings. Gradually, I began to see that she had a flip switch, where her ferocious temper could flare right up at any moment.

It was during that period that I became closer to Marc, my good friend, regular attendee and fan of my Sunday voice group. We were actually a perfect match. He was interested in the same spiritual journey as me, and he was also great fun and easy to be with. He also totally supported me and was a refreshing contrast to the stress with Donna. We got along so well together that I started to question my sexuality. I even thought I had fallen for Marc romantically. One day I asked him if he felt the same way. He admitted that he did and we decided to try dating.

When I broke the news to Donna, she was understandably devastated. She said that, in the past, she would have done something in revenge, like slashing my face with a knife or at least slashing the tyres of my car! I shook inside as she spoke, but then she said, "I suppose I'll let you go, Nikki, as this is probably my payback for all the partners I have cheated on in the past. Up until now, you have been the one who has moved my life forward the most."

I felt really sad when she said this. Although Donna was obviously troubled, there was a warmth and kindness mixed in with her aggression that could be both touching and loving. One time, when I was broke, she said that she would even be willing to go on the game for me to get me some money, and she meant what she said. This was a world I couldn't identify with, but I received her pure intention. I graciously declined her offer and thanked her for her generosity.

Marc and I lasted two months. Despite some obvious compatibility, I was definitely gay. It was a shame because Marc and I had a lovely connection.

We flowed together socially and people said we made a great couple. They could even see us married in the future. However, sadly, we were not to be.

I started feeling an intense desire to be back with Donna. Although I had stopped drinking alcohol, I was not ready to give up the adrenaline of wild relationships. I was still madly attracted to her. I called Donna in tears and said that I missed her. I drove at a ferocious speed to see her again in Gloucester, and I begged her to take me back. She did take me back, but it wasn't the same. In fact, my departure had left Donna mistrusting me. I remember her coming to hear me sing with my soul cover band. If I connected with anybody's eyes in the audience whilst singing solo, she would storm out of the bar in a fit of jealousy. These episodes became increasingly intolerable.

We decided to try and save our relationship by booking a holiday in Greece. It was there that we came to a disastrous finale. One day, Donna thought it would be cool to hire a moped to drive us up to the mountains. We managed to drive to a fishing village for lunch. However, on the way back, the bike went over a loose piece of rock on the road and we skidded and fell off onto the mountain road. Donna scraped her arm and leg badly and I cut my knee. The wheel was bent and Donna began screaming like a crazy lady, blaming me for puttig us in this position. We pushed the bike all the way down the mountain in the blazing heat, as I tried unsuccessfully to reason with her.

"Why is it all my fault?"

"It just is, you bitch," she retorted.

I recognized that the impact of the marijuana Donna smoked would turn her into someone who would, out of the blue, become both paranoid and aggressive. We eventually got back and she ignored me for the last two days of the holiday.

I became more and more frantic inside and when we reached the airport, I said, "Are we really over?"

"I don't want to discuss this," snapped Donna.

We arrived in Gatwick airport and went home to our separate locations.

Donna called me three weeks later, asking me to come and see her. I spoke to friends who supported me with my addiction recovery. They all said that, ultimately, it was my choice. However, they didn't recommend that I stay with her, as the temptation for me to use alcohol and narcotics again was too high. I couldn't face telling Donna. When I finally arrived at her house after a three-hour drive, and as soon as my back was turned, Donna lit up yet another spliff.

My inner voice shouted loudly, "Get out now before it is too late, Nikki."

As she stood puffing in the bathroom, I walked in and said to her, "We are definitely finished Donna. I'm sorry."

Donna was too stoned to follow me. I drove back from Gloucester in tears. In retrospect, Donna had taught me the most valuable and painful lesson yet – to speak up for myself and to have self-respect. She had a good heart and a troubled mind.

जय जय प्रेमानंदा/जय जय मुक्तानंदा

My thirties were a wonderfully inspiring and creative time in the development of the voice work, with 1992-2000 being the period when I laid the foundations for Free the Inner Voice. I was chanting devotedly. Every day, new inspiration would arise within me for facilitating free expression in a conditioned society (especially the UK), where cynical attitudes have stifled the authentic voice for centuries. I would discover each time I facilitated ground-breaking ways to encourage the clients to step out of their comfort zone, they would then discover their authentic sound and take that connection into their daily lives by using the tools that they were born with – their voice and their movement. My inner voice was constantly guiding me to have the courage to risk the work with more and more people. In each group I led, my inner guidance would facilitate a breakthrough in connecting people to their core power. I felt like Michelangelo chipping away at the stuck vibrations until the true masterpiece emerged.

The groups were edgy in the 1990s period. People never knew what would happen next – and neither did I, for that matter. I would implicitly trust my inner voice to give me inspiration. I remember, in one workshop, I had the impulse to invite a woman to sit on the floor and create a ballad on the spot to honour and value herself. I then asked her to do all this in front of a full-length mirror. I remember my heart racing as to whether she would run away. But I held a space bigger than her doubt, until she actually followed through on the exercise. I watched her watching herself in the mirror with mascara running as her contracted heart began melting. She looked radiant afterwards, as a huge weight had clearly lifted.

The next day, she went to work and her manager came downstairs, by sheer coincidence, with a leaflet about natural voice work.

"That's Nikki Slade. I have literally yesterday just done an amazing workshop with her," she said.

"Do you fancy writing an article about her work?" he asked.

I then received a call from her. I hadn't realized that she was a journalist and had come on her day off to free her own inner voice. If I had known in advance she was a journalist, I probably would have felt watched, and perhaps it wouldn't have gone so well.

She said, "I am going to send everyone to you, Nikki," whereupon she wrote a golden review of my work in a mainstream London magazine, which attracted a new flood of clients. She was true to her word.

On the outside, if you were a fly on the wall, the voice groups looked crazy. You really had to participate to experience the extraordinary alchemy that would happen in the sound work. I would always open the evening with a chant that connected the group to their hearts. I was then able to intuit exactly what was required for that specific group and then the inspired exercises would naturally follow. Sometimes, I would invite students to make a sound that they absolutely dreaded making as it reactivated past fears – children should be seen and not heard. Some clients had fears of releasing physically. However, by the time they had impersonated a jelly, their self-consciousness was instantly expelled, or perhaps momentarily worsened, until the red flush had vanished from their cheeks, never to return again.

Sometimes, the guidance was for them to make animal sounds, primal sounds or to let go like a wobbling jelly. Pictures would pop into my mind of inspiring exercises for them to do in pairs for breaking through social inhibitions. I was extremely mindful to announce at the start that this would be a non-judgemental and unconditional space. This being said, the students were truly open to experimentation. I saw clearly that the core issue was people feeling free to express themselves in front of others without barriers. Some clients were freer than others, but every client had a level of vocal connection that they hadn't yet reached. I felt that I was simply a conduit to bring through inspiration for their transformation to happen. I realized, in these privileged moments, that I was witnessing people who hadn't been singing all their lives, as I had. It was a really big deal for them to sing – and especially to chant – for the first time. Their faces would open as the vibrations of the chants touched their hearts and they moved past the shame of being told that they couldn't sing in childhood. Chanting would free them from this burden.

During this evolutionary period, I found a perfect location in North London called Voice Space. This space was a magical basement situated underneath a library in Islington. It was owned by a gay man called Richard who, at one point, had been into the drag scene. There were beaded curtains in the entrance and lots of exotic and eccentric drag costumes hanging on one side of the room, whilst on the other was a free space where Richard held his own vocal workshops. It had a little altar in the corner with Native American medicine cards on it. I would often pick one and they would always give me, and some of the clients, the perfect message for that day.

जय जय प्रेमानंदा/जय जय मुक्तानंदा

Many of my clients from South London followed me to North London. They loved Voice Space – it became their creative den. Some of the stalwart voice workers were Terry, Jay, Caroline, Georgie and Stella. Jay Morris, in particular, totally championed the work, and he turned out to be one of my special angels and holds a very special place in my heart. Jay gave me incredible support in the formative years of Free the Inner Voice. He was my absolute rock, and he tirelessly hosted and spread the word for all my workshops in North London, Norwich and Nottingham. He is also a phenomenal body worker, and his therapeutic massage work kept my body fit for duty. Alternative body work and massage were becoming increasingly popular at that time. Jay and I used to laugh at all the gremlins he was pulling out of my teapot! I am moved and filled with eternal love and gratitude for who Jay was for me during those crucial foundation years.

In this period, Gabriel Roth's 5 Rhythms Dance was becoming all the rage, and Jay was an avid fan. I enjoyed 5 Rhythms, but was less confident about exploring my emotions in movement. I was inspired by her CD called *Initiation* (an ironic title after my journey with the aforementioned book about Egyptian pharaohs by Elizabeth Haich), which I sometimes played for people to warm up to at the start of my groups. A lovely woman called Sue Rickards ran a much-loved group in Tuffnell Park. She generously allowed people to announce their workshops in the space at the end. Jay let people know about my voice work, and many of the early clients that attended were 5 Rhythms dancers. I am thankful to Sue for her generous support of my work. This period enabled me to experiment with new and outside-the-box ideas. My work was known in London circles for being confrontational, yet very freeing. That was the constant feedback that I received. It was evident that people felt safe to experiment there.

Stella, one of my devoted students, was a lovely, vibrant young woman who had a love of 5 Rhythms dance. It was from early on that Stella was one of the apprentices that would surely shine in her own right as a future voice facilitator. Stella came to see me in my private practice in Clissold Park. Stella was a brilliant student with whom I could explore the potential of natural voice work. There was no limit in those sessions. We both had so much fun and would laugh helplessly some days.

I remember when we walked through reception afterwards, the girl at the till would say, "Everyone who comes out of here after chanting always looks amazing. What goes on in there?!"

"You should try it!" said Stella, grinning.

We both became great friends after Stella had completed as my student.

One day, I went for a picnic with Stell, and I asked her where she had grown up.

"Oh, you wouldn't have heard of it, Nikki. It's a tiny village called Send in Surrey," she replied.

"Oh yes, I have. In fact, when I was a student at the Guildford School of Acting, I went to an eighteenth birthday party of a friend of mine who lived there."

"What's her name?" asked Stella.

"Bronwen," I replied.

"Bronwen? That's my sister!" she yelped.

"Oh my god, I've been to your house!" I cried.

"I remember being sent early to bed as it was to be my grown up sister's party," laughed Stella. These moments confirmed, yet again, for me that there is no such thing as a coincidence! Stella and I have been closely linked over the years. We have shared an identical pattern with relationships – discovering that whatever I was going through, she was having the same issue, and vice versa. She, also like me now, is with someone who has a child by a previous marriage.

We laugh about our parallel relationships even to this day. Stella is now a very successful voice facilitator and chant leader in Los Angeles. Terry is now a talented voice facilitator, too, in Europe. One early fan was award-winning life coach Gosia Gorna, who has been a phenomenal champion and angel of my work for over twenty years. She has referred countless clients, and has kept me steadfast on my path with her clear vision of where my career was headed. Everything she predicted would happen for me back when I was thirty-five years old has come to pass. I am eternally grateful to Gosia.

In summary, I regard these wonderful souls as some of the many angels who have helped me to discover my best work by signing up to be my students. I have developed everything over the years through the loyal clients who have entrusted me with their voices. I have seen a pattern from early on in my journey that specific people have been sent by the universe to help me develop some ground-breaking work.

As my career was unfolding, I continued to embrace my own sadhana (the Sanskrit word for spiritual journey) by regularly attending retreats to transform my own stuck patterns. It was on a particular retreat weekend dedicated to *Awakening the Goddess* in 1995 that I met Maliya*. The whole weekend was an "out there" experience, with twenty-five women tapping into their "inner feminine" in wild and wonderful ways. The sequel weekend was in a chateau in France, and I remember, at one point, all of us feeding each other strawberries and grapes with blindfolds on! I was lying next to Maliya; there was an instant chemistry between us. Maliya had mixed-race parents – a Malaysian mother and Irish father. She was striking, with jet-black hair, tall and stunning to behold.

जय जय प्रेमानंदा/जय जय मुक्तानंदा

On the ferry back, we both flirted with each other. I felt a rush of excitement at the power of our connection. I found her irresistible and fascinating. By sheer coincidence, the following day, I happened to be shopping up in Covent Garden. To my amazement, I ran straight into Maliya outside an alternative new-world music shop, which occurred as another divine coincidence. We stood there looking at each other in silence outside the shop.

My heart was racing as I said the classic line, "Fancy meeting you here."

"Yes. Ah well," giggled Maliya.

"So what are you up to today?" I asked her.

"I am going to a Michael Ormiston concert in Islington," Maliya replied. "Wanna come?"

My heart raced again; there was no question that I would not go. Even if I had arranged a prior dinner with the Queen, I was going! Michael Ormiston is an extraordinary musician and sound healer. However, for me, the evening was truly magical for other reasons. We both sat on the floor in the front and Maliya sat behind me with her arms around my waist throughout the performance. The electricity between us was magnetic, and so it was that a six-year romantic roller-coaster relationship began. As I look back, if anyone had showed me a sneak preview of the ride I was about to embark upon, I doubt if I would have had the courage to get on board. In retrospect, I don't regret a single moment, and I probably would do it all over again because the lessons I learned were life-changing. Our relationship took me to the edge of my soul and back, where I felt fully alive every day. It was like being at the edge of the jaws of my inner shark and, at the same time, in the height of blissful ecstasy. Our relationship was to be the most passionate and painful journey of my life to date.

Maliya's attraction to me was initially connected to the Shakti (or spiritual energy) I carried from my yoga path. She used to ask me lots of questions about the chanting tapes I played in my car, until one day she asked for the details of the London venue for attending satsangs. Maliya began to share the same path with me and, as she did, we both began to press each other's buttons. We burned in the fire of yoga as our egos bumped up against one another. One day, we both realized that our connection was karmic and no accident when we saw the cosmic coincidence that our fathers had the same name, Adrian, and our mothers' names were respectively Sue and Siu.

There were also other synchronicities. Maliya, too, was a performer. She was an incredible dancer, particularly in the Japanese style of Butoh. She also had a great singing voice. She was eight years younger than me and it felt like she had taken some of the same life steps as me, only eight years later. We smiled ironically one day when she pulled out her sheet music from her performing arts school training. She used to audition with exactly the same song as I auditioned with, entitled *Could I Leave You?* by Stephen Sondheim. This song portrays a roller-coaster relationship whereby, through years of thrashing it out together, the female declares, "YES," she will finally leave him! My journey with Maliya was to be predicted right there in those lyrics.

Our journey felt epic, consisting of being passionately together for six months, then passionately splitting apart for another three, six, or even nine months during our six years together. I recall once being on a chanting retreat in a shamanic dome in Stroud during one of our nine month break ups. Always during these times apart I would think of Maliya every day with obsessive consistency. Where is she? Is she seeing someone else? Why couldn't she just see things my way? Why did she leave me? Will she come back?

She always did come back, and somehow I always knew she would return, however bad we got – and it did get bad. We were caught in a trap. We would war like Trojans, both of us feeling hurt and justified. We both came from families affected by alcoholism, and we were trying to have a relationship with a familial map that just led to total dysfunction between us. Maliya would go through volatile mood swings. When she was up, I was dancing on air, and when she was down, I felt I was there for days digging trenches trying to pull her out. I never thought to examine my own co-dependent dysfunction in this hopeless pattern we shared.

We were not to blame, and neither were our families. The ancestral alcoholism, however, was at fault. Its horrific legacy, unless addressed, whether as addict or co-addict, had the potential to destroy us both. This showed up in our total inability to last more than one day without an argument. That was a good day because, generally, within hours, we were fighting. However, our chemistry together was so exquisite that it genuinely felt well worth going through all the heartache. I remember being in the shamanic dome in the Cotswolds one night when suddenly at ten p.m., my phone flashed up with Maliya's phone number winking at me. I flew out of the door into a field outside and took the call under a sea of stars in the black velvet sky.

जय जय प्रेमानंदा/जय जय मुक्तानंदा

My heart thumped furiously. What did she want? Was she coming back – again?

"Hello, Maliya. How are you?" I asked nervously.

"Listen, Nik, I really miss you. I realize things are not the same without you here," said Maliya in her alluring voice.

"You could say that again," were the words that ran through me. And presto, we were back together again! I motored at eighty miles per hour, breaking speed limits to see her, which could never overtake the speed of my heart in anticipation of seeing her after nine months apart. I arranged to meet her at South Kensington tube station. I pulled up and there was no sign of her for nearly one hour. I eventually called her on her cell phone.

"Where are you, Maliya?" I asked with a panic in my voice.

"I am at Gloucester Road tube. Where are you?" she replied.

"But I said South Kensington tube; you got out one stop too early!"

I replied. In that moment, I felt a knot inside that I was not doing the right thing. In retrospect, the signs from the universe were always there for me not to get back on this ride, which was never easy and never smooth. If I had been rigorously honest with myself, I knew this meeting was going against my guidance. In my relationship to my career, I felt expansive, inspired and free. I felt that the universe was always on my side, encouraging me to move forward. With Maliya, I turned a blind eye to my inner guidance that was repeatedly telling me to let her go. However, I just could not resist her, let alone leave her. Could I leave her, as the song said? Undoubtedly the answer was No!

The crescendo of our journey came in 1996 when I was cast in a production called *The Slow Drag* in the West End. I was portraying the role of Johnny Christmas, based on the Billy Tipton story. Billy Tipton was a trumpeter in the 1930s, and she was born as a woman who had a passion for music. She wanted to play trumpet professionally in a swing band, which in the 1930s was strictly a male domain. She rebelled and stole her brother's security pass. She used his identity and moved across states in the USA, cut her hair and paraded in a suit. She declared herself as Billy Tipton. In the 1930s, if you wore a suit and spoke in a deep voice, you were automatically regarded as male. Billy never underwent surgery and, still, nobody knew of his female origin. His wife, Kitty Oates, swore that her relationship with Billy was strictly platonic. She said that this was due to a car accident that he reported he had endured that forced him to wear bandages around his midriff. In truth, he wore them to flatten his breasts.

This was a fascinating part for me to play. My intuition told me I had gotten the part practically the moment I walked into the audition. I had my trumpet under my arm and I played *I Got Rhythm* by Gershwin and then sang *Night and Day* by Irving Berlin. The director's eyes glistened, and I knew she had chosen me right there and then. I had shoulder-length blonde hair at that time, was more endowed than some, and could have put off a director with less imagination. I felt this casting was a very karmic event in my life.

That summer of 1996, I had thought I might extend my stay in the ashram in America. I had longed to live close to my meditation teacher and to stay in the ashram indefinitely. The pull I had to the inner journey was immense. Nonetheless, there was a contradiction to this in that I was phoning Maliya back in the UK at vast expense daily. I couldn't completely focus on my spiritual practices because her form would keep appearing before me. That summer we were arguing again, but then what was new? I was very nearly set to move into the ashram when I received the news that I had been offered the part of Johnny Christmas in the show from Broadway, *The Slow Drag*. This part for me, as I reflect back, was a scream from my inner voice to leave Maliya. I shocked myself at my decision to stay in London to play what was to be the classic part of my stage career. The arrival of this Billy Tipton-based part altered the course of my life to spend the next fifteen years pursuing my vocation primarily in London.

The show was opening at the Freedom Café in Soho. The first day I moved into my dressing room, there was a translucent blue vase with peacock feathers in it. The previous production had obviously left them there. This was another beautiful coincidence for me. My meditation master always bestowed blessings by brushing her devotees with peacock feathers. I felt this to be a sign of her grace for me to stay in London and to play this part. The play was a three-hander, portraying the stressful romantic relationship between Johnny and his wife June, based on the life of Billy Tipton and his wife Kitty

Oakes. In the play, Johnny and June have a close friend called Chester, who Johnnie suspects is having an affair with June. This makes Johnnie paranoid and finally breaks his heart. Johnnie dies, in the end, of heartbreak and a stomach ulcer, due to years of suppressing his original female identity.

One of the songs in the show that I played on the trumpet was called *Sweet Melinda*, sung by the character Chester. The song tells of the painful journey of a man deserted by his woman, named Melinda, for other men. When the musical director gave me my trumpet part, he had "accidentally" written *Sweet Maliya* on the top.

"Don't you mean *Sweet Melinda*?" I said.

"Oops! I'll cross that out. Sorry. Don't know why I did that," he said.

I, however, knew this wasn't an accident; it was a loud warning from my inner voice for me to see a piece of my future that I was about to play out in real life with Maliya. It was no wonder I wasn't ready to give my life to spiritual practice in an ashram. Maliya took precedence over everything. She was firmly locked into my system, and I was never going to let her go.

जय जय प्रेमानंदा/जय जय मुक्तानंदा

Maliya had always liked the androgyny in me. In fact, when I used to return home each night from the performances with slicked-back hair and walking like Carey Grant, she said that she became even more attracted to me. We were at the height of our passion during this show. I was leading a parallel life – obsessed with June on-stage and with Maliya off-stage. The rehearsal period for me to play Johnnie had been an amazing adventure. I got to watch and study several 1930s movies with male movie stars in their double-breasted suits, sporting cigarette lighters and opening car doors for women. This was to be my homework for enhancing the realism of my character. When the reviews came out after the first night, they were the best of any I had received in my entire career (including one from Nicholas De Jongh, a highly critical reviewer from *The Evening Standard*, who described it as, "Nikki Slade's enthralling performance of Johnny Christmas").

I remember clearly on the opening press night my girlfriend Maliya sitting in the front row with her incredible upright posture from her years of dance training.

After the curtain call, the actor named Chris, who played Chester, said, "Who was that stunning-looking woman in the front row with the incredible posture tonight? Anyone know?" She was a Japanese style butoh dancer. He was right.

"That's my partner!" I said.

"Wow! You got the jackpot there, Nikki," he replied.

In the play, Chris and I, as the characters Johnnie and Chester, had both just enacted a furious fight on stage over which one of us should have June. This was all feeling very symbolic, indeed.

The Slow Drag did become a prophetic experience of my own life. In the summer of 1999, I became more and more paranoid that Maliya would leave me for men. I could feel that the fateful outcome was coming. I witnessed her flirting with men at the yoga centre. I then became acutely and unbearably possessive, which caused Maliya to become cold and distant. We had our worst row yet before I boarded the plane to the ashram for a couple of months.

At the airport, Maliya said, "Nikki, we are finished; this really is done this time!"

"No!" I screamed, resisting getting onto the plane until the very last minute.

Once again at the ashram, I was madly ringing Maliya every day. Most days she wouldn't pick up. If she did, she would immediately put the phone down after I had begged her to come back to me one too many times.

I couldn't wait to return to London to try a final attempt at getting back with Maliya. I remember driving through Camden town to her flat when a thunder storm started outside. I literally felt, on the inside, that I was on a ship in a stormy sea that was about to capsize. I screamed out loud for help as the windscreen wipers barely cleared the windscreen. Suddenly, I saw an acquaintance I had met at a therapy group, who just happened to be on the pavement. What were the chances of that happening?

I swerved over and said, "Please help me!"

He got into my passenger seat as I bawled my eyes out. He began to talk me down calmly as I told him that I was in danger of picking up alcohol on the extreme pain that I felt.

"You will get through this," he said. "This, too, shall pass, as the saying goes."

By the grace of God, his soothing words spared me another day of physical sobriety, despite my head being full of madness.

Before long, however, my worst nightmare came true – Maliya did leave me for a man. Between the end of *The Slow Drag* in 1997 and March 2001, we were to split up and make up several times. It was at the end of one of these insane break ups that we met up intimately and passionately for what was to be the last time in February 2001. The meeting was so amorous and connected that I definitely thought we were back on. Two weeks later, I was invited to go to an alternative nightclub in Hampstead. It was another extremely synchronistic and fateful night, as right outside the venue I bumped into *Natasha, who was my then part time PA. Natasha and I had become very close over that year. She had not told me that she would be going to the same club that night. I also bumped into two very close friends of mine, Charlie and Michelle. Little did I realize that I was about to need all the support from the universe I could get. I decided to have a look at the upstairs dance floor.

The floor was empty – or was it? There, to my horror and trepidation, in the far corner, was Maliya, dancing with a man in full embrace. I froze on the spot, with six years of our relationship flashing before me, including scenes from *The Slow Drag*. How could she? How could she leave me? This was my only mantra. She didn't see me, but I saw it all. This was my movie, not hers, that I was watching. I saw her in full technicolour, as beautiful as ever, but now she was no longer mine. In fact, had she ever been mine? This was the delusion I had suffered, that I could own anyone. Is anybody ever ours? This painful lesson pierced my heart as it sank deeper. I just couldn't accept or believe what I had witnessed.

जय जय प्रेमानंदा/जय जय मुक्तानंदा

I pinched myself to check if this was real. I started shaking and felt sick to the core. I went back downstairs and saw Natasha, who had just arrived in the entrance hall. Later, I recognized that the Universe had sent in the troops for me. Thank God, as I was going down fast!

"Are you okay, Nikki? You look pale."

"No!" I said. "My girlfriend is embraced with a man on the dance floor upstairs."

"Do you want to leave? I can come with you," said Natasha.

"No. I want to face this!" I replied.

I went downstairs to another dance floor, which was now filling up with people. Right at the back, I could see Maliya and the man again. They had come downstairs to join the throb of the party. I knew that I just had to ask her. I needed to know the exact nature of their relationship so that I had proof and could move on without living in hope for the future. I took a deep breath and strode over like the lovesick soldier Joe in the movie *Carmen Jones*. I lightly tapped Maliya on the shoulder, interrupting her dance.

"I have to talk to you, please. Give me just five minutes?"

She looked perturbed and so did he.

"Do you mind? Can't you see we are dancing?" he said to me.

Maliya ushered him to wait for her and said to him awkwardly, "I'll be five minutes, hon."

I felt sick hearing her address him.

There was a quiet lobby area at the back with glass doors you could view the dance floor through. We stepped into that space.

"Are you seeing him?" I asked.

"What do you mean seeing him?" she replied.

"Have you slept with him?"

"Yeah … and actually I want to get back to our dance now!" she said in a matter-of-fact voice.

"I thought we were on again when we last met?" I asked with insecurity rising inside. "We had a beautiful night, I thought. Didn't we? How could you do this? Don't you love me any more?" I couldn't believe that after a night of such passion I could be so cruelly replaced.

"Look, Nikki, please just accept it – we're finished! We were already finished! We really have to stop this now, please. Look, I need to go now!"

I was mortified at how cold and brutal she was, as if I was an irksome stranger. Maliya walked swiftly back to the dance floor. As I watched her join him again, I knew that, right there, we were done forever. I took a deep breath and went back into the dance hall and, strangely, found myself walking straight up to her bloke and patting him on the back.

"Good luck," I said to him as I walked past, acknowledging to myself that finally he was the catalyst for me to finally accept that my future was to be without her.

It was when I got back to the front lobby that my legs began to give way. Michelle and Charlie appeared like angels and were hugely supportive in escorting me out of the building. They gave me lots of reassurance that all would be well in the future, and it was definitely time to let go!

"Chant the Durga mantras," said Michelle (in her strong, Brooklyn, New York accent). "They'll blow this thing outta the water!"

These were vedic mantras of fearlessness to be recited in times of challenge. Natasha then came outside and said she would be happy to accompany me home in my car. Michelle asked if she could have a lift, too.

I talked in a nonstop haze all the way back about Maliya, and they both listened. Until, out of nowhere, Michelle shouted out from the back seat of my car, "STOP NOW, Nikki. It's over! If you don't, you're gonna die!"

I felt like it wasn't Michelle talking. It was a voice of providence and foreboding that this time I just could not ignore. I realized, in that moment, that

Michelle was my inner voice on loud haler that night, and thank God she was there to heed the call. I eventually got home and went to bed. I slept remarkably well and awoke with an amazing sense of clarity. The very next day, I wrote Maliya a letter of closure and posted it through her door. I drove through the rain down Holloway Road. I felt the tears of letting go pour down my face. At the same time, curiously, I felt free, with a brand new future ahead of me.

जय जय प्रेमानंदा/जय जय मुक्तानंदा

Maliya was a monumental and precious catalyst for me in my life. I didn't thank her for being that back then, but I certainly do now. We were both agents for one another, working out familial patterns and waking up to our spiritual growth. I eventually recognized that I had never been able to accept Maliya for the way she was. I always wanted her to change. This led to unbearable possessiveness, which was my part in our drama. Throughout our journey, I experienced being on the edge of my creativity. In all our up and down excitements, I wrote some of my best songs, and my most edgy voice work was born during our turbulent relationship. I am truly grateful for our time together, and she will always have a special place in my heart.

I recall now my vision on the bus to Cardiff, when my spiritual teacher appeared on the screen at the front of the bus, explaining that for each chakra or spiritual energy centre that I would move through there would be a significant relationship for me. As I reflect back, Holly represented the first chakra in my struggle for survival as a young and inexperienced adult; Donna was the second or sex chakra – a largely physical relationship; and Maliya definitely represented chakra number three, the solar plexus – the centre of fire and strength and the ability to take constructive action in the face of volatile emotions. It took six years for me to face my test in the seas of these perilous emotions of jealousy, rage and overwhelming rejection and abandonment. With perfect grace and a miracle/some miracles, perhaps I eventually took the right action and moved forward. Thank you for the ride, Maliya.

You are invited to chant once again!

JAY JAY PREMANANDA / JAY JAY MUKTANANDA to help us to remember that wherever we are in our journey, beyond the drama is a life of inner freedom.

EVENING STANDARD

FANTASIES may, course, get you anywher
But as Carson Kreitzer
haunting little play, T
Slow Drag, suggests, son
people feel fantasising
just not enough and are driven
live their sexual fantasies in re
life. This off-Broadway play dea
with one such example — a woma
living as a married man and dece
ing everyone except his wife.

Miss Kreitzer calls her play
flight of fantasy", inspired by a 19
item in Time Magazine. It w
reported that after the death
Billy Tipton, an old jazz musicia
one of his adopted sons was told
a funeral director that Billy h
really been a woman.

The Slow Drag follows closely
Tipton's footsteps by composing
play in which Johnny Christmas
jazz musician who blows his ow
trumpet, falls for June Wedding
sultry torch singer, and lives qu
happily ever after.

Even prim, squeamish people l

Ratings: No stars — adequate
★ *good,* ★★ *very good,*
★★★ *outstanding,* X *poor*

Christopher Colquhoun   Kim Criswell   Nikki Slade in

THE SLOW DRAG

by Carson Kreitzer

Directed by
Lisa Forrell

"Brilliant...
mesmerising"
Sunday Telegraph

"Alluring...
enthralling"
Evening Standard

"This is great
entertainment"

FRIDAY, 21 FEBRUARY, 1997   **49**

REVIEWS

g of being a
-made man

Drag
Theatre

E JONGH

ucial questions
riage come rush-
The Slow Drag,
sa Forrell's spir-
als with none of

pose and live as
of sex life did the
a closet lesbian
fathered June's
the couple hood-

s about sexual

identity and behaviour are never debated. Instead, a small jazz band counterpoints desultory scenes from the couple's married life, with nostalgic love-songs alluringly delivered by Kim Criswell's June Wedding. Nikki Slade's enthralling performance as Johnny almost makes up for the play's textual thinness. In double-breasted, pin-stripe suit and slicked-back hair, Miss Slade makes a pretty convincing young man. She has the right stuff — a breastless look, a male walk and strut, even a man's voice.

But despite the appearance of Christopher Colquhoun as Johnny's best friend, Chester, who hankers manfully for June's body,

there's no real dramatic pulse. Johnny's laconic, ironic talk — "I was a self-made man" — amuses. And Miss Criswell's big, plush voice soars and stoops all the way from More than You Know to The Way You Look Tonight. And

there's something most poignant about this view of an illicit marriage which defies the odds and survives through Billy's fanatical allegiance to her adopted gender.
● *Until 15 March. Box office: 0171 734 0122*

Return to gender: Nikki Slade as Johnny in The Slow Drag

Hugo Glendinning

ॐ नमो दुर्गा माँ/ॐ नमो लक्ष्मी माँ

Part 4: Om Namo Durga Ma /Om Namo Lakshmi Ma

This chant invokes the protection and blessings of the divine feminine energy.

OM = the supreme one.

NAMO = to honour.

DURGA = is the goddess of courage (as previously mentioned in section 2). She represents the fearless courage that comes from our direct connection to the inner SELF (or universal divine power as we understand it).

As we chant Durga's name, we invoke that courage to move fearlessly through the challenges that are in front of us.

LAKSHMI = is the goddess of sustainment and the provider of our inner and outer abundance. As we chant her name, we become aware of the many blessings we have already received and the many gifts that are yet to come, whilst remaining in the infinite awareness that where there is perfect giving, there is perfect receiving.

MA = Mother. Durga is described as the great mother who protects and guides us. Lakshmi is an aspect of Mother Durga's function to sustain our well-being and to bring us nourishment.

I recommend this chant any time you are in a mindset of lacking, whether it be worry, anxiety or frustration. The vibration of the chant clears the mind and uplifts the spirits to a sense of gratitude for being alive. My experience is that, when I am resonating with gratitude, the blessing of abundance flows towards me, whether it be love, money, opportunities, or friendship.

DOWNLOAD "OM NAMO DURGA MA/OM NAMO LAKSHMI MA" AND CHANT ALONG!

I would love to invite you to join me in chanting as you journey through the next part of my story.

You can download this chant for free by logging on to the following website and entering your details:

www.nikkislade.com/freechants

Let's Chant!

I t was 1999, and a very exciting year for evolving the voice work. That year I received an incredible review by an arts critic to *Time Out* magazine. This review attracted a stream of new and wonderful clients, including Louisa, another stalwart regular at The Voice Space in Islington. She was a puppeteer and phenomenal artist. Louisa asked me if she could work with me privately. We began our journey, which resulted in her gifting voice work sessions to all her family, including her older sister, Natasha. The entrance of Natasha, whom I have mentioned a little in the previous chapter, was to mark the beginning of an incredible relationship that was to accelerate my career and, ultimately, Natasha's destiny, too. Natasha resonated with Free the Inner Voice straight away. For over a year, she attended every class I offered, from North to South London and retreats.

During that period, two movement therapists, Richard and Emma, began to attend the Wednesday evening group. Richard was head of the movement therapy course at the Central School of Speech and Drama called *Sesame*. He loved the voice work, and duly invited me to run some workshops for the school. This was a leading-edge time for me in the early nineties, when there were relatively few natural voice workers facilitating in London. It was exciting to be invited to offer my work in such prestigious schools and to be a part of the evolution of a new era.

Shortly after that, I was also invited by the head of drama in education at Central, Sally MacKee, to lead a voice course for the postgraduate students, too. It was great to be able to offer something back to the drama world, having struggled with my own confidence when I was an actor. Later on, I also received the call from the aforementioned Sue Rassay, my old friend from

The Guildford School of Acting days. She is now the drama director at the London School of Musical Theatre. She invited me to work with the students there, who were at the pre-audition stage for agents.

The London School of Musical Theatre then became an annual engagement for seven years. It has been very rewarding to bring what Sue and I identified from our own acting history as being the missing link in empowering young actors to connect with their core. I recognized from my own experience the benefit of actors connecting to themselves first before getting lost in, or even hiding behind, a character. The impact over the years on the drama students has been amazing to watch, as students move from a state of self-doubt to a newfound inner confidence. The chanting assisted them greatly to open up their hearts to a fearless space of openness and inspiration, as well as bringing out the natural resonance of their authentic voice. It was refreshing to bring students together through the power of chanting and to witness them leaving the luvvie culture momentarily behind to connect within. The majority of the students, at the end of the training, reported that they felt more empowered to stay centred and confident with critical feedback from some directors and agents before entering the pressures of the acting profession.

With Free The inner Voice over the years, what I have loved is bringing chanting into contexts where this might never have happened. One day, I was invited to offer my voice work in Wandsworth men's prison. My friend, Nicholas, was a therapist and he ran the addiction recovery wing there. The men on this wing had committed crimes directly as a result of being obliterated through drugs and alcohol. I spoke to Nicholas and shared about the chanting and natural voice work. First, he suggested that I run a trial workshop for the other therapists on the wing to see whether they felt it could benefit the men. I worked with five of them and, as their hearts opened, some of them were so moved that they cried.

At lunch afterwards, Nicholas said that he was willing to put me in with the "wolves behind bars." I will never forget the ground breaking day, arriving for the first time at this ominous prison. I remembered, as I looked up at the grey walls of the building, that I had often wanted to offer something at Brixton prison when I ran my first ever voice group opposite that building. Well, I got close, for here I was at Wandsworth armed with my instruments: a harmonium, a drum and some Tibetan bowls. As I walked into the clinical reception area with my kit, I was abruptly stopped by security.

A warden in uniform behind a bulletproof window glared at me. "Miss, you can't bring all that into the building," he said brusquely.

"But I have been booked to run a music group this morning under the authorization of Nicholas B.," I replied, dismayed.

"Let's have a look. Well, you are on the list, but there ain't no mention of any instruments coming in," he replied.

"But these are the tools I use to lead the session. I need them," I said anxiously.

"Well, I'm sorry, you can't bring 'em in!" he emphatically replied.

What was I going to do?

ॐ नमो दुर्गा माँ/ॐ नमो लक्ष्मी माँ

My heart pounded. The prospect of leading chanting to prison inmates was already scary enough, let alone leading without my props and doing it a capella! My mind was ticking over fast – how could I do it without? I had come this far, and I definitely was not going to turn back now. I remembered I had a drone CD of an Indian tamboura with me and I also had a tamborine.

"May I bring one CD and a tamborine in, at least?" I asked nervously.

"Mmm, yeah okay then," he replied, apparently enjoying his authority.

He opened the back gate and gestured that I follow on behind him. He led me across a courtyard and up and down stairs and passages where there were endless locks for every corridor. I was expecting to be led into a recreational gym where the men would be able to move freely. Instead, I found myself taken to a pokey cell room with a tiny window only in the corner with four bars across.

"Is this where the session will be?" I asked the warden, feeling surprised at the lack of space.

"Yep. Keep 'em tight!" He smirked.

I walked into the space with my heart pumping. This was the most confronting prospect I had ever experienced, to date. I had twenty minutes before the men were due to arrive. I knew that I needed to trust the guidance of my inner voice more than ever for this gig. I knew I had to let go completely, otherwise fear would overwhelm me. I got down on my knees and repeated some Sanskrit mantras to invoke blessings for the task ahead of me. As I finished, one of the therapists, named Brian, came in and said he would be joining the session to keep an eye out in case of trouble and for my protection.

The men arrived. There were sixteen of them, one therapist and me with a tambourine! They were rowdy and up for a right laugh. I welcomed them all, like they had arrived into my home. I asked them politely to stand in a circle, breathing calmly so as not to be fazed by their raucous behaviour. My inner voice assured me that the only way to win them over was with plenty of humour. I created the absurdity for them that here we all were in a crammed cell about to make chicken noises, but what the heck! Whereupon, they were inspired through gut wrenching laughter to make all manner of noises, sounds and physical manoeuvres. They were doubled over and releasing for sure. I really didn't care at that point whether they got the subtle essence of anything as it was just so wonderful that they were laughing, and by this point I was in hysterics too!

"Awwww, mate you look like a right twat doing that!" "He looks like a fricking yak giving birth", and "Look at Rob, ha ha ha ha!" were the kind of guffaws coming out of them.

It was in that moment that I had huge gratitude for my time at Pimlico comprehensive school, sitting in class for seven years with rebellious boys who were trashing life before they had even started. Somehow, I wasn't fazed by the men, for my past experience assisted me in blending into their reso-nance. Once they had made every daft noise in the universe to warm up, they were ready for something subtler. I was guided to inspire them to compose their own song from the heart.

I invited them to sit on the floor in a circle and close their eyes – to try to connect to their happiest memory from their life on the outside. I invited them then to come up with one lyrical sentence that captured that time for them that could be turned into a collective song.

One of them piped up, in a broad squaddie cockney accent, "I've got a poem!"

"Oh yes," I said.

"It's in my cell," he replied with a deadpan look in his eyes.

All the men put their heads down to shrieks of, "Ah, no this is so embarrassing!"

They obviously had heard his poem and knew the contents of it back-wards! There was a feeling in the room that the men knew that I was about to be fatefully tested upon hearing his offering. I could feel that the men were getting embarrassed on my behalf in case I couldn't handle what I heard.

I braced myself. "Okay then, let's hear your poem."

He left the room and came back with a crumpled piece of paper. There was a pause in the room – you could hear a pin drop.

"Okay, let's hear what you have," I said.

He cleared his throat and looked down at the scrawny piece of paper, mumbling in his broad cockney accent a debauched limerick with lyrics worthy of the squaddies' mess.

He leered at me over the top of his paper and looked me straight in the eyes and said, "How would you turn this into a song, then?" He twinkled with a "gotcha there" type of twang. All the men lent forward and froze to watch how I would react to this crude and bawdy lyric, and to catch what I would say.

I paused for what felt like an age and said a rapid prayer in my mind as I searched in the archives of my life for a speedy retort. I suddenly remembered when I was nineteen, going out with some gay friends to the Vauxhall Tavern (a well-known drag bar in London). They had six-foot men in drag with huge stilettos, giraffe lashes and fishnets singing the greats and turning everything into filthy innuendo! That's it, I got it!

Seizing the moment, I said, "I know how your poem would be best set to music."

I vividly set the scene for all the men, creating for them the drag bar setting and what I was wearing. I then dived into my best impression of one of the roughest drag queens I had seen there. I chose to soften my impression with a touch of Danny la Rue (a famous British drag queen who made it to star at The London Palladium). I stood up in full character as though I was standing in the middle of a drag club stage with sequin curtains behind me. I acted being six foot five in stiletto heels. Suddenly, I broke the long pause by beginning to sing out loud and proud a spontaneous melody I composed on the spot to the inmate's shady verse with a dramatic voice and full on cabaret gestures.

ॐ नमो दुर्गा माँ/ॐ नमो लक्ष्मी माँ

The song reached an outrageous climax, at which point I held the last note and final pose for what felt like forever, whilst wondering for dear life how my performance had gone down? There was another big pause from the men, when suddenly this roar of laughter hit the room, followed by a mighty round of applause. They couldn't believe what was coming out of my mouth! After that, they were like sweet boys – putty in my hands. They were, suddenly, genuinely keen to learn about mantras. They said that they were looking forward to my next visit.

At that point, my keyboard was put through an x-ray machine and it was passed through. I led them in the chant *Kali Durge Namah* (that you have chanted earlier in this book), which began to have them all rocking. There was an atmosphere that afternoon of a musical that had broken on the wing. The wardens came by one by one and stared through our window. They couldn't believe what they were hearing as the men chanted at full volume, "KALI DURGE NAMO NAMAH" (hail to the fearless goddess power within) – like Arsenal were playing Tottenham at home!

After the successful feedback of the work at Wandsworth prison, Nicholas the therapist was offered a management position at the Priory Hospital North London. He asked me if I would like to facilitate my workshops there on the addiction treatment programme. I am still there thirteen years on, and the sessions there are very much one of the highlights of my week. It has been a way for me to pass on what has helped me hugely in my own addiction recovery. The path of addiction has definitely been for me, and I believe for countless other souls, the pursuit of bliss and ecstasy. The only thing amiss being that we sought the ecstasy in all the destructive places.

Chanting, for me, has been the number one transformational practice, and to pass it on to other recovering addicts has been a total joy and blessing over the years. Recovering addicts loved it because they actually got it! Just like I did. The relief and release on their faces as they begin to connect to themselves and their core sound is so rewarding to behold. There is also a lot of humour as we break the initial ice, too.

I remember a patient called Mo, who was a geezer from Shepherd Market. One morning, I announced, "Today we will chant 'Jaya jaya Shiva shambho'."

Mo looked at me deadpan and said, "I haven't heard that one for years."

We all fell about laughing at the idea of "Roll out your Shiva, we'll have a barrel of fun!"

Another patient, called Al, couldn't wait for Jay Bhagawan, which he used to call Jay's Burger Van. In fact, he even asked me to sing it onto his answer phone message, whereupon he said "Jay's burger van. Leave your message after the tone!"

The patients I have worked with are from all backgrounds, ages, cultures and classes – from upper class lawyers to a gangster's moll, renowned singers and wayward teenagers. Once the chanting begins, all their roles and statuses in life fade into insignificance as they unite together as one heart. Afterwards, some even describe their experience as similar to coming up on a pill without the come down.

I often ask the group afterwards, as we look around at the walls of the green house where we have our weekly session, "So, are we in a five-star hotel on a tropical island?"

"No," they reply, as it dawns on them that freedom can be attained naturally on the inside.

In 2000, I was invited by Paul M. who was one of the original members of my Brixton group, to lead a voice group on a voluntary basis at a day care centre for mental health users in Chiswick on Sunday afternoons. When he asked me, I felt compelled to provide a space for people who had faced the psychiatric system, as I had. I wanted to offer some creative release for them. Sean, from my regular group, was a volunteer at the centre and was the first to introduce me to Paul. Both Paul and Sean had been mental health users in their time, too. Paul, ironically, had served time at Brixton Prison due to mental illness.

I will always recall that first Sunday walking through the day centre dining hall in west London. All the members were eating Sunday lunch, and the smell of subsidized cooking was pungent. They all stared at me as I walked in with depressed eyes and varying dishevelled states. There was a lovely woman there, called Carol, who was one of the helpers. We started talking and it turned out that she had met my meditation teacher years ago in India, and we shared a common friend named George. Carol directed me to the corner of the hall where I would be leading the group.

They all walked in, some with lit cigarettes that Carol asked them to finish outside first. All these wild, wonderful characters appeared, including John (a really nice middle aged guy with depression) and Lee (from up north, who had bi-polar disorder and a very serious demeanour). George was a bubbly Jamaican guy who was always singing. He was also schizophrenic and was sustained on medication. Linda was a large lady with bi-polar disorder and a wonderful soprano voice. John and Lee were keen guitarists and Linda loved to sing. Then, there was a very friendly Asian man, called Dom, with a round face and warm smile. Paul and Sean joined us because, although like Carol they were serving at the centre, they had all been patients under the Mental Health Act at some point. Being with Carol, Paul and Sean was very healing for me. It was really nice to meet others who had been there, too.

ॐ नमो दुर्गा माँ/ॐ नमो लक्ष्मी माँ

The group really took off, attracting more and more members, including another older woman, also named Carol, who was in her late sixties, smoked liked a chimney and talked with the sound of a vocal ash tray. She was a scream. She would walk in and out of the session to have lugs of her fag, but she was still really keen to participate. After six months of meeting on Sunday afternoons, we had all written an album's worth of music together. Each person contributed a lyric to each song, and I would thread it all together with chordal accompaniments on my keyboard and record each song in its roughest version for posterity. Sometimes the songs were really moving.

"Ooh, this song makes me want to cry," jolly Linda chortled, and would then immediately laugh out loud after she realized she had said something sad.

Dom would frequently get up and start dancing with joy at the prospect that he was actually having fun for once.

Four months into our sessions, the tragic day came when we heard the news that Dom had died of a heart attack. In commemoration, the core group came together to compose a song for Dom to be sung at his funeral. It began with, "There was always a strange peace that surrounded your pain. Dearest friend, you had the light within, but couldn't face the darkness of the day!"

After Dom's funeral, Sean was so moved by the song that he had the initiative to apply to the MIND Millennia Fund for a maximum grant to professionally record an album of these songs. The application had related that Paul, Sean, Carol and I had come through the mental health system, and Paul from prison, and we were out the other side wanting to make a real difference to other mental health users. The grant they were offering was looking for applicants just like us. I will never forget driving with Paul and Sean to the East End of London to the MIND Millennia Fund main office. The manager in charge twinkled at us as we shared our vision and passed him a rough recording of the songs.

He looked at me directly and said, "I want you all to know that this project has a really strong chance of getting the maximum grant we are offering. Let me take your application to the powers that be!"

As he spoke, I had a chilling feeling as the Shakti pulsated through me. It was the very same feeling I got when I intuitively knew I had gotten the part in *The Slow Drag* before I was actually told.

A month later, we were miraculously awarded the top grant of £20,000 to record our album. Sean came up with an inspired title, CARSOS (Creative Arts Resource for the Sanity of the Soul), as the label name. Carol's neighbour, by an extraordinary coincidence, had once been Ike and Tina's backing vocalist, and he was also a record producer. Jimmy was an African American in his sixties who was so relaxed and laid back that you could almost push him over. He had wonderful tales to tell us of his experiences on the road in the good old days with the Turners. He was in his twenties then, with his whole future ahead. Jimmy lived with his British wife, Kathy, in a bedsit in Shepherd's Bush

London. He was now dedicated to recording and playing the blues. Kathy was deeply into her spiritual master Krishna Murti, and she would talk for hours about him whilst puffing on a spliff with Jimmy.

Jimmy was certainly meant to be for our project. When Carol told him the cause of our project and that there were funds to pay him, he was right there for us. I couldn't believe our luck. Here was someone with years of experience in the USA with the stars. Jimmy brought the project together. After we played him the songs, with me on the keyboards and John and Lez on guitar, he booked an excellent studio off the renowned Portobello Road in London to begin recording. Jimmy and I worked together really well, and we both recognized that it was important that I co-produced the album, as I was so fundamental to its structure. I began to recruit singers for the songs, as some of the original writers didn't want to sing on the recording. I felt it was important for the integrity of the project to invite people who had some prior experience, either directly or indirectly, of mental health issues.

It came to me in a flash that I should approach Holly. After at least ten years of no contact, we arranged to meet in a café in Islington. It was extraordinary to see her again. She arrived in the same "I'm here" kind of vibe she had always had with her black leather jacket and headband. I could also tell that she had been through a rough ride and was still a regular user of lithium for her manic depression. Her illness had taken her to the psychiatric hospital five times in total. Her saving grace was a care worker she had met on the ward, called Mary, who was truly there for her. After she was released, they got together and they have been life partners for many years now.

We caught up for a while about old times. I could feel Holly flirting with me a little as we looked back on our old romance, in the way that old flames do sometimes. I then told her about the CARSOS project and asked her if she would be interested in singing on the album. Holly said she would be delighted.

ॐ नमो दुर्गा माँ/ॐ नमो लक्ष्मी माँ

The first day of recording was magical. The studio in the Portobello Road was upstairs, opposite a trendy bangers and mash shop. Sean, Paul, Len and John attended the first session. The first song we recorded was Dom's song. Jimmy brought in amazing musicians to play each song. This wonderful musician called Karl turned up; he was a wonderful bass player. He also added a particular flare to Dom's song with a haunting solo on the mouth organ, which was so very touching. Each day, we recorded one new number.

Steve showed up the second day. He was one of the mental health users from the centre who was actually willing to sing on the recording. He had composed a unique original song entitled *Section 3* about the confinement he had endured being banged up on a mental health section.

He addressed the question that was core to all of us, "Are the ones who are banged up really the mad ones?"

The song reminded me of some of the sick staff from Epsom Hospital, including the dreaded night duty nurse, Rosemary. Steve's rendition was both absolutely hilarious and candid at the same time. He screamed out the song in Ian Drury meets Joe Cocker style. Steve was a real character with a broad cockney accent. He suffered from schizophrenia. Often he couldn't face coming outside but, whenever he did, he was priceless. We recorded him in just one take with purely his acoustic guitar and voice. To this day, his offering is the most remarked upon song on the CARSOS album. Tragically, Steve was discovered dead due to drowning in the River Thames one year later. He could not bear another day with the torment of those voices, God rest his soul.

The day came for Holly to record one of the group's home-grown classic ballads. Holly was as incredible as ever when she sang. She still had the same brilliance and charisma. She gave a phenomenal performance of the song that night. Everyone's hair stood on end as she sang those first notes in the studio, like Grace Jones or similar.

"Now that's what I call singing," said Jimmy, who was long in the tooth when it came to recognizing brilliant artists.

Unfortunately, Holly had not taken her lithium that day, and was talking ten to the dozen to Jimmy after she had finished singing. He was totally exhausted by the end from trying to calm her down. All of us involved with CARSOS were talented, though troubled in some way.

George, who also suffered with schizophrenia, came to record his song entitled *Feeling Free*. He came from an Afro-Caribbean background, and the melody had a real carnival feeling. George was always cheerful. One day he told me he had served time in prison for knocking someone out cold in a pub due to the voices he heard inside his head. He said that sometimes the voices were evil, but many of them were good. He told me that a Native chief had channelled through to him and showed him that you could read the energy of any outside land by listening to the energy emanating from your navel. He showed me a natural dowsing exercise the native had told him to do, standing in the north, south, east and west, and then tuning into the navel energy.

As George spoke, it felt that what he was saying was somehow plausible. In fact, it sounded to me like George was a kind of trance medium. As I previously mentioned, I discussed this subject with a well-known psychiatrist at the Royal College of Psychiatry called Dr. Andrew Powell. He was a spiritually-minded man who said, indeed, schizophrenia could well be related to mediumship. The only difference, he said, is that a medium can remain centred and in control when the spirits come through, and he/she is not compelled to act out on the voices. A schizophrenic, however, does not have the capacity to differentiate with what is real, and frequently carries out into action the negative, sometimes fatal, requests of the spirits who speak to them. George was a success story. His medication was working well for him, he was in a halfway house, and he was getting ready to apply for a job in the real world. His song *Feeling Free* was sung in true sunshine style on the day.

The final recording day eventually came. The whole day centre group showed up, including "fag ash" Carol. They were all excited at the prospect of singing the final song all together. Each member was given his or her own solo or duet part to sing. Linda sang in her best soprano, and a Middle Eastern man, called Ali, sang his line in every key except the one we were in – but it just didn't matter. We were all in it together. The song was called *IF*, and it was a real Live Aid kind of song. Listening back, it is a touching memento for all the people involved.

The album was eventually entitled *Breakthrough*. We also made a video of some of the process, and it was amazing to watch the video later of everyone coming in and recording their parts just like on Live Aid. There are some terrific songs on the CD, and it is definitely a classic result. We thank MIND, to this day, for giving us the award and for believing in us.

ॐ नमो दुर्गा माँ/ॐ नमो लक्ष्मी माँ

Two years later, I was singing in a concert in Brighton with Chloe Goodchild. I had copies of *Breakthrough* on display for people to buy to raise funds for the CARSOS charity. There was a man in the crowd, named Larry Culliford, who was a psychiatrist with a very spiritual outlook. His friend noticed the CD and pointed it out to Larry, who purchased a copy. A week later, I received a lovely email from Larry commending the CARSOS project. He asked if I would like to meet him for tea. He had white hair and glasses, and he was refreshingly different from the cold Charles Gray character I had been examined by at Springfield hospital.

"The lyrics are amazing on *Breakthrough*," he said enthusiastically. "In fact, there is something wonderful about all the songs. Tell me about your journey."

I began to share with him about my Kundalini awakening, where it had taken me and how it was now.

"Would you like to come and share your experiences with some consultant psychiatrists at our annual 2002 conference?" he asked. "I think you could really open their eyes to some of the misdiagnoses that can occur with patients with psychosis and the links with spiritual emergency."

It was such a relief to hear a western professional really hearing and acknowledging my experience as being something other than merely psychosis.

I acknowledged to Larry that, in India, it is a fact that if you go through a Kundalini awakening, such as I experienced, you are regarded as undergoing a beneficial fever. People, in fact, swoon around you to mop your brow, massage your feet and feed you until you move through it. Larry and I formed a bond and, after a few months, he invited me to speak in 2002 at The Royal College of Psychiatry conference, which was to be held in a conference centre in Cardiff – of all places, where I had experienced the peak of my spiritual emergency. This was miraculous synchronicity, and I knew in my heart that I had come full circle.

In 2001, I spent my summer in the ashram, once again. I was invited to offer service in the young people's department. I had spent so many happy retreats in both ashrams. When I was there, I was totally at home – immersed in the practices of yoga, chanting, meditation, and selfless service. I met so many incredible people there, including a wonderful human being, called Ericka. Ericka had been a revered freedom fighter in the 1970s. Her husband was an active campaigner who was tragically killed. Ericka told me her extraordinary story of being falsely arrested when she was innocent, and how she was imprisoned when her baby was only three weeks old. She told me that, inside prison, she began to meditate and she had visions of a great yogic master who came to her whilst she was in her meditation practice. One day, after serving fourteen months of her sentence, she was finally proven innocent.

Ericka related to me the incredible story of how, after being released, a friend of hers took her to a meditation programme where she saw the same spiritual master in person that she had seen in her visions in prison. This was a miraculous and beautiful story, and it gave me immense hope. Ericka is a great soul, and I have loved and admired her ever since. Ericka's name is a significant one for me, because I had been bullied at school by the other

Ericka when I was eleven years old. Ericka's friendship definitely helped me to heal the scars from my school years. I did not realize, at that time, that I would meet yet another Ericka a few years later, who would be my future life partner.

Ericka was both a soul sister and Mother Earth figure for me. We would have lunch every day and share our experiences of selfless service together. We would laugh and cry, sometimes, as we shared the challenges we faced. We spent many hours talking together during our lunch breaks. We found, with each other, an ease and mutual rapport. That summer, on a level, it felt like we were falling in love. However, it was a deep spiritual love that was to go no further. We are now lifelong friends.

The ashram was a wellspring of rejuvenation for me. The word ashram is a Sanskrit word for "without worldly fatigue." It was here that my love of chanting blossomed over the years. There were several devotional chants sung throughout the day in the daily schedule that we could participate in. Chanting was much easier for me than silent meditation. As a recovering addict with an overactive mind, I found that having mantras to focus on made it easier to turn within. The chanting released an ecstatic energy that would build inside to such heights. Whenever I was in the ashram, I felt supremely connected to my heart. I had many beautiful experiences of tingling energy moving through me. I had many inner revelations and incredible heart connections with other devotees. Everywhere I walked in the grounds, I would stop to have a brief exchange with someone. There would always be a message for me as though God was speaking to me through other devotees.

ॐ नमो दुर्गा माँ/ॐ नमो लक्ष्मी माँ

Both ashrams I stayed in between 1992-2001 were like paradise on Earth. The whole environment there is tended to with devotion, whether it be the lush green gardens with multiple trees, lakes, flowers or the temples and courtyards that scintillate with divine energy (Shakti). Everyone came to spend time there to accelerate their sadhana (path of spiritual discipline). Whatever each soul was resisting, avoiding or dealing with in their life would come up with piercing accuracy in the ashram. This, for me, meant that, eventually, I had to face where I was holding onto past grudges, regrets and, in general, stuck ways of being. After ten years of going every summer holiday, sometimes for winter retreats in California or Easter retreats in Europe, I had my biggest test to date. I had a painful clash with the head of the young people's department in America. His name was Robert*, and he reminded me of the previous clash I wrote about before with Chris, ironically another Australian.

During the time 1996-2001, I would serve every summer in the youth department, and Robert was our supervisor. I was excited by what I felt I could contribute. I had a full theatrical and musical background and loads to offer in that respect. Initially, I had a whale of a time composing upbeat songs for kids with the aforementioned Shelley, my lifelong friend. We created some inspirational activities for children over five consecutive summers, and the children loved them. Each year, we would escort the kids on a shuttle bus to sing the songs they had composed for our spiritual teacher. This was always the highlight of the summer for the children and for all of us who assisted.

However, in the midst of all the joy, my biggest obstacle was my Australian supervisor, Robert*. My experience was that he would unfairly criticize my creative efforts. I had the impression that he didn't want me to develop my ideas. Initially, I managed to move beyond his feedback until, in 2001, the situation worsened. I felt creatively stifled and my old wound of voicelessness hit me again.

I returned to the UK in the summer of 2001 feeling at rock bottom, and I began to sink into a deep depression. After eleven years of sobriety, I even feared that I would relapse. I felt disempowered. I was hurting badly and I chose to take a break from the ashram. It was when I returned to the UK in September 2001 that I met an amazing American man, an older guy called Jamie (another synchronicity with names, as it had been the previous James who helped to get me sober), back in London. He had a solid recovery from alcoholism and I told him how bad I felt. He said I needed to address my resentments, otherwise I would drink again. He encouraged me to go back through my life and clean house until I got to the root causes of my fears and resentments. It took many months to do this thoroughly.

When I finally looked honestly at my painful journey with Robert, I realized that, spiritually, Robert was a tremendous gift to me because he had triggered an old wound that I was holding onto. I had still not yet forgiven my father for all the artistic criticism he had given me as a child. Robert was, in fact, a direct mirror and a gift for me to heal this unresolved resentment.

All my life up to that point, I had always loved my father, but it had always hurt me when I felt he didn't validate my acting or appear to respect my spiritual choices. Naturally, the choices I made were important to me. I realized that the time had come for me to deal with my reactions to my father and, in fact, all of my relationships in which I had held onto resentments. I began to thoroughly and fearlessly look at my part in all the relationships that were causing me a disturbance inside. If I seriously wanted to be well and free within, this was essential.

It sometimes felt ironic that I had started a business called Free the Inner Voice, and yet I was far from free. Yet, to call myself a fraud would not be fair. There is an expression that says we get to teach "that which we most need to learn!" I realized that so long as I was one step ahead of my students in cleaning up my own path and experience of darkness, I surely had something valid to pass onto them. The client could always sense, on a subtle level, whether I had already been through my own darkness because of the way I could hear them in their darkest places.

For me, inner freedom was always my deepest longing. Chanting had unlocked a pathway inside for me to have direct access to experiences of inner ecstasy and liberation. At the same time, chanting would always put the spotlight on relationships and situations in my life that I was yet to transform. These blocks would arise inside and my chanting practice would always make it crystal clear for me that I just had to face them. Chanting would always reveal to me that unconditional love and compassion for myself and everyone was the only way forward, although, with some resentments – my ego was more stubborn.

ॐ नमो दुर्गा माँ/ॐ नमो लक्ष्मी माँ

I was bitter and judgemental towards Robert. I started to chant every day for the answer to transform this bitterness that I felt. My prayer was answered. I received a call one morning, right after my chant, from my recovery mentor, Jamie. He told me about a transformational weekend course he had done called the Landmark Forum.

"If you really need a radical path to forgive Robert, do the Landmark Forum, Nikki," said Jamie.

In the same two weeks, two dear friends from my yoga path, Gerry and Shelley from the ashram, also mentioned the same course.

The Landmark Forum was a life-changing and transformational experience for me. The major thing I finally realized, aged forty years, was that *my* perception of *my* parents was totally messed up. In truth, I recognized that everything they ever did for me was because they loved me, and it was my interpretation of events that had caused my suffering.

I saw by the end of the weekend how self-righteous and judgemental I was. I got in touch with both my mum and dad and apologized for how I had not bothered to understand their journey and perspective in life. I saw how hard it must have been for them bringing me and my brother into the world with very little wealth or life experience. My father had always tried to explain to me the value of money, and he had often been furious when I fell into debt. I always thought he never understood me and judged me when, in fact, all he was trying to do was to help me get onto a secure financial path. I realized that the artistic criticism he gave me as an actor was coming from his fear that I would fail in that area, as he had judged his own acting ability.

Parents are always concerned that their children don't repeat their patterns and want their children to succeed in life. I also cried as I acknowledged my mum, who carried me at twenty-three years old, having been through a childhood of her own dealing with her alcoholic mother. I apologized for not making the effort to understand her life. We spoke woman to woman for the first time, rather than me as a blaming child to her parent.

I learned in the Landmark Forum that we are all human beings doing our best with the scripts we have. My mum and dad gave me all the love they had to give and, sadly, for a large portion of my early adulthood due to my struggle with alcoholism, I was unable to appreciate all they had done for me. However, I am also clear that without the early life tensions I had with my family, I would not have taken the path to the destiny I have now with sound. I would probably have had a much more harmonious ride with my parents, but I am clear my life would have been bland in comparison. Looking back, although it was tough for us all throughout the period from twenty to thirty-five years, our relationship is, today, far richer and stronger than it ever was. I now regard my parents as great friends, allies on my spiritual journey, and I love them both dearly. They have given me everything. This beautiful healing with my parents was one of the many extraordinary results I got out of my participation in the Landmark Forum.

I subsequently resolved the never-ending drama with Robert through the training. Spectacularly, my Forum leader was Australian, an ironic and perfect completion to the circle with Robert. He coached me to see that self-righteousness was what had blocked me. He got me to see that I had not respected that Robert was my supervisor at the time. If I didn't like his feedback, until I was supervisor, I should align with his guidelines. Otherwise, I did have the choice to move on. Suddenly I heard a ping inside. Oh my god. So simple. Why had I fought so hard?!

The moment came for me to finally make my peace with Robert. Jamie said I should be willing to go to any lengths to resolve the situation.

"You should take a flight to New York," he said.

I was shocked that he meant those kind of lengths! I was really resistant at first. Nonetheless, this was crucial for me, so I looked into flights. Ironically, in the end, I discovered that Robert was no longer in the ashram but was, in fact, in Hungary. Jamie said that, as I had been willing to go to the lengths of flying to the USA, my reward was that I could simply call Robert, who was now staying in Budapest. The next day, I managed to track Robert down over the phone.

My heart shuddered as I dialled his number. He was amazed to hear from me. On the call, I apologized to him for having failed to respect his leadership position in the ashram and, even though I might not have agreed with the way in which he ran the department, it wasn't my place to gossip negatively about his ways or to resist his authority quite so overtly. I told him that I realized that when I am someday the supervisor of a department, I will be the one who makes the final decisions. However, if I am in someone else's department, then I must align with what they ultimately order, or choose to move on. Robert accepted my apology and we both now have moved on in our lives. We have since exchanged emails about a book he wrote and a CD I released, encouraging one another's success. It is a miracle in action that we are now at peace. I thank the power of chanting for opening my heart, Jamie for his mentoring, Shelley and Gerry for their friendships, and the Landmark Forum for these transformational breakthroughs in my life.

ॐ नमो दुर्गा माँ/ॐ नमो लक्ष्मी माँ

I now recognize in life that it is important to keep our apparent enemies in life close to our chest. They are ultimately in our life to strengthen us in our faith. When these dark teachers appear, the best thing to do is chant.

Whenever we chant Durga's name, we are connected to the infinite power of the Shakti, which gives us the Grace to face our inner enemies. We then come to realize that our outer enemies are, in truth, our greatest teachers.

> Bring the face of anyone who is challenging you in your life right now and surrender all your concerns to the chant. Over time, you will be naturally guided from within as to how to face the situation.

In August 2001, after a challenging summer, I left the ashram early for a big conference. This was to be my first-ever corporate gig in the UK, and was for Ashridge Business College. I was invited to lead a voice workshop at the grand finale of their conference entitled *Finding Your Leadership Voice*.

I had been recommended to them by a loyal client named Susie Kershaw, who I acknowledge with gratitude to this day as being my first advocate for corporate engagements.

I remember the excitement and expectation I felt when I arrived at Ashridge. I had no idea what to expect and, therefore, I had prepared nothing. Intuitively, I knew that all I had to do was trust my inner voice and all would be well. When I arrived, I was directed to an area called The Open Space, where a man called Albert was leading a Q&A session that was about to draw to a close. At the end, a drummer began playing a drum roll on her djembe drum to call all the delegates into the finale room where my workshop was to start. My heart beat fast in time with her drum.

"This is it!" I thought. "Sink or swim, for better or for worse!"

As they came in, I invited them all to take off their shoes and to find a space in the room. I still had no idea what I was doing, and there were already raised eyebrows at my request to remove all shoes. I suddenly received an inspirational download to divide them into groups of men and women. I remembered a ska reggae song that we had been singing at the ashram. The song originally had spiritual lyrics about meditation when the children had sung it previously, whereupon, I had the brain wave to change the words to fit the conference theme. Hence, the word meditation was replaced with celebration for their finale.

I asked the men to sing one refrain whilst the women sang the other. I invited the men to be on one side of the room and the women on the opposite side. I started the reggae track on my keyboard and asked the men to come up with their own groovy moves whilst the women came up with their own moves. They started to sing whilst dancing towards each other, and it was hilarious as well as joyful to behold. It reminded me of watching the Jets and the Sharks sing *America* in *West Side Story*. The words were celebratory, and the beat and melody were so catchy that the energy built higher and higher until they all clapped effusively. I knew, at that point, that they were open for anything. I invited them all to sit cross-legged on the floor and to take a partner and hold hands with each other. Many of the couples were two men. I invited them to look into each other's eyes and to chant mantras for connecting to the heart. The men were initially in hysterics as their nervous energy dispelled. When, suddenly, they shifted and settled into a strong and open connection with their partner.

I kept tuning into my inner voice that guided me to keep risking everything with this group. I listened and invited them all to chant a tribal version of the mantra Om Namah Shivaya. As I started to chant, one by one they started to stand like they were tribal warriors saluting the sun, empowered and proud to be standing fully connected to their bodies. They chanted full out with great devotion. My heart burst with love as I watched them all.

"Wow, this is my first ever corporate gig," I thought.

I just knew, in that moment, that everything I had ever been through, good or bad, had brought me to this exquisite point of sharing my work with leaders. At the end, there was a whoop of appreciation and a ripple went through the conference. On the way out, at the bar, many of them reported to those outside that they had just come out of a great session and how they regarded me as being "the energy woman." I felt thrilled that it had gone off so well. Many of the leaders asked me for my card and promised future offers. In that moment, I felt fulfilled, on purpose, and that I had made a real difference.

Finding Your Leadership Voice was a memorable gig that led to several offers at Ashridge College over the next six years, courtesy of a lovely man there called Bob Fergusson, who has subsequently retired. One such occasion was a memorable event when I facilitated for 100 men for an Eco based company from Europe. At first, I tried the tribal warrior gung ho approach with them, which didn't work so well. I realized I hadn't tuned in deeply enough when I suddenly received a strong intuition to lead these men, instead, in a beautiful chant to connect them to their divine feminine energy. I abruptly stopped the raucous noise in the room and asked these suited and booted men to sit on the floor all around the stage. I taught them the words Jay Jaya Devi Matha, which translates to "I surrender to the divine mother principal within."

As the chant started, I invited them to put their hands on their hearts and to envision the future of their company as being centred right there in the heart. As I looked out upon this sea of men, I suddenly saw the innocent young boy in all of them. Many of them were crying as they connected to the tenderness in their own hearts. In that moment, I had a vision of the consciousness of the feminine prevailing in the future of business. This day may only arrive when I am old and grey, but I felt that a tiny seed was definitely sown in the hearts of those men that day. All this I owe with gratitude to the power of chanting, which has connected me to divine grace in my life.

ॐ नमो दुर्गा माँ/ॐ नमो लक्ष्मी माँ

One of the most challenging invitations I received as a result of the Ashridge leadership conference was from a well-known chocolate company. They were having their annual conference at Derby Football Club. They asked if I could facilitate an energetic vocal session for four hundred people since there would be no coffee break due to the room's spatial constraints. The conference room overlooked Derby football pitch, and there were prominent pillars inside that made it hard to move everyone easily from their seats. I will never forget arriving and looking out of the glass windows onto the pitch. I imagined how fantastic it could be to lead a chant one day with the crowd, or even to warm up the England team in the World Cup.

In the conference suite, there was a raised T-bar stage with grid-like screens at the back. My heart thumped as I walked in at 7:30 a.m. to behold Cirque du Soleil dancers in rehearsal, acrobatically dancing to Robbie Williams' track *Let Me Entertain You* while displaying giant chocolate boxes. My heart shuddered. I knew this would be the most out-of-my-comfort-zone event that I would lead, to date.

I did my sound check. At 9:00 a.m. sharp, all 400 delegates poured into the room and took their seats expectantly as they glanced at the video screens displaying all the different ranges of chocolate that had come out that year. As the audience filled up, bright lights and booming music began to strike, and the dancers I had seen earlier emerged in full costume, wowing the crowd with their spectacular moves. As the music stopped, so did their routine, when suddenly a drum roll thundered and the host of the event stepped onto the stage. She spoke in a broad northern accent and proudly began to acknowledge the company's achievements for that year, and let the audience know what an uplifting day lay ahead. She then introduced the first of various leaders from different regions of the UK who spoke that day.

They were mainly women, making speeches about the sales margins that year UK wide, and the promises they held for the future. After each woman spoke, there was rapturous applause. The clock slowly ticked towards the coffee hour, and I shook nervously at the back of the stage as I stood with my headset on standby.

I thought to myself, "Okay, Nikki, here we go. Once again, we either sink or swim!"

The host announced in her broad northern accent, "Okay, everyone, you thought you were gonna get coffee now but, instead, to wake you all up we have for you... Nikki Slade!"

Boom, boom, boom, went my heart.

The crowd clapped outwardly whilst inwardly, I'm sure, initially, they were disappointed that they wouldn't get their caffeine hit. The lights were so bright in my eyes as I stepped out front that I felt like I imagine comedians must feel stepping out into the bright lights of a Las Vegas stage.

I felt like a runway model on that T-bar and exclaimed, "Morning, Derby. Sorry about your coffee break, but the good news is you've got me!"

In meditation the night before, I was guided to begin with singing something with them all that was earthy and in their comfort zone. I, thus, boldly invited them to join me in a rousing version of the Sister Sledge song *We are Family*. There were hundreds of northern women out there who couldn't wait to sing the refrain, and I felt relief as I managed to inspire 380 women and twenty men to all dive into the refrain with full lungs. There was a tremendous spirit in the room, and thank God I trusted my inner voice and didn't go straight in with a Sanskrit chant.

The Sister Sledge song went down a storm, and I could feel the momentum gathering. I knew the room was with me, so I decided to take a bold risk. I invited them all to stand and I then directed them to express themselves with all manner of vocal noises and movements in pairs with the person beside them. They all began laughing hysterically out loud. There was a tremendous atmosphere at that point, such that I felt they would now be open for anything.

"Seize the moment," I thought. "I'm now going to risk a Sanskrit chant with them."

I had my harmonium on stage with me. "Does anyone know what this instrument is?"

"That is a harmonium," piped up an Indian gentleman at the back of the room.

The rest of them were unfamiliar with the instrument.

"I'm going to lead you in a chant, similar idea to the ones you chant on the terraces down there on the pitch," I said. "Only this time, the intention is to connect your team to the heart vibration of your vision. Are you up for it?" I shouted.

"Ay up," they yelled back.

Soon, all 400 of them were chanting Om Namah Shivaya, which translates to "I honour the one SELF within me." We did it with tribal drums, and everyone really got into it. So much so that, after the gig, I received reports that they simply couldn't keep the women off the karaoke mics in the conference party later that evening. I travelled back on the train from Derby pinching myself that I had the courage to follow my inner voice and go way out of my comfort zone voice to share the power of chanting with the corporate world.

ॐ नमो दुर्गा माँ/ॐ नमो लक्ष्मी माँ

The year 2001 was an expansive one for me, both professionally and personally. My relationship with my assistant Natasha had become very close, and we realized our connection was far deeper than purely professional. This revealed itself the day Natasha handed in her notice as my personal assistant. That day we both got overly upset in a way that was exaggerated for colleagues. We realized, some days later, that we had fallen in love. Shortly after, my next relationship began. Natasha and I had a full and enriching journey that, for me, represented the relationship that opened my heart chakra. Natasha had the gift of being able to speak directly to people's hearts and to really "hear" where they were. I hadn't laughed out loud for a long time, and Natasha unlocked my ability to belly laugh – something I treasured about her.

Once again, there were many cosmic coincidences with us. For example, family birthdays – her brother shared the same birthday as my father; her parents' anniversary was the same day as my mum's birthday; her father's birthday was the same as my grandmother's; and she and her sister Louisa went to the same school and university as my cousins. Natasha grew up two miles up the road from me, only twelve years later. My birthday was only three days apart from her mother's. With all these subtle signs, we soon recognized we were working out family karma together.

Natasha was bold and brave and travelled to the depths of Africa and India by herself in her early twenties. She was tall and statuesque with a mane of frizzy hair that gave her the aura of a lioness. She was a natural leader. She was always popular with people she met. Natasha was, initially, attracted to my work. Like Maliya, she was drawn to my spiritual path, which she also now follows. Natasha was also a keen apprentice of my voice work. She encouraged me greatly to keep going with Free the Inner Voice – especially in the barren times. Natasha also assisted me with administration and promotion of my courses. She was also instrumental in championing and grounding my voice facilitators training in 2006/2007 along with Emma Westcott, a loyal previous client and friend. Natasha massively believed in the voice work, and I will always thank her for the immense support that she gave me during those years.

After three years, our relationship had blossomed and we decided to take the bold step of having a commitment ceremony. We declared to family and friends our intentions and we announced our ceremony date on September 18th, 2004. Ironically, four months after our special day, civil partnerships became legal in December 2004.

Our ceremony was a wedding, in truth, and it was a really big deal for us. We had a lot of apprehension about what people would think, especially family relations, if we were to tie the knot. However, we were strongly encouraged by friends, and in particular Natasha's sister Louisa. We duly arranged a supper party for our parents to meet each other in advance of the wedding. This was a nerve-wracking moment. Happily, however, they all got on very well.

Natasha's parents said to me after my folks had gone home, "You didn't tell us your parents would be like that – what a relief!"

My parents were very uncomfortable with the idea of a gay wedding. Not because they didn't embrace our relationship, but more from the view of "What will the family think?"

My father said it would be too much for a lot of the extended family to attend. I reluctantly went along with his wishes, but stood firm in inviting my Uncle Julian and my cousin Humphrey, who were both gay. It meant a great deal to me that they both came.

Natasha's family were incredible in helping us find a location to marry. We chose Lady Margaret's school hall in Parsons Green, which was often used for functions. It had a large kitchen at the back for receptions and a delightful garden as you stepped out of the French windows at the side. Natasha's parents and a great team of friends literally transformed the hall into a wedding temple.

Our friend, Annabel, made a beautiful puja (altar) for us with a statue of Kuan Yin, who was a special divine goddess for us. I had a good friend at the time, named Jas, who was a Buddhist. He was also a seer and channel for Kuan Yin, and he told us that Kuan Yin had blessed our relationship. We had received many channelled messages from Kuan Yin throughout our relationship.

ॐ नमो दुर्गा माँ/ॐ नमो लक्ष्मी माँ

In the summer of 2001, Natasha and I both went together to the ashram. Whilst there, we were invited by our friend Serge to a Japanese tea ceremony in a woodland just outside the centre. Originally, he invited several people. However, one by one, they all dropped out until it was just us three. We went to a beautiful house at the edge of the woods and were greeted by the ceremonial host. She was dressed in oriental satin green with a pristine sash and beautifully swept-back hair in a bun with a comb and chopsticks. She was American and glowing with radiance.

"Walk with me" she said.

It was just myself, Natasha and Serge. She led us to a bamboo hut in the middle of the woods. It was so serene and magical.

She opened the door; Natasha and I both gasped. The back of the hut was a five-foot statue of the mother Goddess Kuan Yin carved completely out of beech wood. It was absolutely beautiful, and we felt that Kuan Yin herself had invited us to be there. There were several tiny pots of tea at her feet awaiting our focus.

"This hut is where the Brahmin priests perform wedding ceremony blessings. At these ceremonies, there is traditionally one witness for the occasion," said the host.

Natasha and I gasped inside again, as we realized that the universe had arranged a miraculous marriage blessing for us. The host didn't realize that she had been cast as the priest and Serge had been perfectly cast as our witness! We understood that the power of grace had removed everyone else from the tea ceremony so that we could have our own unique blessing.

We returned to England excited about our big wedding day. The happy day was announced on September 18th, 2004. We had 250 guests, which was an incredible turn-out. We had all ages, cultures, backgrounds and walks of life there. We stood at the foot of the aisle in our specially tailored Indian silk robes. Natasha was so nervous that I held her hand all the way up the aisle. We had the still drone of an Indian tambora playing as we slowly walked together. The atmosphere was electric as everybody watched history in the making!

Our celebrant was awaiting us. We had composed our very own vows, then we faced one another and began to speak them out loud. My parents were sitting at the front on my family side and Natasha's folks on the other side. I could see my parents out of the corner of my eye; my dad was sitting, arms folded, looking at the floor apprehensively.

Natasha and I faced each other for our vows. As the last vow was spoken, the wonderful Chloe Goodchild sang Jay Bhagavan ("thy will be done" in Sanskrit) as we exchanged rings. She was then joined by a radiant choir of friends who sang divine mantras led by Jay's wife, Janice. Masashi Minagawa, a Tai Kwon Do master and colleague of Chloe's, did some incredible martial movements whilst the choir sang to invoke auspicious blessings. It was a truly glorious service.

At the end, my brother made a moving and glorious speech. Then, to our amazement, both our fathers stood up unannounced and began to sing!

Natasha and I looked at each other with utter amazement as they chanted, "Good afternoon. We're the two daddies, the fathers of Nikki and Tash. We are not sure what we're supposed to be doing, but we're glad to be here at this bash!"

The song was set to the melody of *What ever Happened to Baby Jane?* that I had sung for my father's fundraiser at Drury Lane all those years ago. The circles were completing themselves. The song continued with incredible, poignant and witty lyrics – some touching ones, too. At the end, the whole congregation stood up and roared into rapturous electric applause! I was so moved by both the daddies, but especially my own father. This was a beautiful and heart-melting moment that brought us both full circle to a space where we could express total and unconditional love. From that moment on, the wedding party went higher and higher. The food was incredible, the musicians and artists were fabulous, and the dancing was nonstop.

People said that, without a doubt, this was the best wedding they had ever been to. It was "where love was truly present" a guest exalted, where all barriers of opinion dissolve, leaving one united world! The day after our wedding, we looked at our wedding book at the inscriptions that the people in the congregation had personally written inside to us.

Natasha turned to me and said, "Nik, did you notice how many of the people mentioned in this book that your work has profoundly touched their lives? You need to acknowledge that, you know."

I had always found it hard to receive complements.

Natasha and I had a powerful life-changing journey together that spanned nine years, playing many roles: first as my student, then later as my colleague, and finally as my wife. In 2007, the tides began to change, and our lives were moving in different directions. In January 2008, we both reviewed the Landmark Forum together, which gave us the clarity and courage to part with love and affinity fully present.

We chose to have an acknowledgement ceremony to separate powerfully with a witness, just like the tea ceremony with Serge, only this time with Dave (our next door neighbour) as a witness. We wanted to respectfully untie the agreements between us and to create a great space for our future journeys apart. We went to the oldest tree in England, in Barnes London, and brought two pieces of cloth from our wedding gowns and a small statue of Kuan Yin. We acknowledged each other in turn for everything we had received, including all the gifts and the challenges we had given each other. We blessed each other in moving forward freely with love in our hearts. Natasha is now happily married and a successful voice facilitator in Ireland and Europe.

ॐ नमो दुर्गा माँ/ॐ नमो लक्ष्मी माँ

In 2001, I met the man who opened up many professional opportunities for me in Europe. He was an American by the name of JC Mac. He was also a bold risk-taker who was great fun to work with, and he had a wild rebellious streak that I loved. He was willing to risk taking my work into banks and into the IT industry. So it was, in 2005, John invited me to lead an energizing team building session in Romania for a renowned European bank. I had never been to Romania, and the first gig I did there was with a bank in Brasov in a forest surrounded by mountains. I felt like I had just arrived onto the film set from the movie *Heidi*.

At nine o'clock the next morning, I walked into the conference hall with its blue chairs and forest view with all my instruments mic'd up and set to go. My heart was pounding with excitement as I was about to step into the unknown. 150 Romanians bankers walked into the hall and took their seats. There were an even number of men and women in the room.

The host welcomed everybody in preparation for an enriching day ahead.

He then introduced John, who stood up with his laid back American accent straight out of a cop show and said, "Hey, guys, how ya doin? Okay, good. So, this morning I thought we'd get straight to a very important part of today, and that is energy. Without energy, nothing really comes to life. So to energize us all today, I am going to invite Nikki to come up to lead us all in a little chanting, so let's welcome Nikki!"

"This is it," I thought to myself, "There is nothing to lose – just go for it!"

I played the first chord on my harmonium and then invited them all to put their hands on their hearts and chant OM together a few times. I then taught them the words to the chant, which were "Jay Bhagawan," which means "I surrender to the divine". I invited them to chant in call and response. As soon as we started, they all participated with full enthusiasm. As I looked out into the room, they all had smiling and happy faces. I suddenly had flashes of their recent history in bondage to the communist regime. I could feel their appreciation in the chanting, perhaps even releasing some of their past. All of a sudden, their gypsy Romanian roots kicked in and they all started clapping along with enthusiasm. It was extraordinary to witness them, and it felt both eccentric and amazing to be chanting in this exquisite setting with bankers. As I flew back to the UK, I felt an incredible grace and awe of my destiny to be serving as an instrument for global chanting work.

In 2005, in the summer of that year, due to the success of the first gig, we were flown out to Romania again for a large mobile phone company conference. As I arrived in Bucharest Airport, a customs official stopped me.

"Have you heard about London?" he said in his broad Romanian accent.

"You mean winning the Olympic bid? It's great, isn't it?" I replied.

"No." He shook his head sternly. "No, terrorists attacked London Underground!"

I went numb as I heard the news. Natasha went through my mind. Was she on the tube? Who else did I know who took the tube at Aldgate or Kings Cross? I began to feel sick inside. As I came through the airport arrival gates, TV cameras and mics were immediately thrust in my face.

"Are you scared, are you scared?" they chanted at me.

This was because I was one of the first British tourists who came through the barriers of Bucharest Airport that morning.

I was irritated by the question being asked of me, so I replied sharply, "Wouldn't you be?"

When I finally arrived in the mountains of Brassov, it was so surreal to see news clips flashing in the hotel lobby of me being interviewed on national TV. I called home and, thank God, everyone I knew was safe. It was truly heartbreaking and devastating to watch the rolling CNN news footage of the tragedies that had occurred that day.

I returned to the conference by day and led one of my best ever energizers with 300 delegates. John decided to build on the energy theme that we had touched on at the previous bank conference after their positive response to chanting. There were three other speakers that day. By lunchtime, after listening to a lot of speaking, the group was visibly heavy and exhausted in their energy. They were very resistant to the high-end coaching they were receiving. It was as though they needed to be led, rather than be motivated, to be the one and take action in their own right. This was very much a leftover conditioning of communism, to follow and not lead.

I spoke to JC and said, "I think I can do something to wake them all up."

"Nik, if you can shift these dead folks, you got it!" he said with a playful glint.

It was a huge challenge, but I took the bull by the horns in the graveyard slot right after lunch and got them all playing vocal martial arts and edgy voice and movement games. I invited them to go way out of their comfort zones, concluding in a rousing chant. I left Romania feeling that I had made a big breakthrough with my work, and I was very excited by the potential of bringing more and more business teams together through the power of chanting and voice work. I thank JC for giving me the platform to connect business people to a high vibration energy, which enabled them to see greater possibilities in their leadership.

ॐ नमो दुर्गा माँ/ॐ नमो लक्ष्मी माँ

During that period, the corporate opportunities continued to flow in, including an invitation from a global IT company. It was there that I met Igor, who was a senior manager in Europe at that time. He was a leader who was ahead of his time and who totally embraced the holistic approach to living. He loved the fact that my work took people out of their comfort zones and into their energy bodies. I remember the resistance of some of the delegates that first morning. I really didn't know if I could make a difference in that cold hall at 9:00 on a Monday morning. They were locked into their heads and highly confronted at being asked to make sounds, let alone move at the same time.

My drummer started playing and I began to play the harmonium. As I gave them the Sanskrit sounds that went with the movements, I could feel this wall of cynicism spread through pockets of the room like I had confronted a serpent that was hissing, "Don't you dare take this any further!"

Their egos were screaming. As a facilitator, I had to remain centred and focussed on the free vision I had for them all that they couldn't yet see. That first day was really hard, as they projected their awkward way of being onto the session.

Later that afternoon, a drumming facilitator got them all going with world drumming. He brought in several drums, and his session was much more comfortable for them because they could hide behind the drums.

Igor, their manager, came up to me at the end of the day and said, "Nikki, your session was extraordinary; it was a real breakthrough and, although hard for them to open up, they stepped out of their comfort zone today." He said this with surprising enthusiasm. I, on the other hand, felt like I had just walked through a bog backwards.

That night, I knew that from a shamanic perspective I needed to ensure that they all left the second day with an uplifting sense of having a break-through. I could feel the serpent of their resistance coursing through me that night. I had the fear arising within me of a general who is about to enter into battle. I phoned Cyril, one of my friends and allies, en route to the venue. He managed to bring a fresh perspective to my ears of embracing fearless-ness, and to see the situation as an opportunity for my growth. I walked into the venue with the energy of Bodacea that second morning, with an expansion within me that would take no passengers. I wasn't going to allow anyone's inner serpent to have victory over the day, and I now felt completely unstoppable.

At 9:00 a.m., as I once again invited them to stand in a circle, I saw the sceptical faces of half the group with, "Oh no, not this again!"

One man was constantly fiddling with his Blackberry in one hand and a breakfast banana in the other. I told him with light humour that he wouldn't require a banana for the morning warm up! Everyone laughed, and slowly the ice melted as the group moved from resistance to appreciation. The man was left looking at his banana, that was intended to be his weapon of satirical sabotage, when he suddenly realized he was losing his control. He put the banana and Blackberry down and, rather like a dog with an alpha trainer, he began to align with the workshop.

My inner voice whispered that if I kept my heart open and remained totally non-judgemental throughout the day, I could take the group anywhere I wanted – and that was exactly what happened. It was wonderful to see IT people come into their bodies and actually enjoy it as the vibration in the room spontaneously lifted, leading to lightness and laughter in the room. By the end of the day, they were chanting from the heart, and many of their faces were unrecognizable – even glowing. Igor came up to me and insisted that we run the same workshop in Brussels the following week for his IT team in Europe. I felt excitement and a sense of a real accomplishment that I had worked through the challenges and made a real difference.

Brussels was a breeze compared to London. The Europeans were far less rigid, and they embraced the vocal sessions with joyous enthusiasm and a gratitude that they were away from their computer for the day. I risked taking them much deeper into the chanting, and they truly loved it. Igor was thrilled, and I knew that we would definitely work together again.

In March, 2008, I turned forty-five years old and, for the first time in fifteen years, I was a single woman. After much anxiety at the prospect of living alone for the first time, I moved into the most perfect place for me, right in the heart of Pimlico on the Victoria side. It was a gorgeous, light apartment that belonged to a yoga teacher who was moving to India to study Kirtan (devotional Sanskrit chanting). This was a miraculous synchronicity. My dear friend Michael James discovered the place for me. We were dining one night and I hadn't yet moved out of my place in Chiswick. I was anxious about my future. I told him that I had never lived alone before and wanted somewhere nice to live. That night he received a general email from Sasha, a yoga teacher he knew (it was ironic to me that her name rhymed with Natasha), saying she was looking for somebody who was interested in yoga that didn't smoke or drink to rent her apartment for minimum of a year.

ॐ नमो दुर्गा माँ/ॐ नमो लक्ष्मी माँ

Michael called me straight away. In my gut, I absolutely knew this was my new home to be. I wrote to Sasha immediately and said that I could pay her six months' rent in advance. By uncanny coincidence, it turned out that Sasha knew me already. Apparently, she had attended one of my Kirtan classes at Triyoga in Primrose Hill when she was working part-time in reception there. We spoke and laughed at how magical the synchronicity was between us. It was like we were swapping lives with her studying Kirtan in India and me being in her flat and teaching in London. I even ended up teaching for a short while in the same centre where she taught yoga in Victoria.

I finally moved in to Denbigh Street and took a little while adjusting to living on my own. There was an eccentric lady, called Clare, downstairs who was a well-to-do secretary of a senior firm. We would pass pleasantries on the stairs, except when it came to vacuuming the stairs outside.

She would make barbed remarks about, "Whose were the black hairs on the stairs?"

We never did discover, although Clare was convinced that they were connected with my flat.

Michael James was an incredible friend to me throughout that period, and remains loyal to this day. He would frequently visit and give me incredible support in that lonely period. I used to describe him as Archangel Michael when I spoke of him. For my first year living alone, it felt strange not being in a relationship. I had always been in a relationship since I was nineteen, and here I was at forty-five years living on my own and single for the very first time. I am so grateful to Michael for his companionship during that time and his constant friendship today, hence, my invitation to him to write this forward.

However, I soon had a strong crush on a beautiful Asian Muslim woman called Sana who I had met on a course. I felt like a lovesick teenager. We became flirtatious friends for two years. However, sadly, her feelings for me were not as strong as mine were for her, and she chose to end our brief romantic moment. I thank Sana for the very short, but powerful, journey we had. She represented for me my throat chakra relationship, because it was her influence that inspired me to expand my self-expression as a leader.

The first night that I came home to my new flat on my own I felt unsure. However, after the first few nights alone, I began to feel strangely excited at my new lease of independence. The world was suddenly my oyster. I could go anywhere, do anything, and meet anyone – how exciting! I began to do things just for me. I booked myself a yoga holiday in Turkey and a holiday to my favourite island in Greece with a friend. I then decided to make the most of this solo period by signing up for team leadership training. I felt this would be productive, as I had a solo business and it was very much up to me to drive it. I knew it was important for me to be connected to a group that supported me at that time. The course was a wonderful life-expanding training. It stretched my comfort zone significantly in that, throughout that year, we all had to create projects that would make a difference out there in the world. I decided to offer an event on the controversial subject of Spiritual Emergence – a subject deep in my heart.

After my own spiritual emergence experience, the universe sent me a number of souls who were misdiagnosed as being psychotic and who were, in fact, in the intense process of spiritual emergence. In many cases, I was the only person who could hear them in their hour of need. Spiritual emergence was a subject that health professionals barely knew anything about, and it was much simpler to diagnose these cases as having a "mental health issue." One friend, Lisa*, went through a radical Kundalini awakening that was as dramatic as my experience.

Natasha and I had looked after Lisa at our flat whilst she was in the height of her experience. We would come home and the TV would be on and it was the European Cup. Lisa would say what the scores of each game would be at the start of each match. Every time she was right! This was because she would receive constant universal downloads from the future that were accurate. For example, I asked her about my episode with Robert at the ashram and she knew everything about him without, in reality, knowing anything. Her channel was so open that she was at one with source energy (the global encyclopaedia to all knowledge when we are clear enough to tap into it). Lisa began to travel through time just as I had done during my awakening.

One night, Lisa called me from a London park bench to tell me that she was communing with UFOs!

"Nik, they are so beautiful. They are communicating with me. It's amazing out here," she said with so much love in her voice it was entrancing to listen to.

I knew she was telling the truth based on my own vivid Kundalini experience. A number of people in spiritual emergency would call me because they knew I had been there, too. Unfortunately, at present, these Kundalini experiences are not always recognized in the West and are often labelled as psychosis by mental health institutions. Lisa would be no exception. Natasha and I couldn't house her long term. Unfortunately, one fateful night she went on a walk about in Chelsea and ended up at the home of a mutual friend, Harry.

ॐ नमो दुर्गा माँ/ॐ नमो लक्ष्मी माँ

Harry called me in desperation saying, "You have to come! Lisa has been walking around Chelsea in her dressing gown and turned up on the doorstop of my family home. My parents want her removed from here immediately; either you come, or they will call the police!"

"Oh, my god!" I thought. If she was taken by the police, that would make her scared and paranoid. I was fully aware of the subtlety of her state. I recalled my spiritual teacher's words of how episodes like these were regarded as beneficial fever in India, as the Kundalini energy would work its power in expelling blockages to inner freedom.

In India, people actually stop in the street and mop your brow and massage your feet with reverence and honour at the spiritual process you are going through until you are well. I, therefore, knew that Natasha and I would have to fetch her. As we arrived, she had been made captive in a posh Chelsea terrace house dining room.

As she saw Natasha and me, her face lit up and she said with great intensity and wide eyes, "Listen, there are twelve chosen apostles and you are two of them; the others will reveal themselves soon. We are all going to Australia. That is where the energy is most connected now!"

As I heard her words, I recalled being in the psychiatric ward with my friend Sue as I took her through Nazi Germany on the dining room floor. I realized through Lisa how crazy I must have looked, and how, in my case, I had no one who believed me. I felt like a godmother, somehow, urgently being called to help Lisa in her hour of need as she was being perilously judged by the aristocrats of Chelsea. Lisa ended up, for a brief period, just like me, in psychiatric hospital. She, similarly, threw away her medication and discharged herself within a month. Lisa was initially a student and is now a successful voice facilitator and chant leader in her own right.

The Spiritual Emergency project was successful. Of the 100 guests attending, fifty percent of them had either experienced emergency or were relatives of someone who had. Dr. Andrew Powell attended from the Royal College of Psychiatry. He was the aforementioned leading edge thinker who created the Special Interest group at the Royal College of Psychiatry dedicated to exploring all aspects of mental health and, particularly, the part that spirituality plays in mental well-being. I invited JC to be the main speaker on this night because, shortly after some of the corporate gigs we did together, he, ironically, went through a major spiritual awakening which was monumental and very similar to my Kundalini awakening.

It was at this point that I recognized that there were no support structures in the UK for people going through spiritual emergence, hence, my inspiration to run such an event. JC would call me daily as he found himself frozen in aisle seven of Sainsbury's, trying to understand the cosmic connection between where he was in relation to a can of baked beans! On another occasion, he was in his car and, for him, time had stopped. He suddenly realized that thirty cars were behind him slamming on their horns. He thought he was doing thirty miles per hour when, in fact, he was only doing five miles per hour. He had actually shifted into timeless awareness, when all the cars behind him were in linear time.

On one occasion when he called me, I totally related to the space he was in, moving between being the finite and the infinite all in one moment. A Kundalini awakening can, initially, be a turbulent and sometimes terrifying experience. It is then followed by waves upon waves of bliss, until the next cycle of movement, from the unconscious, bubbles to the surface. JC told me that my voice at the end of the line was like an anchor in a wild sea.

The Spiritual Emergency Event turned out great. It was an immense achievement and team effort in creating the first event of its kind on this taboo subject for the general public. People in the audience got to be heard as they shared their vulnerable experiences from the floor in response to JC's sharing of his experience. It felt like a seed was being sown for the future – for new structures that will come into existence in the future, perhaps even spiritual hospitals.

In 2002, a professor of psychology approached me. Dr. Phillip Barker asked if I would write a chapter for a book that he was compiling called *Spirituality and Mental Health* subtitled *Breakthrough*. This was a book compiling the mystical awakenings of people who had been restrained by the mental health act due to the doctor's lack of understanding about their experience. My chapter was entitled *Heaven-bound*. This title was inspired by that fateful February in 1989 when I saw written on the front of a commuter train "Heaven-bound" at East Putney station. I was in a heightened state of consciousness. Suddenly, an Up-minister train was taking me to heaven. I will never forget stepping onto that train and seeing everyone as souls for the first time. I saw the oneness connecting one pair of eyes to the other person sitting beside them. This was a profound realization, and I definitely felt I was heaven-bound.

ॐ नमो दुर्गा माँ/ॐ नमो लक्ष्मी माँ

The period from 2005-2015 has been a ripening of magical connections, both personally and professionally. In 2007, Graham Fink, who was the one of the art directors of M+C Saatchi at that time, came to explore his voice on a private basis. Graham is a rare leader with the highest integrity, and he is also a generous and inspirational person. He recognized the value of my work, and he gave me a great opportunity to run a team building session (for twenty-three of his account holders) in their main branch on Golden Square in Soho. Graham wanted to surprise his staff, so he chose not to warn them all in advance as to the nature of the session they were coming to. He instructed the maintenance men to roll up the boardroom carpet especially that morning, and to move out the furniture so we could have a spacious floor for the session. They then transported twenty-three upright chairs from the basement.

My drummer, Mark, and I set up the space for the workshop. As I sat in my chair in anticipation of these high end media people arriving, I took a moment to take in the atmosphere. Here I was, in one of the top advertising firms in the world, about to risk my voice work with potential sceptics. I looked at the white leather and plasma screens and the buzz of London Soho outside the window, aware that this would probably be the first occasion in history in London that a media company would experience a workshop quite like this. Suddenly, I could hear them all lining up outside the boardroom door. The team was instructed to leave their shoes outside before they entered. My adrenalin soared as they came in. They looked somewhat surprised and sceptical to see all the instruments set in front of the wall-to-wall windows. We had put on the sound of an electronic drone in the background and a circle of chairs lay ready for them.

Graham had debriefed me that, in recent months, he had divided his team into pods. He wanted to create an atmosphere of everyone working in harmony together. This was the perfect intention for me to work with. I looked around at the group of an even balance of men and women. I began with introductions, going around the circle, and I asked them their first impressions of what they thought was about to happen. I clocked immediately who the jokesters and more cynical media people were. I have always found that those characters, if you tune in, can really get the group going (if you play your cards right). I chose one of them, with overnight stubble on his chin and a small beer belly, to lead a physical warm up. This man was a joker and he led it full-out like Ricky Gervais playing David Brent in the series *The Office*. He was very funny and he got to unleash all his star personality energy by motivating the group.

We then divided the room into their pods, as per their department, and we did several voice and movement energizers, the culmination of which was the Zulu charge. In this moment, all the participants lined up at one end of the room with secretaries rolling up their pencil skirts and men rolling their shirt sleeves as they all charged towards the plasma TV screen. The other side were putting the full weight of their bodies and voices towards their future goals and aspirations! The release in the room was tangible. They were surely now ready and open to chant, I thought.

I invited them back into a circle to lead them in a call and response chant of Jay Bhagwan, which means, "I surrender to the supreme principle." The momentum built and the energy in the room went to golden heights on Golden Square. It was magical to watch their peaceful and free faces and their bodies gently swaying as the vibrations of the chant began to affect them. They loved the overall experience. Many of them queued up afterwards to express how much they enjoyed their experience and to say thank you. For two days after, I received testimonials from the participants reading, "After six months of sharing an open plan office with these people, I have gotten to know them better in just one hour with Nikki – amazing!" or, "I feel that I can now fly to Scotland and back!" or, "I wish we could have this every time just before we make a creative pitch!"

Graham was enormously supportive. He said he could recognize the challenge I had in advertising my voice work. He generously offered, in gratitude for my workshop, the opportunity for me to work with six of his top creative team members to come up with a promotional pitch for the work. The team proposed that they would design my brand so that I could easily present it to finance managers (who were the toughest people to enroll), and which would make the energy work that I provided both credible and grounded. Incredibly, they gave me six months of their precious time for free. Finally, the day came when they unveiled my new brand to me. It was to be Nikki Slade/Chemistry at Work. It promised to ignite chemistry between people in teams, creating an alchemical shift that wasn't present before, leading to increased energy, teamwork and great results. I felt so fortunate and blessed that day to have my new brand out there in the world.

ॐ नमो दुर्गा माँ/ॐ नमो लक्ष्मी माँ

After the M+C Saatchi launch, I was invited to some incredible opportunities to lead chanting and voice workshops with companies around the world. One memory stands out for me, in particular, which was being invited to energize a group of bankers from all over Europe at Deutsche Bank on London wall. I will never forget walking into their regal building with startling marble plinths and plaques lining the foyer. As I walked into the lift, looking somewhat incongruous with my instruments, I got some surprised looks from staff. I boldly walked into the conference room and began to set everything up. At 9:00 a.m., the pin-striped suits all began to walk into the room, whereupon some of them walked up to my drum and began to play beats like children messing around.

These bankers had never been all together in one room before. They had only ever spoken on Skype or video conferencing. It was like the Eurovision Song Contest – they had representatives from all over Europe. To break the ice, I had the inspiration to invite them all to lead the group one at a time in the middle of the circle in a movement session with a particular flavour from their country, both physical and vocal. These men were totally up for it. They rolled up their sleeves, as the Italian let rip his lyrical opera with everyone following. The French sang with full *amour*, then the German in military style and finally a Canadian banker cast off his pristine jacket and loosened his silk red tie and began break dancing in the middle of the circle with everyone clapping in rhythm around him. Suddenly, I became aware, out of the corner of my eye, of a couple of maids in black uniforms with white hats peering around the door with their tea trolley. Their jaws dropped at history in the making! It reminded me of the scene in the sweet factory from the film *Chitty Chitty Bang Bang* when all the factory and office workers stopped what they were doing to sing *Toot Sweets*. The ice had well and truly melted and, by this point, the bankers were up for anything. Nothing was too touchy-feely for them now. They even held hands whilst chanting heart-opening mantras.

As I went home that day, I felt privileged and grateful for this fulfilling vocation to bring people together through the power of chanting. In the taxi back, I flashed back to singing in the woods as a child and imagining orchestras playing in the trees, being in make believe about ordinary people bursting into song wherever they happened to be. I smiled to myself, for that had actually happened that day. It completed a circle for me right back to the day when I inspired all the children to sing together in my primary school playground when I was only ten years old. That day I felt I was fulfilling my purpose – it felt like a divine fruit.

In 2002-2013, I was blessed with incredible new and exciting connections, including Yogi Cameron, an Ayuvedic coach to the stars, who included my chants on his documentary DVD, which was then shown on NBC TV. I was also approached by the renowned tabla player and composer Talvin Singh, who exclaimed how much he had enjoyed listening to my CD *Nectarine*. Talvin invited me to his studio and we had a great afternoon of musical improvisation together. There was a very high energy (Shakti) in his space. He opened the door to the corner of his studio where there was a photo of his music Guru, whom he worshipped with reverence each day. As I walked into that space, I felt so uplifted simply being there. Those moments on my journey have felt like feathers on my path giving me faith that I am on the right track.

The year 2010 saw the dawn of my new brand website with the close guidance of holistic PR woman, Andrea Adler from California. She had an excellent eye and was a lover of chanting. She really got what I was offering. I met Andrea for the first time in person when I was invited to open a global conference on sustainability at the Fort Mason Centre, San Francisco in 2010. I will never forget my assistant, Lindsey, spotting this opportunity online and recommending that I apply for it. I was really nervous, as it was a big leap of faith to offer something of this size in the USA that I had never done before. I will never forget walking up to the doors of the Fort Mason Centre with my longstanding percussionist, Mark Fisher, who has accompanied me for ten years. He is a great musician who I have often described as my right arm. Without Mark, the chants would not have been the same. We have travelled far and wide together, and he has made a huge contribution to my professional journey

As we walked into the Fort Mason Centre, my heart was racing in anticipation as to how the event would unfold. At 9:00 a.m., we were the first up on stage to get the audience into the zone of being open, alert and attentive to the speakers who were present on the day. I looked out at a sea of delegates and young students of anthropology. This was it; I had nothing to lose.

I thought, "Just go for it, Nikki!"

I invited them immediately to rise up on their feet, as the hall was chilly and everyone needed warming up. I started to lead them in sounds from behind my harmonium while Mark started to play the beats. I partnered everybody up with their neighbours and they explored expansive sounds and movements as instructed. They loved it. Their spirits were soaring and I found myself watching their smiling faces in slow motion. It was a tangible picture.

Afterwards, they once again took to their seats and it felt completely natural, at this point, to lead them in a chant to the divine mother Kali Durge Namo Namah.

The atmosphere transformed from being cold and distant at 9:00 a.m. to being warm and connected. Transformational leader Barbara Marx Hubbard, who was the main speaker after us, acknowledged to the crowd the extraordinary impact that the chanting session had made on the atmosphere in the room. She said that this approach in sound vibration was the next massive wave in our future evolution for world change. Andrea Adler then took the initiative to successfully ask Barbara afterwards for a testimonial – something I would never have dreamed of doing. I felt truly privileged to have been there.

ॐ नमो दुर्गा माँ/ॐ नमो लक्ष्मी माँ

I am deeply present to my blessed life. Every year my bowl is filled with the fruits of incredible people, clients, friends and opportunities. All these are the unexpected gifts of an awakened life that could only have come to me through the grace of chanting.

There is a saying, "Home is where the heart is," and that is so true. A strong home life literally nourishes and supports the growth of all good things in life. I have learned in the fifty-three years of my life that timing is everything. For the past six years, I have been happily in a very special relationship with Erika, who I mentioned earlier.

Erika has been such an important name in my journey. The first one bullied me at school, the second one was my greatest spiritual ally and friend and, finally, Erika came into my life as a beautiful and unconditionally loving relationship at the perfect time. In my chakra journey, she represents the third eye or adjna chakra – the centre of spirituality and wisdom. Erika is from Mexico, originally, and has a nine-year-old daughter, Lara, by her previous marriage. Erika and I originally met when she attended my chanting group. After three years, she was so inspired by the chanting and voice work that she accepted the offer to become my part-time assistant. After some time, we fell in love and we now have a lovely home in the suburbs of London. Lara lives with us most of the time, and we are very happy. It is a wonderful experience to be a step-parent in my fifties.

Lara is a real gift in my life. She already loves chanting, singing, dancing and musical theatre. We spend quality time together playing the piano and entering the land of make-believe. It is an amazing experience to share highlights from my childhood with her. Children bring so much joy and laughter into home life. Erika has been my rock, and she says the same is true of me. We complement one another on every level. She has helped me hugely with the administrative side of the business and in making great professional connections for me, especially in Mexico. She not only opened doors for me there, but was also phenomenal in translating my work. I, in turn, champion Erika's acting and voice-over career.

At forty-eight years old, when Erika and I had been together for three years, I made a remarkable discovery about myself that I would like to share with you. In the summer of 2009, I was co-facilitating a yoga and chant retreat in Portugal with a great Yogi. He is highly intuitive and I have found him to be psychic. One evening, after an uplifting evening of chanting, he and I had a moment to talk alone. I was curious to ask his wisdom about the karmic journey I had undergone as a lesbian woman.

Yogi looked deep into my soul and said in his Indian accent, "Actually, Nikki, you are not a woman! You are a man in a female body. You see, what actually makes a person male or female is their brain. In fact, that is where their gender and sexual orientation, in truth, comes from. You are like Shikhandi, who is a character in the Mahabharata who was a man born into a female form."

I was staggered as he shared this! In that moment, I completely under-stood my whole life backwards. All my child hood years as a tomboy. It was suddenly clear why I never identified with being a girl and party dresses. I had always felt out of place. In early childhood, I much preferred playing with boys, and I always wanted to play the father in father and mother make believe games, as I described earlier with my best friend Janie. It also made sense why, as a child, I had always drawn men. I also recalled, in depth, my love of Tommy Steele. He was my role model back then. In truth, I actually wanted to be just like him as Arthur Kipps in the movie *Half a Sixpence*. It was definitely more than a girlhood crush. I have also always had the ability to form strong friendships with men. These friendships have always flourished, so long as they remained platonic.

As Yogi continued speaking to me, I reflected back to playing Billy Tipton (Johnny Christmas) in *The Slow Drag,* when I was required for the role to strap my breasts in every night to portray a man on stage. I had always thought that the universe was giving me a sign in playing this role to connect more with my feminine side. I now see, on the contrary, that playing Johnny Christmas was actually the universe confirming for me the struggle I had felt in my own body, my whole life, of feeling male in a female form. This was a massive and staggering revelation for me to uncover so late in life – the extraordinary realization that I had lived forty-eight years as a male in a female body.

After this revolutionary meeting with Yogi, I spent a year in copious research on this subject. I discovered that, in modern-day terms, I would be transgender and not lesbian at all. I have the utmost awe and respect for all those millions of men and women who have undergone gender reassignment. I am particularly grateful and in awe of the bold journey of a transgender man who I discovered in my research on YouTube who captures his entire transition from female to male over five years. I was so moved by his journey, which was paramount in helping me process whether such a courageous act would ever have been fitting for me.

ॐ नमो दुर्गा माँ/ॐ नमो लक्ष्मी माँ

One day, a wonderful man called Marco* came for a private voice session gifted to him by his girlfriend at the time.

About halfway through the session, he said, "I feel I should share something with you, Nikki. You see, I think I should tell you that I haven't always been a man! I actually started life as a girl! I have transitioned over the past seven years!"

I took a breath and was amazed (as you really couldn't tell). His reassignment surgery and hormone treatment had completely transformed him. He is an incredible man and he was a great mirror for me of meeting, in the flesh, all the wonders of what is possible. The universe was reflecting for me an option that I could have taken if I had chosen to transition.

I wholly acknowledge the beautiful souls who have transitioned with their gender this life. They are torchbearers and amazing examples to us all. They are a pillar of strength for those souls who are still struggling with their gender and are trying to acquire the courage to transition. I would like, at this point, to acknowledge my friend and author, Persia West, who wrote the unique and beautifully written book *The Choice*, exploring her passage through gender and beyond.

I deeply contemplated over many months this mind-blowing revelation of being male in a female form, and began to view my incarnation as a privileged opportunity. I have, today, chosen to embrace my feminine form and inner masculine power. Today, I accept who I am as being a woman on the outside with a strong connection to my inner masculinity and that, for this lifetime, I am perfect just the way I am. I arrived at this place of self-acceptance after the recognition that, in spirit, I am neither male nor female – I am my soul, which transcends gender. For this lifetime, I am learning to embrace this androgyny and, ultimately, to transcend it. Erika, too, embraces who I am completely. She intuitively recognized my masculine energy long before we ever got together. We share a glorious chemistry and soul connection, which we believe spans over many lifetimes, where we both have had visions of when I was externally a man and she was a woman.

After twenty-five years of sadhana – or spiritual discipline – I realize that my gender is merely a part of my karmic journey and I am wholly at peace with that. The Dalai Lama is quoted as saying, "The world will be saved by the western woman." Thus, being androgynous in the form of a Western woman occurs to me now as the perfect incarnation for my journey in this life.

I owe the abundant gifts I have received, and experiences I have had, on my journey to the grace of chanting. I feel truly blessed to have a purpose in sound that each year is expanding. Over twenty-five years, chanting has taken me around the world to Europe, New York, Mexico City, Singapore and Melbourne. My favourite place is California; it feels like my spiritual home and I offer heartfelt thanks to Manizeh Rimer and Toni Cupal for opening doors for me there.

Now celebrate your life, wherever you may be, by chanting for the final time:

OM NAMO DURGA MA/OM NAMO LAKSHMI MA

Conclusion

"Amazing Grace, how sweet the sound, that saved a soul like me;
I once was lost, but now I am found, was blind but now I see."

John Newton

Chanting has revealed an understanding about the purpose of every intimate relationship I have experienced on my path. Each precious partner has represented, and given me, the opportunity to learn about a particular chakra on my personal growth journey. Only supreme Grace knows what lessons I still need to learn before one day, one lifetime, I will merge with my inner self. Chanting has shown me the perfection of my family of origin and how I incarnated into my specific family in order to grow on a soul level.

Chanting has given me the strength to march forward in the face of a history of bullying in early life. When the negative voices hound me on the inside, or conflict comes towards me on the outside, chanting lifts me out of the bog of darkness. Through revelations, it has led me to the perfect environments and teachers to help me develop as a human being and leader. It has put me in a vibrational alignment with daily synchronicities, whether with people or places. It has opened my eyes to the divine flow of life. Chanting has been my direct access to inner freedom and has been a major factor in my daily reprieve from alcoholism over twenty-five years.

Finally, chanting has opened up a priceless destiny – the honour and privilege of sharing this practice with a broad range of people worldwide, including recovering addicts, prison inmates, business leaders, performers, yoga students, teachers, householders and teams in business and in the workplace.

I have shared my story with you in the hope that you, too, may be inspired to chant. My heartfelt desire is to see a world filled with chanting. Chanting connects everyone to the power of love – that incredible feeling that, once the chant starts, we are transported home inside to the realm of inner bliss. As we all chant together, there is no sense of separation – only love prevails.

Chanting has brought the power of Grace into my life. It has given me the key to joy and inner bliss. I hope that my story has been of value and that you are enjoying chanting along with these tracks. May the nectar of chanting continue to expand for you always. I leave you with a recording of the first song I ever sang in public when I was ten years old – *Amazing Grace*.

Chant for your life

and

enter the bliss of the heart.

Download Amazing Grace at www.nikkislade.com/freechants

HAPPY CHANTING, EVERYONE!

Quotes

"I was born a tomboy; I'm a girl, too."
Anonymous

"By singing God's name, become completely desire-less and delight in the inner self."
Manpuri, Eleventh Century Saint

"But courage, child: We are all between the paws of the true Aslan."
C. S. Lewis, The Last Battle in Narnia

"Not being liked was so much worse than being invisible."
Rebecca Donovan

"If one throws salt at thee, thou wilt receive no harm unless one has sore places."
Latin Proverb

"Oh Arjuna, I am attained by one who sings my name steadfastly and ceaselessly."
Bhagavad Gita

"'As long as you have desires about how it ought to be, you can't see how it is."
Ramdass

"Bless us with a divine voice and may we tune the harp strings of our life to sing songs of love to you."
Rig Veda

"Chanting the name of God is a yoga. It has great Shakti. That Shakti stills the mind and fills the heart with love."
Swami Muktananda

"I'm singing a song for my daddy."
Bette Davis, *What Ever Happened to Baby Jane?*

"The most intriguing people you will encounter in this life are the people who had insights about you that you didn't know about yourself."
Shannon L. Alder

"Learn the true alchemy human beings know: The moment you accept what troubles you've been given, the door will open."
Rumi

"The earth, the sea, the sky, the stars are all woven together by the soft strains of the divine music."
Sama Veda

"Mira says no one can stop her, Mira says no one can criticize her or stand in her way; intoxicated with divine love, she sings the names of the Lord."
Mirabai

"The self is the hub of all sacred places. Go there and roam."
Bhagawan Nityananda

"Like the joyful streams gushing from the mountains so do our hymns sound forth to the Lord."
Rig Veda

"Imagine there's no heaven; it's easy if you try; no hell below us, above us, only sky."
John Lennon

"Your name alone has me brought back lustre to my soul."
Tukaram Maharaj

"I am purified. Because of the power of chanting all my karmas are washed away."

Tukaram Maharaj

"Any moment spent without singing the name of Gods glory should be regarded as a great loss."

Hanuman in the Ramyana

"I have become alive."

Swami Muktananda'

"Its vibrations echo through the corridors of time in the endless canopy of the sky."

Sama Veda

"When we quit thinking primarily about ourselves and our own self-preservation, we undergo a truly heroic transformation of consciousness."

Joseph Campbell

"The perfect spiritual practice for this age is to chant the holy name and to make others chant the name of the Lord."

Anon

"The greatest thing a human soul ever does in this world is to see clearly is poetry, prophecy and religion all in one."

John Ruskin

"Every once in a while, people need to be in the presence of things that are really far away."

Ian Frazier

"With the shelter found in your Grace, life has become ever grateful. My heart is brimming over with the light of gratitude."

Unknown

"Do not give what is holy to the dogs; nor cast your pearls before swine, lest they trample them under their feet, and turn and tear you in pieces."

Mathew 7:6 New Testament

"The yogi dyes his garments red, but if she knows naught of that colour of love, what does it avail though her garments be tainted?"
Kabir

"Whatever you can do, or dream you can do, begin it now. Boldness has genius, power, and magic in it."
Goethe

"When we go into the inner chamber and shut the door to every sound that comes from the life without, then will the voice of God speak to our soul and we will know the keynote of our life."
Hazrat Inayat Khan

"If we do not change where we are headed, we are likely to end up where we are headed."
Chinese Proverb

"Opportunities are like sunrises: if you wait too long, you miss them."
William Arthur Ward

"Life is a risky business and if we put up too many fences against risk one ends by shutting out life itself."
Anonymous

"The most intense conflicts, if overcome, leave behind a sense of security and calm that is not easily disturbed. It is just these intense conflicts and their conflagration which are needed to produce valuable and lasting results."
Carl Jung

"That which is dreamed can never be lost, can never be undreamed."
Neil Gaiman, The Sandman, Vol. 10: The Wake

"If you ever find yourself in the wrong story, leave."
Mo Williams

"You introduced me to bliss, now I see love everywhere and the world is a happy place."
Mukta Passi

"When my mind became pure, like a mirror free of dust, I found the self within myself."
Lalleshwari

"Sometimes the person you want the most is the person you're best without."
Anonymous

"The growth and development of people is the highest calling of leadership."
Harvey S. Firestone

"Life is a full circle, widening until it joins the circle motions of the infinite."
Anais Nin

"Only with the virtue of enthusiasm can one make the impossible possible."
Valmiki Ramayan

"The dark thought, the shame the malice, meet them at the door laughing and invite them in be grateful for whoever comes because each has been sent as a guide from beyond."
Rumi

"A ship is safe in the harbor, but that's not what ships are built for."
William Shepp

"Love is the absence of judgement."
Dalai Lama

"When you do what you fear most, then you can do anything."
Stephen Richards

"Life is not merely a series of meaningless accidents or coincidences, but rather, it is a tapestry of events that culminate into an exquisite, sublime plan."
Anonymous

Acknowledgments

I wish to acknowledge many people, especially my spiritual meditation master teacher for guiding me home. I have no words to express my gratitude other than Om Namah Shivaya. My deepest gratitude to Erika Sanchez Luna for our unconditionally loving partnership and your infinite stand for my career. I love you. I want to thank my mum and dad for being brave teachers for me in so many ways, and a constant loving support throughout my life. Thank you for your love and generosity. I love you both. Thank you Rupert, my dear brother, for being my first champion and cheering my singing since our childhood. To my cousin, Humphrey Barclay, for all the support you gave me. To my grandmother, May Slade, Christopher and Jane Slade and Pauline Hamilton-Russell for solid values that have lit my life.

There are so many people who fill my heart with gratitude. To Sophie Beswick (Doherty), my teenage friend. To Nousjka Thomas, my lovely eternal friend, we will always be in each other's hearts. You have been a constant, like an evergreen; however much I change, you have always embraced me just the same. James Mconnel, without your support I would have sunk in those early storms. I can never, ever thank you enough. You are my "honeysuckle rose". Lulu, you were the first miracle for me. When you came into my life, miracles happened. Thank you for opening the door for me and for being a generous star so rare!

Michael James, you are my soul brother, friend, eternal champion and an angel. Thank you for your steadfast kindness and guidance in all storms. Lara Lolly B, I love you, magical child. Thank you for the lessons you have taught me and the many gifts you have brought me. To Chloe Goodchild, for being my champion guide and divine maternal mentor. I do not have enough words to express my infinite gratitude for all you have gifted me. I love you always. Thank you, Helena Shenel, for being my incredible vocal teacher – the best in the world. You changed my vocal technique forever and gave me wings to fly. You literally saved my voice. I could not have done it without you. Devon

Buchannan, magical spiritual friend, an angel of light in my era of darkness, that the dark somehow shimmered and fell away.

Gosia Gorna, you were there rooting for me at the start. Your intuition is extraordinary. Everything you spoke came to pass, and you have been unwavering in your faith in me. Thank you. To Nick Williams, for being there from the beginning and for always cheering me on and being a male mentor to me with such feminine sensitivity. Thank you for all the opportunities you gave me to shine. Thank you, Ericka Huggins, for being the kind of friend that I have to pinch myself to think "did I really attract someone as magnificent into my life?" You saw me through the worst of it. I could not have made it without you. You have had a major impact on my life for the better. I love you always. To Shelley Wilner, for being an incredible and unforgettable friend for a major part of my journey. You are always with me, even though we live so far apart. Only love remains. Louisa White Lovely, soul sister and friend, you are a very special person in my life. Thank you for trusting my work in the formative years and for being the channel for major connections.

I would also like to thank Yasia Leiserach. We have shared a monumental journey. Thank you for being the earth to my fire, for ensuring the birth of a new era of voice. We have been alchemists for one another. Richard Hougham, for the openings you gave me. Em Westcott, for being a dear friend and advocate for my work and the mother of an angel. Thank you to Gabe, my lovely timeless child friend. The precious moments we have shared will stay with me forever. Thank you to Ilana and Bodhi, for being my beautiful God children. Thank you to Sylvia and Jonathan Leiserach for your loving care, interest and support always.

Yogi Ashokanada, you are a true guide and cosmic friend. Thank you for seeing me in all the blind spots where I have not been able to see myself. Thank you for your faith in my journey, and for giving me hope always. Dr. Larry Culliford, thank you for being one of the luminaries in the field of psychiatry, and for recognizing and validating my spiritual emergency. Theresa Symes, your ability to see futures blows me away. You are on the button every time and are right there whenever I call to guide me through the storms. Thank you.

Davina Mackail, fabulous friend, shamanic guide and sister forever, I adore you. Marie Claire Carlyle, thank you for being a passionate and loyal advocate of my work. Your passion and enthusiasm has moved me greatly. Rachel Elnaugh, for great opportunities and lessons learned. Kat Dever, for your magical mirror of what's possible. Mark Eynon, for your belief in me and for being there when you knew it mattered. Sofie Haag, for the ride of our lives!

Giles Petit, thank you for your unique training in northern Indian raga. Your approach gave me the inspiration and incentive to take my chanting voice to the next level. Yogi Manicka Yogeshwarn, for your kind and gentle guidance with southern Indian raga for opening my voice in new and wonderful ways.

Charlotte Pulver, another soul sister with the wisdom of the ancients. You have always seen me. Thank you, Sarbdeep Swan. Son, you are like a Royal bouncer who is always in the shadows watching out for me. I love you. Anne Nowell, you are an extraordinary oracle. You have been there to guide me in critical moments. I think of you as being like Hera was to Jason in *Jason and the Golden Fleece*. Bobby Nowell, thank you for your steadfast faith in me when I struggled to believe in myself. Your gentle strength and healing wisdom inspired me on my path. Jas Singh, thank you for bringing Kuan Yin into my life, and for the hours and hours of guidance you gave me when I was drowning in maya. I owe you one. Andrea Adler, thank you for seeing me and championing me, and for bringing positive gifts to my chanting journey.

Annie Ashdown, for your Thelma and Louise style companionship, the laughs, the camaraderie and unbelievable channelling. I miss you. Manizeh Rimer, for being one of my favourite Americans, who gave me openings that have led to magical connections. Thank you, dear one. Toni Cupal, thank you for opening the gates for me in your homeland. Your generosity has gone a long way and you will always be in heart. Adrian Kowal, you have the same name as my father and, even though you are a shining young man, thank you for being an elder, father earth, father sky and a sweet and gentle champion. Corinne Kowal, thank you for the space you gave me to evolve the work. EVOLVE is a reflection of yours and Adrian's steadfast vision and love. Thank you for the honour of marrying you both. It has been special knowing you. Anna Ziman, you have been a cheerleader from the beginning. You have made me cry with laughter, and moved me in your unstoppable commitment to my work by showing up when least expected.

A big thank you to Marc Mortiboys, for your "storming" support, for being there at the start as I turned the key to the door of the biggest adventure of my life. Jay Morris, you have moved me to tears by the way you were there when I most needed support. You put yourself out there because you believed in me. Unforgettable and priceless, brother. Thank you. I love you. Heather, you were my first messenger for the work, a lucky feather on my path. Bless you. Nigel Sadler, thank you for grounding the vision for me, when technology was more of an enigma even than it is now, and for helping me when you didn't have to. Your belief in me always stays in my heart. Jonathan Sattin, you have been there since the start, believing in my voice and the song of my heart. I am moved and eternally thankful for all you have brought me. TRIYOGA is a pond of nectar. Thank you. Jamie Moon, your selfless service leaves me humble and in awe of the legacy you have left. Thank you for being there on Christmas Day that year. Dr. Larry Culliford, for your enriching stand in awakening the psychiatric field to the power of spiritual emergence, and for your constant friendship. Peter Larsen, how I have loved our recording collaborations – not only musically, but the laughs, the in-depth sharings and general love of life together. You are the best. Mel Larsen, generous authentic loving champion, always quietly cheering from the wings.

Chris Gibbons, for happy musical collaborations and cosmic chats in your alphasud along the hedge rows of Devon. Sue Kalincinska, for being a constant steadfast presence as a loyal client, friend and medicine woman. Michael Ormiston, for happy memories in concert together with your light, talent and humility that touched me in the early days and inspired me to deepen my own voice path. Chris James, for inspiring a whole new approach. Edwin Coppard, for the generous time you and Cheryl gave me in Vancouver in 1999, and for those unforgettable songs we developed together. Lisa Eldridge, for having the vision I couldn't see for my change in vocation. Josie and Smudger Smith, for being dear friends and spiritual elders who feel like eternal family. You have always been there. I love you. Mark Fisher, for a musical marriage that lasted a decade. You are a unique treasure and in all my best gigs, you were there. Thank you with all my heart. Mike Forde, for your passion, enthusiasm and vital rhythms. You are a bright light and joy to play with, and you have a heart of gold. Kelly Smith, for the incredible energy, commitment and talent you have brought to all my recordings, and an eternal priceless friendship.

Thank you to Kirby. The spaces we played together are unforgettable. You witnessed my most courageous work, and your love, support and unbelievable rhythms were the icing on the cake at all those corporate events. You were a huge part of an important era and you rock! Afra Bell, thank you for the Goddess you are, and the subtle magic you have brought over the years that only you can. Anna Ashby, thank you for your loyal and special partnership over the years. I have loved our collaborations and have produced some of my best work with you. And we have laughed a lot, haven't we? Katy Appleton, you are an amazing woman, a treasure to work with, and a total inspiration. I am blessed to have you in my life. Suzie Kershaw, you were the match that lit the fire for my work with companies. From that one flame, so much has grown. Thank you for paving the way and for always being there. Patrick Holford, for championing my singing and bringing me opportunities. Tony Coope, for believing in me. Lynne Nesbit, for your loving friendship and spiritual friendship. George Masri, for being a true example, elder and guide throughout the years. Annie and John Grieg, for your loving support in the early days of my Sadhana.

Lindsay Robertson, for being the voice of technology – a language I couldn't speak – for ensuring the visibility of my vision and for the loving way with which you laboured. Thank you. JC Mac, for the visionary opportunities you gave me and for trusting me to deliver. Lindsay Willcox, for the special times we shared chanting in your home and for being such an incredible minister. Rev. Nev Annie Neville, for cheering me on in the early days and for seeing me clearly. Hillary Wilson, for celebrating my chanting journey in the early years and for lots of laughter along the way. Gary Purser, thank you for the breaks you gave me and the companionship. Although we have only been together a few times, each meeting has been as rare as gold. Chris Waters, for opening doors for me at the beginning. Life Times was a special time. Maya Parker, for helping me to unravel it all. Charles Montague, for your unconditional love and encouragement. Nikki Redmond, for encouraging my soul song. Maggie Eyre, I will never forget our journey. You were heaven sent to me, and I could not have done it without you.

Nerina Ramlakhan, for your unshakeable vote of confidence and generosity in putting me forward and leading me to Kim. Dr. Kim Jobst, for leading me to Emily and for the adventure we are on together. Kerri-Lyn Stanton Downes, for your advocacy and grounded empowerment. Claudina Elliott, for your championing of the work. Angus Fergusson, for all your inspired support at the end of the phone. Gita Jeeraj, for your loyal friendship. Ze Roberts, for your incredible friendship and support. Cloud Taylor, for your loyal friendship and for sharing my work in the LGBT community. Thao Dang, for a connection that feels like we agreed to meet this time around in a previous life and support one another. I love your energy, and you have made an outstanding contribution to my career.

Thank you to Alison Murtough, your profound M.O.T.s! Thank you to Carmel Morrisey for helping me to grow the work in the early days. Tracy Starreveld, for those rich, creative years we spent together. I will never forget you. Pauline McCrann, for your loyal support. Julianne Miller, for your bright enthusiasm and guidance. Thank you to Landmark Worldwide for opening up a whole new realm for me, and particular gratitude to Per Holgren and Pip Gardiner. Thank you, Triwidyatmaka, for your great work on the front cover, and Jerzy Kokurewicz for capturing the Arunchala mountain. Samjhana Moon, for that classic portrait and David Lau, for the cover shot.

Thank you to Kamali Allnut for your steadfast friendship and enthusiasm.

To Amba Gatherum, thank you for being one of my angels!

To Julia McCutchen, I cannot thank you enough for the time, support and dedication that you gave me at the start.

I would like to thank Gina Lazenby for her early belief in me and for nominating me for the Women of Spirit award.

And finally, an ode to my clients. You know who you are. I thank each and every single one of you. It appeared that I was teaching you, but you taught me so much more. Thank you, generous souls, for helping me evolve. To Christopher Hareesh Wallis, for guiding me into the next level of knowledge and understanding of the power of mantra, and for always being an inspiration.

Glossary

Ananda: Sanskrit word for bliss and happiness.

Ankh: Ancient Egyptian symbol for fertility.

Dyspraxia: Developmental coordination disorder.

Durga: The Goddess of courage and steadfastness.

Jay: Sanskrit word for hail or praise.

Kali: The Goddess known as "the black one the death of time". She frees devotees from ego and the cycle of birth and death.

Lakshmi: The Goddess for prosperity derived from the Sanskrit meaning "goal".

Muktananda: Sanskrit word for the bliss of freedom.

Namah: Sanskrit word for honour or salutations.

Namo: Sanskrit word for "to bow" "to honour".

Om: Sanskrit word for ultimate reality supreme soul.

Sanskrit: An ancient Indo-European language of India, in which the Hindu scriptures and classical Indian epic poems are written, and from which many northern Indian (Indic) languages are derived. It is refined and celestial language.

Satsang: The Sanskrit definition for gathering in the company of the truth.

Shakti: Sanskrit for primordial cosmic feminine energy.

Shivaya: Sanskrit for divine inner Self.

Shiva: Sanskrit for "the Auspcious one", the destroyer of evil.

Seva: Sanskrit word for selfless service.

Vedas: Ancient texts composed in Vedic Sanskrit. The texts constitute the oldest layer of Sanskrit literature and the oldest scriptures of Hinduism.

About the Author

Nikki Slade is one of the leading pioneers in the field of voice, chanting and sound work in the UK. As founder of Free the Inner Voice and Chemistry at Work, she has inspired corporate groups, including M+C Saatchi, Deutcshe Bank and Cisco, and she is the Resident Kirtan leader at Triyoga, London. Nikki has recorded four highly acclaimed CDs: Nectarine, Monsoon, Soundscape and Epiphany.

Nikki's cutting-edge approach to working with "the voice" has also been experienced at Wandsworth Prison and at The Priory Hospital in North London, where she has impacted the recovery of hundreds of addicts for over a decade. Nikki has led chants with more than a thousand people at 11.11.11 at the Mind Body Spirit Festival, and The Hilton Metropole for Oneness 12.12.12. She has also led for The Prosperity conference at The Barbican in 2013 and for Just This Day at St. Martins in the Fields in Trafalgar Square. In 2015, she led the finale chanting celebration at the Plaza Ballroom for Emily Gowor's Inspiration Bible book launch in Melbourne.

"I am passionate about vibrational harmony. There is a note within the heart of each individual which, when played, releases expansive joy and inner fulfilment, inspiring the highest expression of who we truly are. I devote my life to this possibility for all I have the privilege to work with."

www.nikkislade.com

Chanting CDs by Nikki

THE ALCHEMY OF WHOLENESS is a collection of Nikki's own songs reflecting the journey of her awakening between 1989 and 2004.

NECTARINE is Nikki's first ever Kirtan/chanting CD recorded in 2005 with original melodies.

MONSOON is Nikki's second Kirtan/chanting CD inspired by the Monsoon season in India recorded in 2007 with original melodies.

SOUNDSCAPE is a collection of four channelled pieces for meditation inspired by footage of the Arizonain mountains and The Colorado River. This popular CD has been widely used in Yoga classes and for meditation in connection with the law of attraction academy in London.

EPIPHANY is Nikki's third chanting CD, a double album collection of chants with original melodies in celebration of the blessings she has received through chanting over the years.

NIKKI SLADE
FREE THE INNER VOICE PUBLISHING

Lightning Source UK Ltd.
Milton Keynes UK
UKHW022006220519
343156UK00005B/296/P

9 780995 766617